Cybercrime and Digital Forensics

Cybercrime and Digital Forensics

Edited by Jason Wayne

CLANRYE
INTERNATIONAL
www.clanryeinternational.com

Clanrye International,
750 Third Avenue, 9th Floor,
New York, NY 10017, USA

ISBN: 978-1-63240-725-2

Cataloging-in-Publication Data

Cybercrime and digital forensics / edited by Jason Wayne.
p. cm.
Includes bibliographical references and index.
ISBN 978-1-63240-725-2
1. Computer crimes. 2. Forensic sciences. 3. Computer crimes--Investigation.
4. Forensic engineering. I. Wayne, Jason.
HV8079.C65 C93 2018
363.259 68--dc23

For information on all Clanrye International publications
visit our website at www.clanryeinternational.com

Contents

Preface

As the use of Internet is rapidly growing from the past few years, so is the rate of crime related to it. Today cybercrime has become one of the most threatening crimes in the world. Cybercrime refers to any crime which has been committed via Internet and on the computer. It includes copyright infringement, child pornography, hacking or unwarranted mass surveillance, etc. Digital forensics refers to that subfield of forensics which investigates the digital space and digital devices from which the crime has been committed. This textbook discusses in detail about the concepts, technologies, methods and laws used in this field. It includes topics concerned with the techniques and theories used in the subject. This book, with its detailed analyses and data, will prove immensely beneficial to professionals and students involved in this area at various levels.

A short introduction to every chapter is written below to provide an overview of the content of the book:

Chapter 1 - The offences committed against individuals or any group of people by using computers and networks is known as cybercrime. It can cause a threat to a person's life or to the security of a company. A security hacker is someone who violates and exploits the loopholes found in computer networks and security. This chapter will provide an integrated understanding of cybercrime and digital forensics; **Chapter 2 -** An Internet fraud is a scam which takes place by using the Internet. It usually occurs via the email, message boards or through websites. Some of the topics explained are cyberterrorism, cyberwarfare, international cybercrime and malware. The major components of cybercrime are discussed in this chapter; **Chapter 3 -** One of the common forms of bullying is cyberbullying. It includes spreading rumors, abusing, making sexual remarks, hateful comments and disclosing an individual's personal information. Bullying can harm a person to an extent where they can develop suicidal tendencies. Cybercrime is best understood in confluence with the major topics listed in the following chapter; **Chapter 4 -** Digital forensics is the method of interpreting electronic data. It is mainly used in courts to approve or disapprove a hypothesis. There are several sub-branches of the subject like network forensics, mobile device forensics, computer forensics and mobile device forensics. The topics discussed in the chapter are of great importance to broaden the existing knowledge on cybercrime and digital forensics.

I extend my sincere thanks to the publisher for considering me worthy of this task. Finally, I thank my family for being a source of support and help.

Editor

An Introduction to Cybercrime

The offences committed against individuals or any group of people by using computers and networks is known as cybercrime. It can cause a threat to a person's life or to the security of a company. A security hacker is someone who violates and exploits the loopholes found in computer networks and security. This chapter will provide an integrated understanding of cybercrime and digital forensics.

Cybercrime

Cyber crime, or computer related crime, is crime that involves a computer and a network. The computer may have been used in the commission of a crime, or it may be the target. Bhanges Fernandez and Shuhag Sukla and Kiachaur Jaishankar define cybercrimes as: "Offences that are committed against individuals or groups of individuals with a criminal motive to intentionally harm the reputation of the victim or cause physical or mental harm, or loss, to the victim directly or indirectly, using modern telecommunication networks such as Internet (networks including but not limited to Chat rooms, emails, notice boards and groups) and mobile phones (Bluetooth/SMS/MMS)". Cybercrime may threaten a person or a nation's security and financial health. Issues surrounding these types of crimes have become high-profile, particularly those surrounding hacking, copyright infringement, unwarranted mass-surveillance, child pornography, and child grooming. There are also problems of privacy when confidential information is intercepted or disclosed, lawfully or otherwise. Debarati Halder and K. Jaishankar further define cybercrime from the perspective of gender and defined 'cybercrime against women' as "Crimes targeted against women with a motive to intentionally harm the victim psychologically and physically, using modern telecommunication networks such as internet and mobile phones". Internationally, both governmental and non-state actors engage in cybercrimes, including espionage, financial theft, and other cross-border crimes. Activity crossing international borders and involving the interests of at least one nation state is sometimes referred to as cyberwarfare.

A report (sponsored by McAfee) estimates that the annual damage to the global economy is at $445 billion; however, a Microsoft report shows that such survey-based estimates are "hopelessly flawed" and exaggerate the true losses by orders of magnitude. Approximately $1.5 billion was lost in 2012 to online credit and debit card fraud in the US. In 2016, a study by Juniper Research estimated that the costs of cybercrime could be as high as 2.1 trillion by 2019.

Classification

Computer crime encompasses a broad range of activities.

Fraud and Financial Crimes

Computer fraud is any dishonest misrepresentation of fact intended to let another to do or refrain from doing something which causes loss. In this context, the fraud will result in obtaining a benefit by:

- Altering in an unauthorized way. This requires little technical expertise and is common form of theft by employees altering the data before entry or entering false data, or by entering unauthorized instructions or using unauthorized processes;

- Altering, destroying, suppressing, or stealing output, usually to conceal unauthorized transactions. This is difficult to detect;

- Altering or deleting stored data;

Other forms of fraud may be facilitated using computer systems, including bank fraud, carding, identity theft, extortion, and theft of classified information.

A variety of internet scams, many based on phishing and social engineering, target consumers and businesses.

Cyberterrorism

Government officials and information technology security specialists have documented a significant increase in Internet problems and server scans since early 2001. But there is a growing concern among federal officials that such intrusions are part of an organized effort by cyberterrorists, foreign intelligence services, or other groups to map potential security holes in critical systems. A cyberterrorist is someone who intimidates or coerces a government or organization to advance his or her political or social objectives by launching a computer-based attack against computers, networks, or the information stored on them.

Cyberterrorism in general can be defined as an act of terrorism committed through the use of cyberspace or computer resources (Parker 1983). As such, a simple propaganda piece in the Internet that there will be bomb attacks during the holidays can be considered cyberterrorism. There are also hacking activities directed towards individuals, families, organized by groups within networks, tending to cause fear among people, demonstrate power, collecting information relevant for ruining peoples' lives, robberies, blackmailing etc.

Cyberextortion

Cyberextortion occurs when a website, e-mail server, or computer system is subjected to or threatened with repeated denial of service or other attacks by malicious hackers. These hackers demand money in return for promising to stop the attacks and to offer "protection". According to the Federal Bureau of Investigation, cyberextortionists are increasingly attacking corporate websites and networks, crippling their ability to operate and demanding payments to restore their service. More than 20 cases are reported each month to the FBI and many go unreported in order to keep the victim's name out of the public domain. Perpetrators typically use a distributed denial-of-service attack.

An example of cyberextortion was the attack on Sony Pictures of 2014.

Cyberwarfare

The U.S. Department of Defense (DoD) notes that the cyberspace has emerged as a national-level concern through several recent events of geo-strategic significance. Among those are included, the attack on Estonia's infrastructure in 2007, allegedly by Russian hackers. "In August 2008, Russia again allegedly conducted cyberattacks, this time in a coordinated and synchronized kinetic and non-kinetic campaign against the country of Georgia. Fearing that such attacks may become the norm in future warfare among nation-states, the concept of cyberspace operations impacts and will be adapted by warfighting military commanders in the future.

Sailors analyze, detect and defensively respond to unauthorized activity within U.S. Navy information systems and computer networks

Computer as a Target

These crimes are committed by a selected group of criminals. Unlike crimes using the computer as a tool, these crimes require the technical knowledge of the perpetrators. As such, as technology evolves, so too does the nature of the crime. These crimes are relatively new, having been in existence for only as long as computers have—which explains how unprepared society and the world in general is towards combating these crimes. There are numerous crimes of this nature committed daily on the internet:

Crimes that primarily target computer networks or devices include:

- Computer viruses

- Denial-of-service attacks

- Malware (malicious code)

Computer as a Tool

When the individual is the main target of cybercrime, the computer can be considered as the tool rather than the target. These crimes generally involve less technical expertise. Human weaknesses are generally exploited. The damage dealt is largely psychological and intangible, making legal action against the variants more difficult. These are the crimes which have existed for centuries in the offline world. Scams, theft, and the likes have existed even before the development in high-tech equipment. The same criminal has simply been given a tool which increases his potential pool of victims and makes him all the harder to trace and apprehend.

Crimes that use computer networks or devices to advance other ends include:

- Fraud and identity theft (although this increasingly uses malware, hacking and/or phishing, making it an example of both "computer as target" and "computer as tool" crime)

- Information warfare

- Phishing scams

- Spam

- Propagation of illegal obscene or offensive content, including harassment and threats

The unsolicited sending of bulk email for commercial purposes (spam) is unlawful in some jurisdictions.

Phishing is mostly propagated via email. Phishing emails may contain links to other websites that are affected by malware. Or, they may contain links to fake online banking or other websites used to steal private account information.

Obscene or Offensive Content

The content of websites and other electronic communications may be distasteful, obscene or offensive for a variety of reasons. In some instances these communications may be legal.

The extent to which these communications are unlawful varies greatly between countries, and even within nations. It is a sensitive area in which the courts can become involved in arbitrating between groups with strong beliefs.

One area of Internet pornography that has been the target of the strongest efforts at curtailment is child pornography.

Harassment

Various aspects needed to be considered when understanding harassment online.

Whereas content may be offensive in a non-specific way, harassment directs obscenities and derogatory comments at specific individuals focusing for example on gender, race, religion, nationality, sexual orientation. This often occurs in chat rooms, through newsgroups, and by sending hate e-mail to interested parties. Harassment on the internet also includes revenge porn.

There are instances where committing a crime using a computer can lead to an enhanced sentence. For example, in the case of United States v. Neil Scott Kramer, Kramer was served an enhanced sentence according to the U.S. Sentencing Guidelines Manual 2G1.3(b)(3) for his use of a cell phone to "persuade, induce, entice, coerce, or facilitate the travel of, the minor to engage in prohibited sexual conduct." Kramer argued that this claim was insufficient because his charge included persuading through a computer device and his cellular phone technically is not a computer. Although Kramer tried to argue this point, U.S. Sentencing Guidelines Manual states that the term computer "means an electronic, magnetic, optical, electrochemically, or other high speed data processing device performing logical, arithmetic, or storage functions, and includes any data storage facility or communications facility directly related to or operating in conjunction with such device."

Connecticut was the U.S. state to pass a statute making it a criminal offense to harass someone by computer. Michigan, Arizona, and Virginia and South Carolina have also passed laws banning harassment by electronic means.

Harassment as defined in the U.S. computer statutes is typically distinct from cyberbullying, in that the former usually relates to a person's "use a computer or computer network to communicate obscene, vulgar, profane, lewd, lascivious, or indecent language, or make any suggestion or proposal of an obscene nature, or threaten any illegal or immoral act," while the latter need not involve anything of a sexual nature.

Although freedom of speech is protected by law in most democratic societies (in the US this is done by the First Amendment), it does not include all types of speech. In fact spoken or written "true threat" speech/text is criminalized because of "intent to harm or intimidate", that also applies for online or any type of network related threats in written text or speech. The US Supreme Court definition of "true threat" is "statements where the speaker means to communicate a serious expression of an intent to commit an act of unlawful violence to a particular individual or group".

Drug Trafficking

Darknet markets are used to buy and sell recreational drugs online. Some drug traffickers use encrypted messaging tools to communicate with drug mules. The dark web site Silk Road was a major online marketplace for drugs before it was shut down by law enforcement (then reopened under new management, and then shut down by law enforcement again). After Silk Road 2.0 went down, Silk Road 3 Reloaded emerged. However, it was just an older marketplace named Diabolus Market, that used the name for more exposure from the brand's previous success.

Documented Cases

- One of the highest profiled banking computer crime occurred during a course of three years beginning in 1970. The chief teller at the Park Avenue branch of New York's Union Dime Savings Bank embezzled over $1.5 million from hundreds of accounts.

- A hacking group called MOD (Masters of Deception), allegedly stole passwords and technical data from Pacific Bell, Nynex, and other telephone companies as well as several big credit agencies and two major universities. The damage caused was extensive, one company, Southwestern Bell suffered losses of $370,000 alone.

- In 1983, a nineteen-year-old UCLA student used his PC to break into a Defense Department international communications system.

- Between 1995 and 1998 the Newscorp satellite pay to view encrypted SKY-TV service was hacked several times during an ongoing technological arms race between a pan-European hacking group and Newscorp. The original motivation of the hackers was to watch Star Trek re-runs in Germany; which was something which Newscorp did not have the copyright to allow.

- On 26 March 1999, the Melissa worm infected a document on a victim's computer, then automatically sent that document and a copy of the virus spread via e-mail to other people.

- In February 2000, an individual going by the alias of MafiaBoy began a series denial-of-service attacks against high-profile websites, including Yahoo!, Amazon.com, Dell, Inc., E*TRADE, eBay, and CNN. About fifty computers at Stanford University, and also computers at the University of California at Santa Barbara, were amongst the zombie computers sending pings in DDoS attacks. On 3 August 2000, Canadian federal prosecutors charged MafiaBoy with 54 counts of illegal access to computers, plus a total of ten counts of mischief to data for his attacks.

- The Russian Business Network (RBN) was registered as an internet site in 2006. Initially, much of its activity was legitimate. But apparently the founders soon discovered that it was more profitable to host illegitimate activities and started hiring its services to criminals. The RBN has been described by VeriSign as "the baddest of the bad". It offers web hosting services and internet access to all kinds of criminal and objectionable activities, with an individual activities earning up to $150 million in one year. It specialized in and in some cases monopolized personal identity theft for resale. It is the originator of MPack and an alleged operator of the now defunct Storm botnet.

- On 2 March 2010, Spanish investigators arrested 3 in infection of over 13 million computers around the world. The "botnet" of infected computers included PCs inside more than half of the Fortune 1000 companies and more than 40 major banks, according to investigators.

- In August 2010 the international investigation Operation Delego, operating under the aegis of the Department of Homeland Security, shut down the international pedophile ring Dreamboard. The website had approximately 600 members, and may have distributed up to 123 terabytes of child pornography (roughly equivalent to 16,000 DVDs). To date this is the single largest U.S. prosecution of an international child pornography ring; 52 arrests were made worldwide.

- In January 2012 Zappos.com experienced a security breach after as many as 24 million customers' credit card numbers, personal information, billing and shipping addresses had been compromised.

- In June 2012 LinkedIn and eHarmony were attacked, compromising 65 million password hashes. 30,000 passwords were cracked and 1.5 million EHarmony passwords were posted online.

- December 2012 Wells Fargo website experienced a denial of service attack. Potentially compromising 70 million customers and 8.5 million active viewers. Other banks thought to be compromised: Bank of America, J. P. Morgan U.S. Bank, and PNC Financial Services.

- April 23, 2013 saw the Associated Press' Twitter account's hacked - the hacker posted a hoax tweet about fictitious attacks in the White House that they claimed left President Obama injured. This hoax tweet resulted in a brief plunge of 130 points from the Dow

Jones Industrial Average, removal of $136 billion from S&P 500 index, and the temporary suspension of AP's Twitter account. The Dow Jones later restored its session gains.

- In October, 2013 Ingenico's Indian subsidiary EBS (E-Billing Solutions) software was used/abused by cybercriminals to prevent the payment for the IT service of renewal of the domain name, or nodename, Hydro Dot Net. The web address Hydro Dot Net was then deleted by the IT services company rather than renewed, and immediately re-registered by BigRock (India) to be sold at auction to the highest bidder on the SnapNames website, in what some consider to be domain hijacking. Due to the fact that both PDR and BigRock are registrars and are subsidiaries of Directi, the standard "dispute" procedures for contested domains were circumvented. The registrant had successfully completed the payment for renewal via EBS (Ingenico), and additionally paid via wire-transfer bank-to-bank, from Japan Post Savings to Axis Bank at Jaipur Raj, but the cybercriminals had already committed themselves to completing the various legal violations (including a clause of the Companies Act of India concerning CEO's and IT), held the wrongfully lost web address at Directi's BigRock, having maintained the registrar of record (PublicDomainRegistry.com, also of Directi) until after the auction. The wrongfully taken web-address was then laundered via GoDaddy in the US. In this case, although both ICANN and IANA had been alerted to the cybercrime, the "Emergency Action Channel" was not effective, and the cybercrime case remains unsolved. In May of 2009, United States law enforcement served a criminal indictment followed by the world's first arrest for domain hijacking as cybercrime. Although most of the procedures of domain registration and transfer are common, the case of Hydro Dot Net was a case in which the domain-hosting backend was exploited at the point of payment for its renewal, thereby causing its wrongful loss.

- In May 2017, 74 countries logged a ransomware cybercrime, called "WannaCry"

Combating Computer Crime

Diffusion of Cybercrime

The broad diffusion of cybercriminal activities is an issue in computer crimes detection and prosecution. According to Jean-Loup Richet (Research Fellow at ESSEC ISIS), technical expertise and accessibility no longer act as barriers to entry into cybercrime. Indeed, hacking is much less complex than it was a few years ago, as hacking communities have greatly diffused their knowledge through the Internet. Blogs and communities have hugely contributed to information sharing: beginners could benefit from older hackers' knowledge and advice. Furthermore, Hacking is cheaper than ever: before the cloud computing era, in order to spam or scam one needed a dedicated server, skills in server management, network configuration, and maintenance, knowledge of Internet service provider standards, etc. By comparison, a mail software-as-a-service is a scalable, inexpensive, bulk, and transactional e-mail-sending service for marketing purposes and could be easily set up for spam. Jean-Loup Richet explains that cloud computing could be helpful for a cybercriminal as a way to leverage his attack – brute-forcing a password, improve the reach of a botnet, or facilitating a spamming campaign.

Investigation

A computer can be a source of evidence. Even where a computer is not directly used for criminal purposes, it may contain records of value to criminal investigators in the form of a logfile. In most countries Internet Service Providers are required, by law, to keep their logfiles for a predetermined amount of time. For example; a European wide Data Retention Directive (applicable to all EU member states) states that all E-mail traffic should be retained for a minimum of 12 months.

Legislation

Due to easily exploitable laws, cybercriminals use developing countries in order to evade detection and prosecution from law enforcement. In developing countries, such as the Philippines, laws against cybercrime are weak or sometimes nonexistent. These weak laws allow cybercriminals to strike from international borders and remain undetected. Even when identified, these criminals avoid being punished or extradited to a country, such as the United States, that has developed laws that allow for prosecution. While this proves difficult in some cases, agencies, such as the FBI, have used deception and subterfuge to catch criminals. For example, two Russian hackers had been evading the FBI for some time. The FBI set up a fake computing company based in Seattle, Washington. They proceeded to lure the two Russian men into the United States by offering them work with this company. Upon completion of the interview, the suspects were arrested outside of the building. Clever tricks like this are sometimes a necessary part of catching cybercriminals when weak legislation makes it impossible otherwise.

President Barack Obama released in an executive order in April 2015 to combat cybercrime. The executive order allows the United States to freeze assets of convicted cybercriminals and block their economic activity within the United States. This is some of the first solid legislation that combats cybercrime in this way.

The European Union adopted directive 2013/40/EU. All offences of the directive, and other definitions and procedural institutions are also in the Council of Europe's Convention on Cybercrime.

Penalties

Penalties for computer related crimes in New York State can range from a fine and a short period of jail time for a Class A misdemeanor such as unauthorized use of a computer up to computer tampering in the first degree which is a Class C felony and can carry 3 to 15 years in prison.

However, some hackers have been hired as information security experts by private companies due to their inside knowledge of computer crime, a phenomenon which theoretically could create perverse incentives. A possible counter to this is for courts to ban convicted hackers from using the Internet or computers, even after they have been released from prison – though as computers and the Internet become more and more central to everyday life, this type of punishment may be viewed as more and more harsh and draconian. However, nuanced approaches have been developed that manage cyberoffender behavior without resorting to total computer and/or Internet bans. These approaches involve restricting individuals to specific devices which are subject to computer monitoring and/or computer searches by probation and/or parole officers.

Awareness

As technology advances and more people rely on the internet to store sensitive information such as banking or credit card information, criminals are going to attempt to steal that information. Cyber-crime is becoming more of a threat to people across the world. Raising awareness about how information is being protected and the tactics criminals use to steal that information is important in today's world. According to the FBI's Internet Crime Complaint Center in 2014 there were 269,422 complaints filed. With all the claims combined there was a reported total loss of $800,492,073. But yet cyber-crime doesn't seem to be on the average person's radar. There are 1.5 million cyber-attacks annually, that means that there are over 4,000 attacks a day, 170 attacks every hour, or nearly three attacks every minute, with studies showing us that only 16% of victims had asked the people who were carrying out the attacks to stop. Anybody who uses the internet for any reason can be a victim, which is why it is important to be aware of how one is being protected while online.

Agencies

- Australian High Tech Crime Centre

- National White Collar Crime Center

Security Hacker

A security hacker is someone who seeks to breach defenses and exploit weaknesses in a computer system or network. Hackers may be motivated by a multitude of reasons, such as profit, protest, information gathering, challenge, recreation, or to evaluate system weaknesses to assist in formulating defenses against potential hackers. The subculture that has evolved around hackers is often referred to as the computer underground.

There is a longstanding controversy about the term's true meaning. In this controversy, the term *hacker* is reclaimed by computer programmers who argue that it refers simply to someone with an advanced understanding of computers and computer networks, and that *cracker* is the more appropriate term for those who break into computers, whether computer criminal (black hats) or computer security expert (white hats). A 2014 article concluded that "... the black-hat meaning still prevails among the general public".

History

Bruce Sterling, author of *The Hacker Crackdown*

In computer security, a hacker is someone who focuses on security mechanisms of computer and network systems. While including those who endeavor to strengthen such mechanisms, it is more often used by the mass media and popular culture to refer to those who seek access despite these security measures. That is, the media portrays the 'hacker' as a villain. Nevertheless, parts of the subculture see their aim in correcting security problems and use the word in a positive sense. White hat is the name given to ethical computer hackers, who utilize hacking in a helpful way. White hats are becoming a necessary part of the information security field. They operate under a code, which acknowledges that breaking into other people's computers is bad, but that discovering and exploiting security mechanisms and breaking into computers is still an interesting activity that can be done ethically and legally. Accordingly, the term bears strong connotations that are favorable or pejorative, depending on the context.

The subculture around such hackers is termed network hacker subculture, hacker scene or computer underground. It initially developed in the context of phreaking during the 1960s and the microcomputer BBS scene of the 1980s. It is implicated with *2600: The Hacker Quarterly* and the *alt.2600* newsgroup.

In 1980, an article in the August issue of *Psychology Today* (with commentary by Philip Zimbardo) used the term "hacker" in its title: "The Hacker Papers". It was an excerpt from a Stanford Bulletin Board discussion on the addictive nature of computer use. In the 1982 film *Tron*, Kevin Flynn (Jeff Bridges) describes his intentions to break into ENCOM's computer system, saying "I've been doing a little hacking here". CLU is the software he uses for this. By 1983, hacking in the sense of breaking computer security had already been in use as computer jargon, but there was no public awareness about such activities. However, the release of the film *WarGames* that year, featuring a computer intrusion into NORAD, raised the public belief that computer security hackers (especially teenagers) could be a threat to national security. This concern became real when, in the same year, a gang of teenage hackers in Milwaukee, Wisconsin, known as The 414s, broke into computer systems throughout the United States and Canada, including those of Los Alamos National Laboratory, Sloan-Kettering Cancer Center and Security Pacific Bank. The case quickly grew media attention, and 17-year-old Neal Patrick emerged as the spokesman for the gang, including a cover story in *Newsweek* entitled "Beware: Hackers at play", with Patrick's photograph on the cover. The *Newsweek* article appears to be the first use of the word *hacker* by the mainstream media in the pejorative sense.

Pressured by media coverage, congressman Dan Glickman called for an investigation and began work on new laws against computer hacking. Neal Patrick testified before the U.S. House of Representatives on September 26, 1983, about the dangers of computer hacking, and six bills concerning computer crime were introduced in the House that year. As a result of these laws against computer criminality, white hat, grey hat and black hat hackers try to distinguish themselves from each other, depending on the legality of their activities. These moral conflicts are expressed in The Mentor's "The Hacker Manifesto", published 1986 in *Phrack*.

Use of the term hacker meaning computer criminal was also advanced by the title "Stalking the Wily Hacker", an article by Clifford Stoll in the May 1988 issue of the *Communications of the ACM*. Later that year, the release by Robert Tappan Morris, Jr. of the so-called Morris worm provoked the popular media to spread this usage. The popularity of Stoll's book *The Cuckoo's Egg*, published one year later, further entrenched the term in the public's consciousness.

Classifications

Several subgroups of the computer underground with different attitudes use different terms to demarcate themselves from each other, or try to exclude some specific group with whom they do not agree.

Eric S. Raymond, author of *The New Hacker's Dictionary*, advocates that members of the computer underground should be called crackers. Yet, those people see themselves as hackers and even try to include the views of Raymond in what they see as a wider hacker culture, a view that Raymond has harshly rejected. Instead of a hacker/cracker dichotomy, they emphasize a spectrum of different categories, such as white hat, grey hat, black hat and script kiddie. In contrast to Raymond, they usually reserve the term *cracker* for more malicious activity.

According to Ralph D. Clifford, a *cracker* or *cracking* is to "gain unauthorized access to a computer in order to commit another crime such as destroying information contained in that system". These subgroups may also be defined by the legal status of their activities.

White Hat

A white hat hacker breaks security for non-malicious reasons, either to test their own security system, perform penetration tests or vulnerability assessments for a client - or while working for a security company which makes security software. The term is generally synonymous with ethical hacker, and the EC-Council, among others, have developed certifications, courseware, classes, and online training covering the diverse arena of ethical hacking.

Black Hat

A "black hat" hacker is a hacker who "violates computer security for little reason beyond maliciousness or for personal gain" (Moore, 2005). The term was coined by Richard Stallman, to contrast the maliciousness of a criminal hacker versus the spirit of playfulness and exploration in hacker culture, or the ethos of the white hat hacker who performs hacking duties to identify places to repair or as a means of legitimate employment. Black hat hackers form the stereotypical, illegal hacking groups often portrayed in popular culture, and are "the epitome of all that the public fears in a computer criminal".

Grey Hat

A grey hat hacker lies between a black hat and a white hat hacker. A grey hat hacker may surf the Internet and hack into a computer system for the sole purpose of notifying the administrator that their system has a security defect, for example. They may then offer to correct the defect for a fee. Grey hat hackers sometimes find the defect of a system and publish the facts to the world instead of a group of people. Even though grey hat hackers may not necessarily perform hacking for their personal gain, unauthorized access to a system can be considered illegal and unethical.

Elite Hacker

A social status among hackers, *elite* is used to describe the most skilled. Newly discovered exploits circulate among these hackers. Elite groups such as Masters of Deception conferred a kind of credibility on their members.

Script Kiddie

A script kiddie (also known as a *skid* or *skiddie*) is an unskilled hacker who breaks into computer systems by using automated tools written by others (usually by other black hat hackers), hence the term script (i.e. a prearranged plan or set of activities) kiddie (i.e. kid, child—an individual lacking knowledge and experience, immature), usually with little understanding of the underlying concept.

Neophyte

A neophyte ("newbie", or "noob") is someone who is new to hacking or phreaking and has almost no knowledge or experience of the workings of technology and hacking.

Blue Hat

A blue hat hacker is someone outside computer security consulting firms who is used to bug-test a system prior to its launch, looking for exploits so they can be closed. Microsoft also uses the term *BlueHat* to represent a series of security briefing events.

Hacktivist

A hacktivist is a hacker who utilizes technology to publicize a social, ideological, religious or political message.

Hacktivism can be divided into two main groups:

- Cyberterrorism — Activities involving website defacement or denial-of-service attacks; and,

- Freedom of information — Making information that is not public, or is public in non-machine-readable formats, accessible to the public.

Nation state

Intelligence agencies and cyberwarfare operatives of nation states.

Organized Criminal Gangs

Groups of hackers that carry out organized criminal activities for profit.

Attacks

A typical approach in an attack on Internet-connected system is:

1. Network enumeration: Discovering information about the intended target.

2. Vulnerability analysis: Identifying potential ways of attack.

3. Exploitation: Attempting to compromise the system by employing the vulnerabilities found through the vulnerability analysis.

In order to do so, there are several recurring tools of the trade and techniques used by computer criminals and security experts.

Security Exploits

A security exploit is a prepared application that takes advantage of a known weakness. Common examples of security exploits are SQL injection, cross-site scripting and cross-site request forgery which abuse security holes that may result from substandard programming practice. Other exploits would be able to be used through File Transfer Protocol (FTP), Hypertext Transfer Protocol (HTTP), PHP, SSH, Telnet and some Web pages. These are very common in Web site and Web domain hacking.

Techniques

Vulnerability scanner

> A vulnerability scanner is a tool used to quickly check computers on a network for known weaknesses. Hackers also commonly use port scanners. These check to see which ports on a specified computer are "open" or available to access the computer, and sometimes will detect what program or service is listening on that port, and its version number. (Firewalls defend computers from intruders by limiting access to ports and machines, but they can still be circumvented.)

Finding vulnerabilities

> Hackers may also attempt to find vulnerabilities manually. A common approach is to search for possible vulnerabilities in the code of the computer system then test them, sometimes reverse engineering the software if the code is not provided.

Brute-force attack

> Password guessing. This method is very fast when used to check all short passwords, but for longer passwords other methods such as the dictionary attack are used, because of the time a brute-force search takes.

Password cracking

> Password cracking is the process of recovering passwords from data that has been stored in or transmitted by a computer system. Common approaches include repeatedly trying guesses for the password, trying the most common passwords by hand, and repeatedly trying passwords from a "dictionary", or a text file with many passwords.

Packet analyzer

> A packet analyzer ("packet sniffer") is an application that captures data packets, which can be used to capture passwords and other data in transit over the network.

Spoofing attack (phishing)

> A spoofing attack involves one program, system or website that successfully masquerades as another by falsifying data and is thereby treated as a trusted system by a user or another program — usually to fool programs, systems or users into revealing confidential information, such as user names and passwords.

Rootkit

A rootkit is a program that uses low-level, hard-to-detect methods to subvert control of an operating system from its legitimate operators. Rootkits usually obscure their installation and attempt to prevent their removal through a subversion of standard system security. They may include replacements for system binaries, making it virtually impossible for them to be detected by checking process tables.

Social engineering

In the second stage of the targeting process, hackers often use Social engineering tactics to get enough information to access the network. They may contact the system administrator and pose as a user who cannot get access to his or her system. This technique is portrayed in the 1995 film *Hackers*, when protagonist Dade "Zero Cool" Murphy calls a somewhat clueless employee in charge of security at a television network. Posing as an accountant working for the same company, Dade tricks the employee into giving him the phone number of a modem so he can gain access to the company's computer system.

Hackers who use this technique must have cool personalities, and be familiar with their target's security practices, in order to trick the system administrator into giving them information. In some cases, a help-desk employee with limited security experience will answer the phone and be relatively easy to trick. Another approach is for the hacker to pose as an angry supervisor, and when his/her authority is questioned, threaten to fire the help-desk worker. Social engineering is very effective, because users are the most vulnerable part of an organization. No security devices or programs can keep an organization safe if an employee reveals a password to an unauthorized person.

Social engineering can be broken down into four sub-groups:

- *Intimidation* As in the "angry supervisor" technique above, the hacker convinces the person who answers the phone that their job is in danger unless they help them. At this point, many people accept that the hacker is a supervisor and give them the information they seek.

- *Helpfulness* The opposite of intimidation, helpfulness exploits many people's natural instinct to help others solve problems. Rather than acting angry, the hacker acts distressed and concerned. The help desk is the most vulnerable to this type of social engineering, as (a.) its general purpose is to help people; and (b.) it usually has the authority to change or reset passwords, which is exactly what the hacker wants.

- *Name-dropping* The hacker uses names of authorized users to convince the person who answers the phone that the hacker is a legitimate user him or herself. Some of these names, such as those of webpage owners or company officers, can easily be obtained online. Hackers have also been known to obtain names by examining discarded documents (so-called "dumpster diving").

- *Technical* Using technology is also a way to get information. A hacker can send a fax or email to a legitimate user, seeking a response that contains vital information.

The hacker may claim that he or she is involved in law enforcement and needs certain data for an investigation, or for record-keeping purposes.

Trojan horses

A Trojan horse is a program that seems to be doing one thing but is actually doing another. It can be used to set up a back door in a computer system, enabling the intruder to gain access later. (The name refers to the horse from the Trojan War, with the conceptually similar function of deceiving defenders into bringing an intruder into a protected area.)

Computer virus

A virus is a self-replicating program that spreads by inserting copies of itself into other executable code or documents. By doing this, it behaves similarly to a biological virus, which spreads by inserting itself into living cells. While some viruses are harmless or mere hoaxes, most are considered malicious.

Computer worm

Like a virus, a worm is also a self-replicating program. It differs from a virus in that (a.) it propagates through computer networks without user intervention; and (b.) does not need to attach itself to an existing program. Nonetheless, many people use the terms "virus" and "worm" interchangeably to describe any self-propagating program.

Keystroke logging

A keylogger is a tool designed to record ("log") every keystroke on an affected machine for later retrieval, usually to allow the user of this tool to gain access to confidential information typed on the affected machine. Some keyloggers use virus-, trojan-, and rootkit-like methods to conceal themselves. However, some of them are used for legitimate purposes, even to enhance computer security. For example, a business may maintain a keylogger on a computer used at a point of sale to detect evidence of employee fraud.

Tools and Procedures

A thorough examination of hacker tools and procedures may be found in Cengage Learning's E|CSA certification workbook.

Notable Intruders and Criminal Hackers

Notable Security Hackers

- Andrew Auernheimer, sentenced to 3 years in prison, is a grey hat hacker whose security group Goatse Security exposed a flaw in AT&T's iPad security.

- Dan Kaminsky is a DNS expert who exposed multiple flaws in the protocol and investigated Sony's rootkit security issues in 2005. He has spoken in front of the United States Senate on technology issues.

- Ed Cummings (also known as Bernie S) is a longstanding writer for *2600: The Hacker Quarterly*. In 1995, he was arrested and charged with possession of technology that could be used for fraudulent purposes, and set legal precedents after being denied both a bail hearing and a speedy trial.

- Eric Corley (also known as Emmanuel Goldstein) is the longstanding publisher of *2600: The Hacker Quarterly*. He is also the founder of the Hackers on Planet Earth (HOPE) conferences. He has been part of the hacker community since the late 1970s.

- Gary McKinnon is a Scottish hacker who was facing extradition to the United States to face criminal charges. Many people in the UK called on the authorities to be lenient with McKinnon, who suffers from Asperger syndrome. The extradition has now been dropped.

- Gordon Lyon, known by the handle Fyodor, authored the Nmap Security Scanner as well as many network security books and web sites. He is a founding member of the Honeynet Project and Vice President of Computer Professionals for Social Responsibility.

- Guccifer 2.0, who claimed that he hacked into the Democratic National Committee (DNC) computer network.

- Jacob Appelbaum is an advocate, security researcher, and developer for the Tor project. He speaks internationally for usage of Tor by human rights groups and others concerned about Internet anonymity and censorship.

- Kevin Mitnick is a computer security consultant and author, formerly the most wanted computer criminal in United States history.

- Len Sassaman was a Belgian computer programmer and technologist who was also a privacy advocate.

- Meredith L. Patterson is a well-known technologist and biohacker who has presented research with Dan Kaminsky and Len Sassaman at many international security and hacker conferences.

- Michał Zalewski (lcamtuf) is a prominent security researcher.

- Rafael Núñez, a.k.a. RaFa, was a notorious hacker who was sought by the Federal Bureau of Investigation in 2001. He has since become a respected computer security consultant and an advocate of children's online safety.

- Solar Designer is the pseudonym of the founder of the Openwall Project.

Customs

The computer underground has produced its own specialized slang, such as 1337speak. Its members often advocate freedom of information, strongly opposing the principles of copyright, as well as the rights of free speech and privacy. Writing software and performing other activities to support these views is referred to as hacktivism. Some consider illegal cracking ethically justified for these goals; a common form is website defacement. The computer underground is frequently compared to the Wild West. It is common for hackers to use aliases to conceal their identities.

Hacker Groups and Conventions

The computer underground is supported by regular real-world gatherings called hacker conventions or "hacker cons". These events include SummerCon (Summer), DEF CON, HoHoCon (Christmas), ShmooCon (February), BlackHat, Chaos Communication Congress, AthCon, Hacker Halted, and HOPE. Local Hackfest groups organize and compete to develop their skills to send a team to a prominent convention to compete in group pentesting, exploit and forensics on a larger scale. Hacker groups became popular in the early 1980s, providing access to hacking information and resources and a place to learn from other members. Computer bulletin board systems (BBSs), such as the Utopias, provided platforms for information-sharing via dial-up modem. Hackers could also gain credibility by being affiliated with elite groups.

Consequences for Malicious Hacking

India

Section	Offence	Punishment
65	*Tampering with computer source documents* – Intentional concealment, destruction or alteration of source code when the computer source code is required to be kept or maintained by law for the time being in force	Imprisonment up to three years, or/and with fine up to 20000 rupees
66	Hacking	Imprisonment up to three years, or/and with fine up to 50000 rupees

Netherlands

- Article 138ab of Wetboek van Strafrecht prohibits *computervredebreuk*, which is defined as intruding an automated work or a part thereof with intention and against the law. Intrusion is defined as access by means of:

    o   Defeating security measures

    o   By technical means

    o   By false signals or a false cryptographic key

    o   By the use of stolen usernames and passwords.

Maximum imprisonment is one year or a fine of the fourth category.

United States

18 U.S.C. 1030, more commonly known as the Computer Fraud and Abuse Act, prohibits unauthorized access or damage of "protected computers". "Protected computers" are defined in 18 U.S.C. 1030(e)(2) as:

- A computer exclusively for the use of a financial institution or the United States Government, or, in the case of a computer not exclusively for such use, used by or for a financial institution or the United States Government and the conduct constituting the offense affects that use by or for the financial institution or the Government.

- A computer which is used in or affecting interstate or foreign commerce or communication, including a computer located outside the United States that is used in a manner that affects interstate or foreign commerce or communication of the United States;

The maximum imprisonment or fine for violations of the *Computer Fraud and Abuse Act* depends on the severity of the violation and the offender's history of violations under the *Act*.

Hacking and the Media

Hacker Magazines

The most notable hacker-oriented print publications are *Phrack*, *Haking9* and *2600: The Hacker Quarterly*. While the information contained in hacker magazines and ezines was often outdated by the time they were published, they enhanced their contributors' reputations by documenting their successes.

Hackers in Fiction

Hackers often show an interest in fictional cyberpunk and cyberculture literature and movies. The adoption of fictional pseudonyms, symbols, values and metaphors from these works is very common.

Books

- The cyberpunk novels of William Gibson—especially the Sprawl trilogy—are very popular with hackers.

- Helba from the *hack* manga and anime series

- Merlin of Amber, the protagonist of the second series in *The Chronicles of Amber* by Roger Zelazny, is a young immortal hacker-mage prince who has the ability to traverse shadow dimensions.

- Lisbeth Salander in *The Girl with the Dragon Tattoo* by Stieg Larsson

- Alice from *Heaven's Memo Pad*

- *Ender's Game* by Orson Scott Card

- *Evil Genius* by Catherine Jinks

- *Hackers* (anthology) by Jack Dann and Gardner Dozois

- *Little Brother* by Cory Doctorow

- *Neuromancer* by William Gibson

- *Snow Crash* by Neal Stephenson

Films

- *Antitrust*

- *Blackhat*

- *Cypher*
- *Eagle Eye*
- *Enemy of the State*
- *Firewall*
- *Girl With The Dragon Tattoo*
- *Hackers*
- *Live Free or Die Hard*
- *The Matrix* series
- *The Net*
- *The Net 2.0*
- *Pirates of Silicon Valley*
- *Skyfall*
- *Sneakers*
- *Swordfish*
- *Take Down*
- *Tron*
- *Tron: Legacy*
- *Untraceable*
- *WarGames*
- *Weird Science*
- *The Fifth Estate*
- *Who Am I – No System Is Safe (film)*

Non-fiction books

- *The Art of Deception* by Kevin Mitnick
- *The Art of Intrusion* by Kevin Mitnick
- *The Cuckoo's Egg* by Clifford Stoll
- *Ghost in the Wires: My Adventures as the World's Most Wanted Hacker* by Kevin Mitnick
- *The Hacker Crackdown* by Bruce Sterling
- *The Hacker's Handbook* by Hugo Cornwall (Peter Sommer)
- *Hacking: The Art of Exploitation Second Edition* by Jon Erickson

- *Out of the Inner Circle* by Bill Landreth and Howard Rheingold

- *Underground* by Suelette Dreyfus

Copyright Infringement

An advertisement for copyright and patent preparation services from 1906, when copyright
registration formalities were still required in the US

Copyright infringement is the use of works protected by copyright law without permission, infringing certain exclusive rights granted to the copyright holder, such as the right to reproduce, distribute, display or perform the protected work, or to make derivative works. The copyright holder is typically the work's creator, or a publisher or other business to whom copyright has been assigned. Copyright holders routinely invoke legal and technological measures to prevent and penalize copyright infringement.

Copyright infringement disputes are usually resolved through direct negotiation, a notice and take down process, or litigation in civil court. Egregious or large-scale commercial infringement, especially when it involves counterfeiting, is sometimes prosecuted via the criminal justice system. Shifting public expectations, advances in digital technology, and the increasing reach of the Internet have led to such widespread, anonymous infringement that copyright-dependent industries now focus less on pursuing individuals who seek and share copyright-protected content online, and more on expanding copyright law to recognize and penalize – as "indirect" infringers – the service providers and software distributors which are said to facilitate and encourage individual acts of infringement by others.

Estimates of the actual economic impact of copyright infringement vary widely and depend on many factors. Nevertheless, copyright holders, industry representatives, and legislators have long characterized copyright infringement as *piracy* or *theft* – language which some U.S. courts now regard as pejorative or otherwise contentious.

Terminology

The terms *piracy* and *theft* are often associated with copyright infringement. The original meaning of *piracy* is "robbery or illegal violence at sea", but the term has been in use for centuries as a synonym for acts of copyright infringement. *Theft*, meanwhile, emphasizes the potential commercial harm of infringement to copyright holders. However, copyright is a type of intellectual property, an area of law distinct from that which covers robbery or theft, offenses related only to tangible property. Not all copyright infringement results in commercial loss, and the U.S. Supreme Court ruled in 1985 that infringement does not *easily* equate with theft.

"Piracy"

Pirated edition of German philosopher Alfred Schmidt (Amsterdam, ca. 1970)

The term "piracy" has been used to refer to the unauthorized copying, distribution and selling of works in copyright. The practice of labelling the infringement of exclusive rights in creative works as "piracy" predates statutory copyright law. Prior to the Statute of Anne in 1710, the Stationers' Company of London in 1557, received a Royal Charter giving the company a monopoly on publication and tasking it with enforcing the charter. Those who violated the charter were labelled pirates as early as 1603. Article 12 of the 1886 Berne Convention for the Protection of Literary and Artistic Works uses the term "piracy" in relation to copyright infringement, stating "Pirated works may be seized on importation into those countries of the Union where the original work enjoys legal protection." Article 61 of the 1994 Agreement on Trade-Related Aspects of Intellectual Property Rights (TRIPs) requires criminal procedures and penalties in cases of "willful trademark counterfeiting or copyright piracy on a commercial scale." Piracy traditionally refers to acts of copyright infringement intentionally committed for financial gain, though more recently, copyright holders have described online copyright infringement, particularly in relation to peer-to-peer file sharing networks, as "piracy."

Richard Stallman and the GNU Project have criticized the use of the word "piracy" in these situations, saying that publishers use the word to refer to "copying they don't approve of" and that "they [publishers] imply that it is ethically equivalent to attacking ships on the high seas, kidnapping and murdering the people on them."

"Theft"

Copyright holders frequently refer to copyright infringement as theft. In copyright law, infringement does not refer to theft of physical objects that take away the owner's possession, but an instance where a person exercises one of the exclusive rights of the copyright holder without authorization. Courts have distinguished between copyright infringement and theft. For instance, the United States Supreme Court held in *Dowling v. United States* (1985) that bootleg phonorecords did not constitute stolen property. Instead,

"interference with copyright does not easily equate with theft, conversion, or fraud. The Copyright Act even employs a separate term of art to define one who misappropriates a copyright: '[...] an infringer of the copyright.'"

The court said that in the case of copyright infringement, the province guaranteed to the copyright holder by copyright law – certain exclusive rights – is invaded, but no control, physical or otherwise, is taken over the copyright, nor is the copyright holder wholly deprived of using the copyrighted work or exercising the exclusive rights held.

"Freebooting"

The term "freebooting" has been used to describe the unauthorized rehosting of online media, particularly videos. The term was coined by YouTuber Brady Haran in the podcast *Hello Internet*, which he co-hosts. Haran reappropriated the term in an attempt to find a phrase more emotive than "copyright infringement," yet more appropriate than "theft."

Motivation

Some of the motives for engaging in copyright infringement are the following:

- Pricing – unwillingness or inability to pay the price requested by the legitimate sellers

- Unavailability – no legitimate sellers providing the product in the country of the end-user: not yet launched there, already withdrawn from sales, never to be sold there, geographical restrictions on online distribution and international shipping

- Usefulness – the legitimate product comes with various means (DRM, region lock, DVD region code, Blu-ray region code) of restricting legitimate use (backups, usage on devices of different vendors, offline usage) or comes with annoying non-skippable advertisements and anti-piracy disclaimers, which are removed in the unauthorized product making it more desirable for the end-user

- Shopping experience – no legitimate sellers providing the product with the required quality through online distribution and through a shopping system with the required level of user-friendliness

- Anonymity – downloading works does not require identification whereas downloads directly from the website of the copyright owner often require a valid email address and/ or other credentials

Sometimes only partial compliance with license agreements is the cause. For example, in 2013, the US Army settled a lawsuit with Texas-based company Apptricity, which makes software that allows the army to track their soldiers in real time. In 2004, the US Army paid US$4.5 million for a license of 500 users, while allegedly installing the software for more than 9000 users; the case was settled for US$50 million. Major anti-piracy organizations, like the BSA, conduct software licensing audits regularly to ensure full compliance.

Cara Cusumano, director of the Tribeca Film Festival, stated in April 2014: "Piracy is less about people not wanting to pay and more about just wanting the immediacy – people saying, 'I want to watch Spiderman right now' and downloading it". The statement occurred during the third year that the festival used the Internet to present its content, while it was the first year that it featured a showcase of content producers who work exclusively online. Cusumano further explained that downloading behavior is not merely conducted by people who merely want to obtain content for free:

I think that if companies were willing to put that material out there, moving forward, consumers will follow. It's just that they [consumers] want to consume films online and they're ready to consume films that way and we're not necessarily offering them in that way. So it's the distribution models that need to catch up. People will pay for the content.

In response to Cusumano's perspective, Screen Producers Australia executive director Matt Deaner clarified the motivation of the film industry: "Distributors are usually wanting to encourage cinema-going as part of this process [monetizing through returns] and restrict the immediate access to online so as to encourage the maximum number of people to go to the cinema." Deaner further explained the matter in terms of the Australian film industry, stating: "there are currently restrictions on quantities of tax support that a film can receive unless the film has a traditional cinema release."

In a study published in the *Journal of Behavioural and Experimental Economics*, and reported on in early May 2014, researchers from the University of Portsmouth in the UK discussed findings from examining the illegal downloading behavior of 6,000 Finnish people, aged seven to 84. The list of reasons for downloading given by the study respondents included money saving; the ability to access material not on general release, or before it was released; and assisting artists to avoid involvement with record companies and movie studios.

In a public talk between Bill Gates, Warren Buffett, and Brent Schlender at the University of Washington in 1998, Bill Gates commented on piracy as a means to an end, whereby people who use Microsoft software illegally will eventually pay for it, out of familiarity, as a country's economy develops and legitimate products become more affordable to businesses and consumers:

Although about three million computers get sold every year in China, people don't pay for the software. Someday they will, though. And as long as they're going to steal it, we want them to steal ours. They'll get sort of addicted, and then we'll somehow figure out how to collect sometime in the next decade.

Developing World

In Media Piracy in Emerging Economies, the first independent international comparative study of media piracy with center on Brazil, India, Russia, South Africa, Mexico, Turkey and Bolivia, "high prices for media goods, low incomes, and cheap digital technologies" are the chief factors that lead to the global spread of media piracy, especially in emerging markets.

According to the same study, even though digital piracy inflicts additional costs on the production side of media, it also offers the main access to media goods in developing countries. The strong tradeoffs that favor using digital piracy in developing economies dictate the current neglected law enforcements toward digital piracy. In China, the issue of digital infringement is not merely legal, but social – originating from the high demand for cheap and affordable goods as well as the governmental connections of the businesses which produce such goods.

Motivations Due to Censorship

There have been instances where a country's government bans a movie, resulting in the spread of copied videos and DVDs. Romanian-born documentary maker Ilinca Calugareanu wrote a *New York Times* article telling the story of Irina Margareta Nistor, a narrator for state TV under Nicolae Ceauşescu's regime. A visitor from the west gave her bootlegged copies of American movies, which she dubbed for secret viewings through Romania. According to the article, she dubbed more than 3,000 movies and became the country's second-most famous voice after Ceauşescu, even though no one knew her name until many years later.

Existing and Proposed Laws

Demonstration in Sweden in support of file sharing, 2006

The Pirate Bay

The Pirate Bay logo, a retaliation to the stereotypical image of piracy

Most countries extend copyright protections to authors of works. In countries with copyright legislation, enforcement of copyright is generally the responsibility of the copyright holder. However, in several jurisdictions there are also criminal penalties for copyright infringement.

Civil Law

Copyright infringement in civil law is any violation of the exclusive rights of the owner. In U.S. law, those rights include reproduction, the preparation of derivative works, distributing copies by sale or rental, and public performance or display.

In the U.S., copyright infringement is sometimes confronted via lawsuits in civil court, against alleged infringers directly, or against providers of services and software that support unauthorized copying. For example, major motion-picture corporation MGM Studios filed suit against P2P file-sharing services Grokster and Streamcast for their contributory role in copyright infringement. In 2005, the Supreme Court ruled in favor of MGM, holding that such services could be held liable for copyright infringement since they functioned and, indeed, willfully marketed themselves as venues for acquiring copyrighted movies. The *MGM v. Grokster* case did not overturn the earlier *Sony* decision, but rather clouded the legal waters; future designers of software capable of being used for copyright infringement were warned.

In the United States, copyright term has been extended many times over from the original term of 14 years with a single renewal allowance of 14 years, to the current term of the life of the author plus 70 years. If the work was produced under corporate authorship it may last 120 years after creation or 95 years after publication, whichever is sooner.

Article 50 of the Agreement on Trade-Related Aspects of Intellectual Property Rights (TRIPs) requires that signatory countries enable courts to remedy copyright infringement with injunctions and the destruction of infringing products, and award damages. Some jurisdictions only allow actual, provable damages, and some, like the U.S., allow for large statutory damage awards intended to deter would-be infringers and allow for compensation in situations where actual damages are difficult to prove.

In some jurisdictions, copyright or the right to enforce it can be contractually assigned to a third party which did not have a role in producing the work. When this outsourced litigator appears to have no intention of taking any copyright infringement cases to trial, but rather only takes them just far enough through the legal system to identify and exact settlements from suspected infringers, critics commonly refer to the party as a "copyright troll." Such practices have had mixed results in the U.S.

Criminal Law

Punishment of copyright infringement varies case-by-case across countries. Convictions may include jail time and/or severe fines for each instance of copyright infringement. In the United States, willful copyright infringement carries a maximum penalty of $150,000 per instance.

Article 61 of the Agreement on Trade-Related Aspects of Intellectual Property Rights (TRIPs) requires that signatory countries establish criminal procedures and penalties in cases of "willful trademark counterfeiting or copyright piracy on a commercial scale". Copyright holders have demanded that states provide criminal sanctions for all types of copyright infringement.

The first criminal provision in U.S. copyright law was added in 1897, which established a misdemeanor penalty for "unlawful performances and representations of copyrighted dramatic and musical compositions" if the violation had been "willful and for profit." Criminal copyright infringement requires that the infringer acted "for the purpose of commercial advantage or private financial gain." 17 U.S.C. 506. To establish criminal liability, the prosecutor must first show the basic elements of copyright infringement: ownership of a valid copyright, and the violation of one or more of the copyright holder's exclusive rights. The government must then establish that defendant willfully infringed or, in other words, possessed the necessary *mens rea*. Misdemeanor infringement has a very low threshold in terms of number of copies and the value of the infringed works.

The ACTA trade agreement, signed in May 2011 by the United States, Japan, and the EU, requires that its parties add criminal penalties, including incarceration and fines, for copyright and trademark infringement, and obligated the parties to actively police for infringement.

United States v. LaMacchia 871 F.Supp. 535 (1994) was a case decided by the United States District Court for the District of Massachusetts which ruled that, under the copyright and cybercrime laws effective at the time, committing copyright infringement for non-commercial motives could not be prosecuted under criminal copyright law. The ruling gave rise to what became known as the "LaMacchia Loophole," wherein criminal charges of fraud or copyright infringement would be dismissed under current legal standards, so long as there was no profit motive involved.

The United States No Electronic Theft Act (NET Act), a federal law passed in 1997, in response to LaMacchia, provides for criminal prosecution of individuals who engage in copyright infringement under certain circumstances, even when there is no monetary profit or commercial benefit from the infringement. Maximum penalties can be five years in prison and up to $250,000 in fines. The NET Act also raised statutory damages by 50%. The court's ruling explicitly drew attention to the shortcomings of current law that allowed people to facilitate mass copyright infringement while being immune to prosecution under the Copyright Act.

Proposed laws such as the Stop Online Piracy Act broaden the definition of "willful infringement", and introduce felony charges for unauthorized media streaming. These bills are aimed towards defeating websites that carry or contain links to infringing content, but have raised concerns about domestic abuse and internet censorship.

Noncommercial File Sharing

Legality of Downloading

To an extent, copyright law in some countries permits downloading copyright-protected content for personal, noncommercial use. Examples include Canada and European Union (EU) member states like Poland, and The Netherlands.

The personal copying exemption in the copyright law of EU member states stems from the EU Copyright Directive of 2001, which is generally devised to allow EU members to enact laws sanctioning making copies without authorization, as long as they are for personal, noncommercial use. The Copyright Directive was not intended to legitimize file-sharing, but rather the common practice of space shifting copyright-protected content from a legally purchased CD (for example) to certain kinds of devices and media, provided rights holders are compensated and no copy protection measures are circumvented. Rights-holder compensation takes various forms, depending on the country, but is generally either a levy on "recording" devices and media, or a tax on the content itself. In some countries, such as Canada, the applicability of such laws to copying onto general-purpose storage devices like computer hard drives, portable media players, and phones, for which no levies are collected, has been the subject of debate and further efforts to reform copyright law.

In some countries, the personal copying exemption explicitly requires that the content being copied was obtained legitimately – i.e., from authorized sources, not file-sharing networks. Other countries, such as the Netherlands, make no such distinction; the exemption there had been assumed, even by the government, to apply to any such copying, even from file-sharing networks. However, in April 2014, the Court of Justice of the European Union ruled that "national legislation which makes no distinction between private copies made from lawful sources and those made from counterfeited or pirated sources cannot be tolerated." Thus, in the Netherlands, for example, downloading from file-sharing networks is no longer legal.

Legality of Uploading

Although downloading or other private copying is sometimes permitted, public distribution – by uploading or otherwise offering to share copyright-protected content – remains illegal in most, if not all countries. For example, in Canada, even though it was once legal to download any copyrighted file as long as it was for noncommercial use, it was still illegal to distribute the copyrighted files (e.g. by uploading them to a P2P network).

Relaxed Penalties

Some countries, like Canada and Germany, have limited the penalties for non-commercial copyright infringement. For example, Germany has passed a bill to limit the fine for individuals accused of sharing music and movies to $200. Canada's Copyright Modernization Act claims that statutory damages for non-commercial copyright infringement are capped at C$5,000 but this only applies to copies that have been made without the breaking of any "digital lock". However, this only applies to "bootleg distribution" and not non-commercial use.

DMCA and Anti-circumvention Laws

Title I of the U.S. DMCA, the WIPO Copyright and Performances and Phonograms Treaties Implementation Act has provisions that prevent persons from "circumvent[ing] a technological measure that effectively controls access to a work". Thus if a distributor of copyrighted works has some kind of software, dongle or password access device installed in instances of the work, any attempt to bypass such a copy protection scheme may be actionable – though the US Copyright Office is currently reviewing anticircumvention rulemaking under DMCA – anti-circumvention exemptions that have been in place under the DMCA include those in software designed to filter websites that are generally seen to be inefficient (child safety and public library website filtering software) and the circumvention of copy protection mechanisms that have malfunctioned, have caused the instance of the work to become inoperable or which are no longer supported by their manufacturers. according to Abby House Media Inc v. Apple Inc it is legal to point users to DRM Stripping software and how to use it because of lack of evidence that DRM Stripping Leads to Copyright Infringement.

Online Intermediary Liability

Whether Internet intermediaries are liable for copyright infringement by their users is a subject of debate and court cases in a number of countries.

Definition of Intermediary

Internet intermediaries were formerly understood to be internet service providers (ISPs). However, questions of liability have also emerged in relation to other Internet infrastructure intermediaries, including Internet backbone providers, cable companies and mobile communications providers.

In addition, intermediaries are now also generally understood to include Internet portals, software and games providers, those providing virtual information such as interactive forums and comment facilities with or without a moderation system, aggregators of various kinds, such as news aggregators, universities, libraries and archives, web search engines, chat rooms, web blogs, mailing lists, and any website which provides access to third party content through, for example, hyperlinks, a crucial element of the World Wide Web.

Litigation and Legislation Concerning Intermediaries

Early court cases focused on the liability of Internet service providers (ISPs) for hosting, transmitting or publishing user-supplied content that could be actioned under civil or criminal law, such as libel, defamation, or pornography. As different content was considered in different legal systems, and in the absence of common definitions for "ISPs," "bulletin boards" or "online publishers," early law on online intermediaries' liability varied widely from country to country. The first laws on online intermediaries' liability were passed from the mid-1990s onwards.

The debate has shifted away from questions about liability for specific content, including that which may infringe copyright, towards whether online intermediaries should be *generally* responsible for content accessible through their services or infrastructure.

The U.S. Digital Millennium Copyright Act (1998) and the European E-Commerce Directive (2000) provide online intermediaries with limited statutory immunity from liability for copyright infringement. Online intermediaries hosting content that infringes copyright are not liable, so long as they do not know about it and take actions once the infringing content is brought to their attention. In U.S. law this is characterized as "safe harbor" provisions. Under European law, the governing principles for Internet Service Providers are "mere conduit", meaning that they are neutral 'pipes' with no knowledge of what they are carrying; and 'no obligation to monitor' meaning that they cannot be given a general mandate by governments to monitor content. These two principles are a barrier for certain forms of online copyright enforcement and they were the reason behind an attempt to amend the European Telecoms Package in 2009 to support new measures against copyright infringement.

Peer-to-peer Issues

Peer-to-peer file sharing intermediaries have been denied access to safe harbor provisions in relation to copyright infringement. Legal action against such intermediaries, such as Napster, are generally brought in relation to principles of secondary liability for copyright infringement, such as contributory liability and vicarious liability.

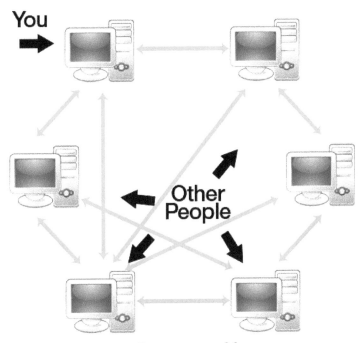

Peer-to-peer model

These types of intermediaries do not host or transmit infringing content, themselves, but may be regarded in some courts as encouraging, enabling or facilitating infringement by users. These intermediaries may include the author, publishers and marketers of peer-to-peer networking software, and the websites that allow users to download such software. In the case of the BitTorrent protocol, intermediaries may include the torrent tracker and any websites or search engines which facilitate access to torrent files. Torrent files don't contain copyrighted content, but they may make reference to files that do, and they may point to trackers which coordinate the sharing of those files. Some torrent indexing and search sites, such as The Pirate Bay, now encourage the use of magnet links, instead of direct links to torrent files, creating another layer of indirection; using such links, torrent files are obtained from other peers, rather than from a particular website.

Since the late 1990s, copyright holders have taken legal actions against a number of peer-to-peer intermediaries, such as pir, Grokster, eMule, SoulSeek, BitTorrent and Limewire, and case law on the liability of Internet service providers (ISPs) in relation to copyright infringement has emerged primarily in relation to these cases.

Nevertheless, whether and to what degree any of these types of intermediaries have secondary liability is the subject of ongoing litigation. The decentralised structure of peer-to-peer networks, in particular, does not sit easily with existing laws on online intermediaries' liability. The BitTorrent protocol established an entirely decentralised network architecture in order to distribute large files effectively. Recent developments in peer-to-peer technology towards more complex network configurations are said to have been driven by a desire to avoid liability as intermediaries under existing laws.

Limitations

Copyright law does not grant authors and publishers absolute control over the use of their work. Only certain types of works and certain kinds of uses are protected; only unauthorized uses of protected works can be said to be infringing.

Non-infringing Uses

Article 10 of the Berne Convention mandates that national laws provide for limitations to copyright, so that copyright protection does not extend to certain kinds of uses that fall under what the treaty calls "fair practice," including but not limited to minimal quotations used in journalism and education. The laws implementing these limitations and exceptions for uses that would otherwise be infringing broadly fall into the categories of either fair use or fair dealing. In common law systems, these fair practice statutes typically enshrine principles underlying many earlier judicial precedents, and are considered essential to freedom of speech.

Another example is the practice of compulsory licensing, which is where the law forbids copyright owners from denying a license for certain uses of certain kinds of works, such as compilations and live performances of music. Compulsory licensing laws generally say that for certain uses of certain works, no infringement occurs as long as a royalty, at a rate determined by law rather than private negotiation, is paid to the copyright owner or representative copyright collective. Some fair dealing laws, such as Canada's, include similar royalty requirements.

In Europe, the copyright infringement case Public Relations Consultants Association Ltd v Newspaper Licensing Agency Ltd had two prongs; one concerned whether a news aggregator service infringed the copyright of the news generators; the other concerned whether the temporary web cache created by the web browser of a consumer of the aggregator's service, *also* infringed the copyright of the news generators. The first prong was decided in favor of the news generators; in June 2014 the second prong was decided by the Court of Justice of the European Union (CJEU), which ruled that the temporary web cache of consumers of the aggregator did not infringe the copyright of the news generators.

Non-infringing Types of Works

In order to qualify for protection, a work must be an expression with a degree of originality, and it must be in a fixed medium, such as written down on paper or recorded digitally. The idea itself is not protected. That is, a copy of someone else's original idea is not infringing unless it copies that person's unique, tangible *expression* of the idea. Some of these limitations, especially regarding what qualifies as original, are embodied only in case law (judicial precedent), rather than in statutes.

In the U.S., for example, copyright case law contains a substantial similarity requirement to determine whether the work was copied. Likewise, courts may require computer software to pass an Abstraction-Filtration-Comparison test (AFC Test) to determine if it is too abstract to qualify for protection, or too dissimilar to an original work to be considered infringing. Software-related case law has also clarified that the amount of R&D, effort and expense put into a work's creation doesn't affect copyright protection.

Evaluation of alleged copyright infringement in a court of law may be substantial; the time and costs required to apply these tests vary based on the size and complexity of the copyrighted material. Furthermore, there is no standard or universally accepted test; some courts have rejected the AFC Test, for example, in favor of narrower criteria.

The POSAR test, a recently devised forensic procedure for establishing software copyright infringement cases, is an extension or an enhancement of the AFC test. POSAR, with its added features and additional facilities, offers something more to the legal and the judicial domain than what the AFC test offers. These additional features and facilities make the test more sensitive to the technical and legal requirements of software copyright infringement.

Preventative Measures

The BSA outlined four strategies that governments can adopt to reduce software piracy rates in its 2011 piracy study results:

- "Increase public education and raise awareness about software piracy and IP rights in cooperation with industry and law enforcement."

- "Modernize protections for software and other copyrighted materials to keep pace with new innovations such as cloud computing and the proliferation of networked mobile devices."

- "Strengthen enforcement of IP laws with dedicated resources, including specialized enforcement units, training for law enforcement and judiciary officials, improved cross-border cooperation among law enforcement agencies, and fulfillment of obligations under the World Trade Organization's Agreement on Trade-Related Aspects of Intellectual Property Rights (TRIPS)."

- "Lead by example by using only fully licensed software, implementing software asset management (SAM) programs, and promoting the use of legal software in state-owned enterprises, and among all contractors and suppliers."

Legal

Corporations and legislatures take different types of preventative measures to deter copyright infringement, with much of the focus since the early 1990s being on preventing or reducing digital methods of infringement. Strategies include education, civil & criminal legislation, and international agreements, as well as publicizing anti-piracy litigation successes and imposing forms of digital media copy protection, such as controversial DRM technology and anti-circumvention laws, which limit the amount of control consumers have over the use of products and content they have purchased.

Legislatures have reduced infringement by narrowing the scope of what is considered infringing. Aside from upholding international copyright treaty obligations to provide general limitations and exceptions, nations have enacted compulsory licensing laws applying specifically to digital works and uses. For example, in the U.S., the DMCA, an implementation of the 1996 WIPO Copyright Treaty, considers digital transmissions of audio recordings to be licensed as long as a designated copyright collective's royalty and reporting requirements are met. The DMCA also provides safe harbor for digital service providers whose users are suspected of copyright infringement, thus reducing the likelihood that the providers themselves will be considered directly infringing.

Some copyright owners voluntarily reduce the scope of what is considered infringement by employing relatively permissive, "open" licensing strategies: rather than privately negotiating license terms with individual users who must first seek out the copyright owner and ask for permission, the copyright owner publishes and distributes the work with a prepared license that anyone can use, as long as they adhere to certain conditions. This has the effect of reducing infringement – and the burden on courts – by simply permitting certain types of uses under terms that the copyright owner considers reasonable. Examples include free software licenses, like the GNU General Public License (GPL), and the Creative Commons licenses, which are predominantly applied to visual and literary works.

Protected Distribution

To prevent piracy of films, the standard drill of film distribution is to have a movie first released through movie theaters (theatrical window), on average approximately 16 and a half weeks, before having it released to Blu-Ray and DVD (entering its video window). During the theatrical window, digital versions of films are often transported in data storage devices by couriers rather than by data transmission. The data can be encrypted, with the key being made to work only at specific times in order to prevent leakage between screens. Coded Anti-Piracy marks can be added to films to identify the source of illegal copies and shut them down.

Economic Impact of Copyright Infringement

Organizations disagree on the scope and magnitude of copyright infringement's free rider economic effects and public support for the copyright regime.

In relation to computer software, the Business Software Alliance (BSA) claimed in its 2011 piracy study: "Public opinion continues to support intellectual property (IP) rights: Seven PC users in 10 support paying innovators to promote more technological advances."

Following consultation with experts on copyright infringement, the United States Government Accountability Office (GAO) clarified in 2010 that "estimating the economic impact of IP [intellectual property] infringements is extremely difficult, and assumptions must be used due to the absence of data," while "it is difficult, if not impossible, to quantify the net effect of counterfeiting and piracy on the economy as a whole."

The U.S. GAO's 2010 findings regarding the great difficulty of accurately gauging the economic impact of copyright infringement was reinforced within the same report by the body's research into three commonly cited estimates that had previously been provided to U.S. agencies. The GAO report explained that the sources – a Federal Bureau of Investigation (FBI) estimate, a Customs and Border Protection (CBP) press release and a Motor and Equipment Manufacturers Association estimate – "cannot be substantiated or traced back to an underlying data source or methodology."

Deaner explained the importance of rewarding the "investment risk" taken by motion picture studios in 2014:

Usually movies are hot because a distributor has spent hundreds of thousands of dollars promoting the product in print and TV and other forms of advertising. The major Hollywood studios spend millions on this process with marketing costs rivalling the costs of production. They are attempting then to monetise through returns that can justify the investment in both the costs of promotion and production.

Motion Picture Industry Estimates

In 2008, the Motion Picture Association of America (MPAA) reported that its six major member companies lost US$6.1 billion to piracy. A 2009 *Los Angeles Daily News* article then cited a loss figure of "roughly $20 billion a year" for Hollywood studios. According to a 2013 Wall Street Journal article, industry estimates in the United States range between $6.1B to $18.5B per year.

In an early May 2014 *Guardian* article, an annual loss figure of US$20.5 billion was cited for the movie industry. The article's basis is the results of a University of Portsmouth study that only involved Finnish participants, aged between seven and 84. The researchers, who worked with 6,000 participants, stated: "Movie pirates are also more likely to cut down their piracy if they feel they are harming the industry compared with people who illegally download music".

Software Industry Estimates

According to a 2007 BSA and International Data Corporation (IDC) study, the five countries with the highest rates of software piracy were: 1. Armenia (93%); 2. Bangladesh (92%); 3. Azerbaijan (92%); 4. Moldova (92%); and 5. Zimbabwe (91%). According to the study's results, the five countries with the lowest piracy rates were: 1. U.S. (20%); 2. Luxembourg (21%); 3. New Zealand (22%); 4. Japan (23%); and 5. Austria (25%). The 2007 report showed that the Asia-Pacific region was associated with the highest amount of loss, in terms of U.S. dollars, with $14,090,000, followed by the European Union, with a loss of $12,383,000; the lowest amount of U.S. dollars was lost in the Middle East/Africa region, where $2,446,000 was documented.

In its 2011 report, conducted in partnership with IDC and Ipsos Public Affairs, the BSA stated: "Over half of the world's personal computer users – 57 percent – admit to pirating software." The ninth annual "BSA Global Software Piracy Study" claims that the "commercial value of this shadow market of pirated software" was worth US$63.4 billion in 2011, with the highest commercial value of pirated PC software existent in the U.S. during that time period (US$9,773,000). According to the 2011 study, Zimbabwe was the nation with the highest piracy rate, at 92%, while the lowest piracy rate was present in the U.S., at 19%.

The GAO noted in 2010 that the BSA's research up until that year defined "piracy as the difference between total installed software and legitimate software sold, and its scope involved only packaged physical software."

Music Industry Estimates

In 2007, the Institute for Policy Innovation (IPI) reported that music piracy took $12.5 billion from the U.S. economy. According to the study, musicians and those involved in the recording industry are not the only ones who experience losses attributed to music piracy. Retailers have lost over a billion dollars, while piracy has resulted in 46,000 fewer production-level jobs and almost 25,000 retail jobs. The U.S. government was also reported to suffer from music piracy, losing $422 million in tax revenue.

A report from 2013, released by the European Commission Joint Research Centre suggests that illegal music downloads have almost no effect on the number of legal music downloads. The study analyzed the behavior of 16,000 European music consumers and found that although music piracy negatively affects offline music sales, illegal music downloads had a positive effect on legal music purchases. Without illegal downloading, legal purchases were about two percent lower.

The study has received criticism, particularly from The International Federation of the Phonographic Industry, which believes the study is flawed and misleading. One argument against the research is that many music consumers only download music illegally. The IFPI also points out that music piracy affects not only online music sales but also multiple facets of the music industry, which is not addressed in the study.

Criticism of Industry Estimates

The methodology of studies utilized by industry spokespeople has been heavily criticized. Inflated claims for damages and allegations of economic harm are common in copyright disputes. Some studies and figures, including those cited by the MPAA and RIAA with regards to the economic effects of film and music downloads, have been widely disputed as based on questionable assumptions which resulted in statistically unsound numbers.

In one extreme example, the RIAA claimed damages against LimeWire totaling $75 trillion – more than the global GDP – and "respectfully" disagreed with the judge's ruling that such claims were "absurd".

However, this $75 trillion figure is obtained through one specific interpretation of copyright law that would count each song downloaded as an infringement of copyright. After the conclusion of the case, LimeWire agreed to pay $105 million to RIAA.

The judicial system has also found flaws in industry estimates and calculations. In one decision, US District Court Judge James P. Jones found that the "RIAA's request problematically assumes that every illegal download resulted in a lost sale," indicating profit-loss estimates were likely extremely off.

Other critics of industry estimates argue that those who use peer-to-peer sharing services, or practice "piracy" are actually more likely to pay for music. A Jupiter Research study in 2000 found that "Napster users were 45 percent more likely to have increased their music purchasing habits than online music fans who don't use the software were." This indicated that users of peer-to-peer sharing didn't hurt the profits of the music industry, but in fact may have increased it.

Professor Aram Sinnreich, in his book *The Piracy Crusade*, states that the connection between declining music sales and the creation of peer to peer file sharing sites such as Napster is tenuous, based on correlation rather than causation. He argues that the industry at the time was undergoing artificial expansion, what he describes as a "'perfect bubble'—a confluence of economic, political, and technological forces that drove the aggregate value of music sales to unprecedented heights at the end of the twentieth century".

Sinnreich cites multiple causes for the economic bubble, including the CD format replacement cycle; the shift from music specialty stores to wholesale suppliers of music and 'minimum advertised pricing'; and the economic expansion of 1991–2001. He believes that with the introduction of new digital technologies, the bubble burst, and the industry suffered as a result.

Economic Impact of Infringement in Emerging Markets

The 2011 Business Software Alliance Piracy Study Standard, estimates the total commercial value of illegally copied software to be at $59 billion in 2010, with emerging markets accounting for $31.9 billion, over half of the total. Furthermore, mature markets for the first time received less PC shipments than emerging economies in 2010, making emerging markets now responsible for more than half of all computers in use worldwide. In addition with software infringement rates of 68 percent comparing to 24 percent of mature markets, emerging markets thus possess the majority of the global increase in the commercial value of counterfeit software. China continues to have the highest commercial value of such software at $8.9 billion among developing countries and second in the world behind the US at $9.7 billion in 2011. In 2011, the Business Software Alliance announced that 83 percent of software deployed on PCs in Africa has been pirated (excluding South Africa).

Some countries distinguish corporate piracy from private use, which is tolerated as a welfare service. This is the leading reason developing countries refuse to accept or respect copyright laws. Traian Băsescu, the president of Romania, stated that "piracy helped the young generation discover computers. It set off the development of the IT industry in Romania."

Pro-open Culture Organizations

- Free Software Foundation (FSF)
- Electronic Frontier Foundation (EFF)
- Creative Commons (CC)
- Demand Progress
- Fight for the Future
- Pirate Party

Anti-copyright Infringement Organizations

- Business Software Alliance (BSA)
- Canadian Alliance Against Software Theft (CAAST)
- Entertainment Software Association (ESA)
- Federation Against Software Theft (FAST)
- International Intellectual Property Alliance (IIPA)
- Association For the Protection Of Internet Copyright (APIC)

- Copyright Alliance

- Fair Use Protection Association (FUPA)

Child Pornography

Child pornography is pornography that exploits children for sexual stimulation. It may be produced with the direct involvement or sexual assault of a child (also known as child sexual abuse images) or it may be simulated child pornography. Abuse of the child occurs during the sexual acts or lascivious exhibitions of genitals or pubic areas which are recorded in the production of child pornography. Child pornography may use a variety of media, including writings, magazines, photos, sculpture, drawing, cartoon, painting, animation, sound recording, film, video, and video games.

Laws regarding child pornography generally include sexual images involving prepubescents, pubescent or post-pubescent minors and computer-generated images that appear to involve them. Most possessors of child pornography who are arrested are found to possess images of prepubescent children; possessors of pornographic images of post-pubescent minors are less likely to be prosecuted, even though those images also fall within the statutes.

Producers of child pornography try to avoid prosecution by distributing their material across national borders, though this issue is increasingly being addressed with regular arrests of suspects from a number of countries occurring over the last few years. The prepubescent pornography is viewed and collected by pedophiles for a variety of purposes, ranging from private sexual uses, trading with other pedophiles, preparing children for sexual abuse as part of the process known as "child grooming", or enticement leading to entrapment for sexual exploitation such as production of new child pornography or child prostitution. Children themselves also sometimes produce child pornography on their own initiative or by the coercion of an adult.

Child pornography is illegal and censored in most jurisdictions in the world. Ninety-four of 187 Interpol member states had laws specifically addressing child pornography as of 2008, though this does not include nations that ban all pornography. Of those 94 countries, 58 criminalized possession of child pornography regardless of intent to distribute. Both distribution and possession are now criminal offenses in almost all Western countries. A wide movement is working to globalize the criminalization of child pornography, including major international organizations such as the United Nations and the European Commission.

Terminology

In the 2000s, use of the term child abuse images increased by both scholars and law enforcement personnel because the term "pornography" can carry the inaccurate implication of consent and create distance from the abusive nature of the material. A similar term, child sexual abuse material, is used by some official bodies, and similar terms such as "child abuse material", "documented child sexual abuse", and "depicted child sexual abuse" are also used, as are the acronyms CAM and CAI. The term "child pornography" retains its legal definitions in various jurisdictions, along with related terms such as "indecent photographs of a child" and others . In 2008, the *World Congress III against the Sexual Exploitation of Children and Adolescents* stated in their formally adopted pact that "Increasingly the term 'child abuse images' is being used to refer to the sexual exploitation of children and adolescents in pornography. This is to reflect the seriousness of the phenomenon and to emphasize that pornographic images of children are in fact records of a crime being committed."

Warning Banner for Operation Protect Our Children

Interpol and policing institutions of various governments, including among others the United States Department of Justice, enforce child pornography laws internationally. Since 1999, the Interpol Standing Working Group on Offenses Against Minors has used the following definition:

Child pornography is the consequence of the exploitation or sexual abuse perpetrated against a child. It can be defined as any means of depicting or promoting sexual abuse of a child, including print and/or audio, centered on sex acts or the genital organs of children.

Child Sexual Abuse in Production and Distribution

Children of all ages, including infants, are abused in the production of pornography. The United States Department of Justice estimates that pornographers have recorded the abuse of more than one million children in the United States alone. There is an increasing trend towards younger victims and greater brutality; according to Flint Waters, an investigator with the federal Internet Crimes Against Children Task Force, "These guys are raping infants and toddlers. You can hear the child crying, pleading for help in the video. It is horrendous." According to the World Congress against Commercial Sexual Exploitation of Children, "While impossible to obtain accurate data, a perusal of the child pornography readily available on the international market indicates that a significant number of children are being sexually exploited through this medium."

The United Kingdom children's charity NCH has stated that demand for child pornography on the internet has led to an increase in sex abuse cases, due to an increase in the number of children abused in the production process. In a study analyzing men arrested for child pornography possession in the United States over a one-year period from 2000 to 2001, most had pornographic images of prepubescent children (83%) and images graphically depicting sexual penetration (80%). Approximately 1 in 5 (21%) had images depicting violence such as bondage, rape, or torture and most of those involved images of children who were gagged, bound, blindfolded, or otherwise enduring sadistic sex. More than 1 in 3 (39%) had child-pornography videos with motion and sound. 79% also had images of nude or semi-nude children, but only 1% possessed such images alone. Law enforcement found about half (48%) had more than 100 graphic still images, and 14% had 1,000 or more graphic images. Forty percent (40%) were "dual offenders," who sexually victimized children and possessed child pornography.

A 2007 study in Ireland, undertaken by the Garda Síochána, revealed the most serious content in a sample of over 100 cases involving indecent images of children. In 44% of cases, the most serious images depicted nudity or erotic posing, in 7% they depicted sexual activity between children, in 7% they depicted non-penetrative sexual activity between adults and children, in 37% they depicted penetrative sexual activity between adults and children, and in 5% they depicted sadism or bestiality.

Masha Allen was adopted at age 5 from the former Soviet Union by an American man who sexually abused her for five years and posted the pictures on the Internet. She testified before the United States Congress about the anguish she has suffered at the continuing circulation of the pictures of her abuse, to "put a face" on a "sad, abstract, and faceless statistic," and to help pass a law named for her. "Masha's Law," included in the Adam Walsh Child Protection and Safety Act passed in 2006, includes a provision which allows young people 18 and over to sue in civil court those who download pornographic images taken of them when they were children. "Downloading" includes viewing without actual download; many successful prosecutions are completed through using residual images left on the viewer's computer.

Relation to Child Molestation and Abuse

Experts differ over any causal link between child pornography and child sexual abuse, with some experts saying that it increases the risk of child sexual abuse, and others saying that use of child pornography reduces the risk of offending. A 2008 American review of the use of Internet communication to lure children outlines the possible links to actual behaviour regarding the effects of Internet child pornography.

According to one paper from the Mayo Clinic of the U.S.A. based on case reports of those under treatment, 30% to 80% of individuals who viewed child pornography and 76% of individuals who were arrested for Internet child pornography had molested a child. As the total number of those who view such images can not be ascertained, the ratio of passive viewing to molestation remains unknown. The report also notes that it is not possible to define the progression from computerized child pornography to physical acts against children. Several professors of psychology state that memories of child abuse are maintained as long as visual records exist, are accessed, and are "exploited perversely."

A study by Wolak, Finkelhor, and Mitchell states that "rates of child sexual abuse have declined substantially since the mid-1990s, a time period that corresponds to the spread of CP online... The fact that this trend is revealed in multiple sources tends to undermine arguments that it is because of reduced reporting or changes in investigatory or statistical procedures. ... [T]o date, there has not been a spike in the rate of child sexual abuse that corresponds with the apparent expansion of online CP."

Typology

In the late 1990s, the COPINE project ("Combating Paedophile Information Networks in Europe") at University College Cork, in cooperation with the Paedophile Unit of the London Metropolitan Police, developed a typology to categorize child abuse images for use in both research and law enforcement. The ten-level typology was based on analysis of images available on websites and internet newsgroups. Other researchers have adopted similar ten-level scales. In 2002 in the UK, the Sentencing Advisory Panel adapted the COPINE scale to five levels and recommended its adoption for sentencing guidelines, omitting levels 1 to 3 and recommending that levels 4 to 6 combine as sentencing level 1 and that the four levels from 7 to 10 each form an individual severity level, for a total of 5 sentencing stages.

The COPINE Scale		
1	**Indicative**	Non-erotic and non-sexualised pictures showing children in their underwear, swimming costumes from either commercial sources or family albums. Pictures of children playing in normal settings, in which the context or organisation of pictures by the collector indicates inappropriateness.
2	**Nudist**	Pictures of naked or semi-naked children in appropriate nudist settings, and from legitimate sources.
3	**Erotica**	Surreptitiously taken photographs of children in play areas or other safe environments showing either underwear or varying degrees of nakedness.
4	**Posing**	Deliberately posed pictures of children fully clothed, partially clothed or naked (where the amount, context and organization suggests sexual interest).
5	**Erotic Posing**	Deliberately posed pictures of fully, partially clothed or naked children in sexualised or provocative poses.
6	**Explicit Erotic Posing**	Pictures emphasising genital areas, where the child is either naked, partially clothed or fully clothed.
7	**Explicit Sexual Activity**	Pictures that depict touching, mutual and self-masturbation, oral sex and intercourse by a child, not involving an adult.
8	**Assault**	Pictures of children being subject to a sexual assault, involving digital touching, involving an adult.
9	**Gross Assault**	Grossly obscene pictures of sexual assault, involving penetrative sex, masturbation or oral sex, involving an adult.
10	**Sadistic/Bestiality**	a. Pictures showing a child being tied, bound, beaten, whipped or otherwise subject to something that implies pain. b. Pictures where an animal is involved in some form of sexual behaviour with a child.

Proliferation

Internet Proliferation

Philip Jenkins notes that there is "overwhelming evidence that [child pornography] is all but impossible to obtain through nonelectronic means." The Internet has radically changed how child pornography is reproduced and disseminated, and, according to the United States Department of Justice, resulted in a massive increase in the "availability, accessibility, and volume of child pornography." The production of child pornography has become very profitable and is no longer limited to paedophiles.

Digital cameras and Internet distribution facilitated by the use of credit cards and the ease of transferring images across national borders has made it easier than ever before for users of child pornography to obtain the photographs and videos. The NCMEC estimated in 2003 that 20% of all pornography traded over the Internet was child pornography, and that since 1997 the number of child pornography images available on the Internet had increased by 1500%.

In 2007, the British-based Internet Watch Foundation reported that child pornography on the Internet is becoming more brutal and graphic, and the number of images depicting violent abuse has risen fourfold since 2003. The CEO stated "The worrying issue is the severity and the gravity of the images is increasing. We're talking about prepubescent children being raped." About 80 percent of the children in the abusive images are female, and 91 percent appear to be children under the age of 12. Prosecution is difficult because multiple international servers are used, sometimes to transmit the images in fragments to evade the law. Some child pornographers also circumvent detection by using viruses to illegally gain control of computers on which they remotely store child pornography. In one case, a Massachusetts man was charged with possession of child pornography when hackers used his computer to access pornographic sites and store pornographic pictures without his knowledge. The U.S. Court of Appeals for the Tenth Circuit has ruled that if a user downloads child pornography from a file sharing network and possesses it in his "shared folder" without configuring the software to not share that content, he can be charged with distributing child pornography.

Regarding internet proliferation, the U.S. Department of Justice states that "At any one time there are estimated to be more than one million pornographic images of children on the Internet, with 200 new images posted daily." They also note that a single offender arrested in the U.K. possessed 450,000 child pornography images, and that a single child pornography site received a million hits in a month. Further, that much of the trade in child pornography takes place at hidden levels of the Internet, and that it has been estimated that there are between 50,000 and 100,000 paedophiles involved in organised pornography rings around the world, and that one third of these operate from the United States.

One massive international child pornography ring was centered in the Netherlands. In the largest ever operation of its kind, police in 30 countries arrested 184 suspects and identified 486 others. Dutch authorities arrested 37-year-old Israeli-born Dutch citizen Amir Ish-Hurwitz, founder and owner of the internet forum Boylover.net, the center of the ring. At its peak, the forum had more than 70,000 members around the world.

In 2008, the Google search engine adapted a software program in order to faster track child pornography accessible through their site. The software is based in a pattern recognition engine.

Collector Behavior and Motives

Viewers of child pornography who are pedophiles are particularly obsessive about collecting, organizing, categorizing, and labeling their child pornography collection according to age, gender, sex act and fantasy. According to FBI agent Ken Lanning, "collecting" pornography does not mean that they merely view pornography, but that they save it, and "it comes to define, fuel, and validate their most cherished sexual fantasies." An extensive collection indicates a strong sexual preference for children, and if a collector of child pornography is also a pedophile, the owned collection is the single best indicator of what he or she wants to do. The National Society for the Prevention of Cruelty to Children describes researchers Taylor and Quayle's analysis of pedophile pornography collecting:

> The obsessive nature of the collecting and the narrative or thematic links for collections, led to the building of social communities on the internet dedicated to extending these collections. Through these "virtual communities" collectors are able to downgrade the content and abusive nature of the collections, see the children involved as objects rather than people, and their own behaviour as normal: It is an expression of 'love' for children rather than abuse.

These offenders are likely to employ elaborate security measures to avoid detection. The US DOJ notes that "there is a core of veteran offenders, some of whom have been active in pedophile news-groups for more than 20 years, who possess high levels of technological expertise," also noting that pedophile bulletin boards often contain technical advice from child pornography users' old hands to newcomers."

A 1986 U.S. Senate report found that motives for people's collecting child pornography include arousal and gratification; validation and justification of pedophile behaviour; to show the images to children to lower their inhibitions to engage in sex; preservation of an image of a child at the age of sexual preference; blackmail of depicted individuals; a medium of exchange and communi-cation with other child pornography consumers; and profit. A 2012 U.S. Sentencing Commission report found that child pornography offenders, while "much more likely to be sexually aroused by children than contact sex offenders or the general population", can also have non-sexual mo-tives for collecting child pornography, including initial curiosity, compulsive collecting behaviors, avoidance of stress and dissatisfaction with life, and an ability to create a new and more socially successful identity (within an online community). Some offenders find collecting child pornogra-phy enjoyable regardless of whether the images are sexually exciting to them; their interest is in assembling complete sets and organizing the material as a pastime, analogously to what a stamp collector might do.

Child Sex Tourism

One source of child pornography distributed worldwide is that created by sex tourists. Most of the victims of child sex tourism reside in the developing countries of the world. In 1996, a court in Thailand convicted a German national of child molestation and production of pornography for commercial purposes; he was involved in a child pornography ring which exploited Thai children. A sizable portion of the pornography seized in Sweden and in the Netherlands in the 1990s was produced by sex tourists visiting Southeast Asia. INTERPOL works with its 190 member countries to combat the problem, and launched its first-ever successful global appeal for assistance in 2007 to identify a Canadian man, Christopher Paul Neil, featured in a series of around 200 photographs in which he was shown sexually abusing young Vietnamese and Cambodian children.

Organized Crime

Organized crime is involved in the production and distribution of child pornography, which is found as a common element of organized crime profiles. Organisation into groups to produce and distribute pornography, they are often called "sex rings." In 2003, an international police investiga-tion uncovered a Germany-based child pornography ring involving 26,500 suspects who swapped illegal images on the Internet in 166 different countries. In a 2006 case, US and international authorities charged 27 people in nine states and three countries in connection with a child pornog-raphy ring that US federal authorities described as "one of the worst" they have discovered. The assistant secretary for Immigration and Customs Enforcement added that the case reflected three larger trends that are becoming more common in child pornography rings. One is the increasing prevalence of "home-grown" pornographic images that are produced by predators themselves, and include live streaming video images of children being abused, not just the circulation of repeated images. Another trend is the growing use of sophisticated security measures and of peer-to-peer networking, in which participants can share files with one another on their computers rather than downloading them from a web site. The group used encryption and data destruction software to protect the files and screening measures to ensure only authorized participants could enter the chat room. A third trend is the increasingly violent and graphic nature of the images involving the abuse of younger children.

According to Jim Gamble, CEO of the Child Exploitation and Online Protection Centre, around 50 per cent of sites showing children being abused are operated on a pay-per-view basis. "The people involved in these sites often aren't doing it because they're deviant by nature. They're doing it because they're business people. It's risk versus profits. We need to reduce the profit motivation." The CEOPP was established in 2006, and targets the finances of organised criminal gangs selling images of child abuse.

The majority of child pornography seized in the United States is not produced or distributed for profit, and there is little evidence that organized criminals operating with a profit motivation are a major source of child pornography's international dissemination.

Laws

History

In the United States, the first federal law to ban the for-profit production and distribution of child pornography was the Protection of Children Against Sexual Exploitation Act of 1977. In response to *New York v. Ferber*, 458 U.S. 747 (1982), a U.S. Supreme Court decision allowing the prohibition of child pornography that did not meet the obscenity standard established in *Miller v. California*, Congress passed the Child Protection Act of 1984, broadening the definition of child pornography and criminalizing nonprofit child pornography trafficking. The 1986 Meese Report found that child pornography was a cause of serious harm; this led to the passage of the Child Sexual Abuse and Pornography Act of 1986, which increased penalties for repeat offenders.

Federal prosecutions of child sex exploitation offenders

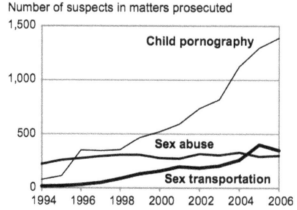

Note: Includes matters with a child sex exploitation offense as lead charge.

The U.S. Supreme Court decision *Osborne v. Ohio*, 495 U.S. 103 (1990), ruled that the U.S. Constitution allowed prohibition of child pornography possession. The High Court noted that at the time of the decision, 19 U.S. states had laws on their books prohibiting child pornography possession. As of 2015, all 50 U.S. states had such laws. Provisions of the Child Pornography Prevention Act of 1996 that banned virtual child pornography were struck down in *Ashcroft v. Free Speech Coalition*, 535 U.S. 234 (2002). Congress passed several laws increasing the penalties for child pornography offenses, so that from 1997 to 2007, the mean sentence of child pornography offenders increased from 20.59 months to 91.30 months of confinement, an increase of 443%. In 2003, Congress passed the PROTECT Act, authorizing lifetime terms of federal supervised release for child pornography offenders; since U.S. Sentencing Guidelines recommend imposing the maximum term of supervised release for all sex offenders, this means that a lifetime term of supervised release is recommended for all child pornography offenders.

During 2006, 3,661 suspects were referred to U.S. attorneys for child sex exploitation offenses. Child pornography constituted 69% of referrals, followed by sex abuse (16%) and sex transportation (14%). In 2006, the median prison sentence imposed was greatest for sex abuse offenses (70 months) followed by child pornography (63 months) and sex transportation (60 months). The median sentenced for sex transportation was 60 months in 2006 and 1996. The median sentence increased from 44 to 70 months for sex abuse and from 15 to 63 months for child pornography. In comparison, median prison terms for drug and weapon offenders remained stable and increased for violent offenses.

A bill named Internet Safety Act, intended to stop child pornography and protect children from online predators by requiring Internet service providers to keep track of data pertaining to users that were assigned a temporarily assigned network address, was introduced in 2009 but was finally not enacted.

In fiscal year 2010, the average term of supervised release for non-production offenders was approximately 20 years; the average term of supervised release for offenders sentenced under the production guideline was nearly 27 years.

International Coordination of Law Enforcement

Investigations include the 1999 Operation Cathedral which resulted in multi-national arrests and 7 convictions as well as uncovering 750,000 images with 1,200 unique identifiable faces being distributed over the web; Operation Amethyst which occurred in the Republic of Ireland; Operation Auxin which occurred in Australia; Operation Avalanche; Operation Ore based in the United Kingdom; Operation Pin; Operation Predator; the 2004 Ukrainian child pornography raids; and the 2007 international child pornography investigation. A three-year Europol investigation, dubbed Operation Rescue, based on the activities of boylover.net, a popular pedophile chat room, netted over 150 arrests and the rescue of 230 children in 2011. The principal of boylover.net, Israeli-born Dutch citizen Amir Ish-Hurwitz, was jailed 17 March 2011 in the Netherlands. Hundreds of additional suspects remain at large.

Even so, the UK based NSPCC said that worldwide an estimated 2% of child pornography websites still had not been removed a year after being identified.

One of the primary mandates of the international policing organization Interpol is the prevention of crimes against children involving the crossing of international borders, including child pornography and all other forms of exploitation and trafficking of children.

The USA Department of Justice coordinates programs to track and prosecute child pornography offenders across all jurisdictions, from local police departments to federal investigations, and international cooperation with other governments. Efforts by the Department to combat child pornography includes the National Child Victim Identification Program, the world's largest database of child pornography, maintained by the Child Exploitation and Obscenity Section of the United States Department of Justice and the National Center for Missing and Exploited Children (NCMEC) for the purpose of identifying victims of child abuse. Police agencies have deployed trained staff to track child pornography files and the computers used to share them as they are distributed on the Internet, and they freely share identifying information for the computers and users internationally.

In Europe the CIRCAMP Law Enforcement project is aimed at reducing the availability of abusive material on the Web, combining traditional police investigative methods and Police/Internet industry cooperation by blocking access to domains containing such files. The result is country specific lists according to national legislation in the participating countries. This police initiative has a worldwide scope in its work but is partly financed by the European Commission.

When child pornography is distributed across international borders, customs agencies also participate in investigations and enforcement, such as in the 2001–2002 cooperative effort between the United States Customs Service and local operational law enforcement agencies in Russia. A search warrant issued in the USA by the Customs Service resulted in seizing of computers and email records by the Russian authorities, and arrests of the pornographers.

In spite of international cooperation, less than 1 percent of children who appear in child pornography are located by law enforcement each year, according to Interpol statistics.

Google announced in 2008 that it is working with NCMEC to help automate and streamline how child protection workers sift through millions of pornographic images to identify victims of abuse. Google has developed video fingerprinting technology and software to automate the review of some 13 million pornographic images and videos that analysts at the center previously had to review manually.

The FBI has begun posting hyperlinks on the Internet that purport to be illegal videos of minors having sex, and then raiding the homes of anyone willing to click on them.

In October 2011, hacking collective Anonymous announced they began taking down child pornography websites on the darknet in a vigilante move, and released alleged user names on a pastebin link.

National and International Law

Child pornography laws provide severe penalties for producers and distributors in almost all societies, usually including incarceration, with shorter duration of sentences for non-commercial distribution depending on the extent and content of the material distributed. Convictions for possessing child pornography also usually include prison sentences, but those sentences are often converted to probation for first-time offenders.

In 2006, the International Centre for Missing & Exploited Children (ICMEC) published a report of findings on the presence of child pornography legislation in the then-184 INTERPOL member countries. It later updated this information, in subsequent editions, to include 196 UN member countries. The report, entitled "Child Pornography: Model Legislation & Global Review," assesses whether national legislation:

(1) exists with specific regard to child pornography; (2) provides a definition of child pornography; (3) expressly criminalizes computer-facilitated offenses; (4) criminalizes the knowing possession of child pornography, regardless of intent to distribute; and (5) requires ISPs to report suspected child pornography to law enforcement or to some other mandated agency.

ICMEC stated that it found in its initial report that only 27 countries had legislation needed to deal with child pornography offenses, while 95 countries did not have any legislation that specifically addressed child pornography, making child pornography a global issue worsened by the inadequacies of domestic legislation. The 7th Edition Report found that still only 69 countries had legislation needed to deal with child pornography offenses, while 53 did not have any legislation specifically addressing the problem. Over seven years of research from 2006–12, ICMEC and its Koons Family Institute on International Law and Policy report that they have worked with 100 countries that have revised or put in place new child pornography laws.

A 2008 review of child pornography laws in 187 countries by the International Centre for Missing & Exploited Children (ICMEC) showed that 93 had no laws that specifically addressed child pornography. Of the 94 that did, 36 did not criminalize possession of child pornography regardless of intent to distribute. This review, however, did not count legislation outlawing *all* pornography as being "specific" to child pornography. It also did not count bans on "the worst forms of child labor." Some societies such as Canada and Australia have laws banning cartoon, manga, or written child pornography and others require ISPs (Internet Service Providers) to monitor internet traffic to detect it.

The United Nations Optional Protocol on the Sale of Children, Child Prostitution and Child Pornography requires parties to outlaw the "producing, distributing, disseminating, importing, exporting, offering, selling or possessing for the above purposes" of child pornography. The Council of Europe's Cybercrime Convention and the EU Framework Decision that became active in 2006 require signatory or member states to criminalize all aspects of child pornography. Article 34 of the United Nations Convention on the Rights of the Child (UNCRC) stated that all signatories shall take appropriate measures to prevent the exploitative use of children in pornographic performances and materials.

Artificially Generated or Simulated Imagery

Simulated child pornography produced without the direct involvement of children in the production process itself includes modified photographs of real children, non-minor teenagers made to look younger (age regression), and fully computer-generated imagery or adults made to look like children. Drawings or animations that depict sexual acts involving children but are not intended to look like photographs may also be regarded as child pornography.

Sexting

Sexting is the practice of using cell phone messaging to send nude or semi-nude images of themselves to others (such as friends or dating partners). These may be passed along to others or be posted on the Internet. In many jurisdictions, the age of consent is lower than the age of majority, and a minor who is over the age of consent can legally have sex with a person of the same age. Many laws on child pornography were passed before cell phone cameras became common among teenagers over the age of consent and sexting was understood as a phenomenon. Because laws were created around the age of majority, teenagers who are legally able to consent to sex can be charged with production and distribution of child pornography if they send naked images of themselves to friends or sex partners of the same age. The University of New Hampshire's Crimes Against Children Research Center estimates that 7 percent of people arrested on suspicion of child pornography production in 2009 were teenagers who shared images with peers consensually. In some countries, mandatory sentencing requires anybody convicted of such an offence to be placed on a sex offender registry.

Legal professionals and academics have criticized the use of child pornography laws with mandatory punishments against teenagers over the age of consent for sex offenses. Florida cyber crimes defense attorney David S. Seltzer wrote of this that "I do not believe that our child pornography laws were designed for these situations ... A conviction for possession of child pornography in Florida draws up to five years in prison for each picture or video, plus a lifelong requirement to register as a sex offender."

In a 2013 interview, assistant professor of communications at the University of Colorado Denver, Amy Adele Hasinoff, who studies the repercussions of sexting has stated that the "very harsh" child pornography laws are "designed to address adults exploiting children" and should not replace better sex education and consent training for teens. She went on to say, "Sexting is a sex act, and if it's consensual, that's fine..." "Anyone who distributes these pictures without consent is doing something malicious and abusive, but child pornography laws are too harsh to address it."

Controversy

In 2010, workers in the United States Department of Defense were found to have downloaded child pornography that caused administrative issues, but the department declined to investigate the incident.

Mass Surveillance

Mass surveillance is the intricate surveillance of an entire or a substantial fraction of a population in order to monitor that group of citizens. The surveillance is often carried out by governments or governmental organisations, but may also be carried out by corporations, either on behalf of governments or at their own initiative. Depending on each nation's laws and judicial systems, the legality of and the permission required to engage in mass surveillance varies. It is often distinguished from targeted surveillance.

Mass surveillance has often been cited as necessary to fight terrorism, to prevent social unrest, to protect national security, to fight child pornography and protect children. Conversely, mass surveillance has equally often been criticized for violating privacy rights, limiting civil and political rights and freedoms, and being illegal under some legal or constitutional systems. Another criticism is that increasing mass surveillance could lead to the development of a surveillance state or an electronic police state where civil liberties are infringed or political dissent is undermined by COINTELPRO-like programs. Such a state could also be referred to as a totalitarian state.

In 2013, the practice of mass surveillance by world governments was called into question after Edward Snowden's 2013 global surveillance disclosure. Reporting based on documents Snowden leaked to various media outlets triggered a debate about civil liberties and the right to privacy in the Digital Age. Mass surveillance is considered a global issue.

By Country

Privacy International's 2007 survey, covering 47 countries, indicated that there had been an increase in surveillance and a decline in the performance of privacy safeguards, compared to the previous year. Balancing these factors, eight countries were rated as being 'endemic surveillance societies'. Of these eight, China, Malaysia and Russia scored lowest, followed jointly by Singapore and the United Kingdom, then jointly by Taiwan, Thailand and the United States. The best ranking was given to Greece, which was judged to have 'adequate safeguards against abuse'.

Many countries throughout the world have already been adding thousands of surveillance cameras to their urban, suburban and even rural areas. For example, in September 2007 the American Civil Liberties Union (ACLU) stated that we are "in danger of tipping into a genuine surveillance society completely alien to American values" with "the potential for a dark future where our every move, our every transaction, our every communication is recorded, compiled, and stored away, ready to be examined and used against us by the authorities whenever they want."

On 12 March 2013 Reporters Without Borders published a *Special report on Internet Surveillance*. The report included a list of "State Enemies of the Internet", countries whose governments are involved in active, intrusive surveillance of news providers, resulting in grave violations of freedom of information and human rights. Five countries were placed on the initial list: Bahrain, China, Iran, Syria, and Vietnam.

Bahrain

Bahrain is one of the five countries on Reporters Without Borders' March 2013 list of "State Enemies of the Internet", countries whose governments are involved in active, intrusive surveillance of news providers, resulting in grave violations of freedom of information and human rights. The level of Internet filtering and surveillance in Bahrain is one of the highest in the world. The royal family is represented in all areas of Internet management and has sophisticated tools at its disposal for spying on its subjects. The online activities of dissidents and news providers are closely monitored and the surveillance is increasing.

China

China is one of the five countries on Reporters Without Borders' March 2013 list of "State Enemies of the Internet", countries whose governments are involved in active, intrusive surveillance of news providers, resulting in grave violations of freedom of information and human rights. All Internet access in China is owned or controlled by the state or the Communist Party. Many foreign journalists in China have said that they take for granted that their telephones are tapped and their email is monitored.

The tools put in place to filter and monitor the Internet are collectively known as the Great Firewall of China. Besides the usual routing regulations that allow access to an IP address or a particular domain name to be blocked, the Great Firewall makes large-scale use of Deep Packet Inspection (DPI) technology to monitor and block access based on keyword detection. The Great Firewall has the ability to dynamically block encrypted connections. One of the country's main ISPs, China Unicom, automatically cuts a connection as soon as it is used to transmit encrypted content.

The monitoring system developed by China is not confined to the Great Firewall, monitoring is also built into social networks, chat services and VoIP. Private companies are directly responsible to the Chinese authorities for surveillance of their networks to ensure banned messages are not circulated. The QQ application, owned by the firm Tencent, allows the authorities to monitor in detail exchanges between Internet users by seeking certain keywords and expressions. The author of each message can be identified by his or her user number. The QQ application is effectively a giant Trojan horse. And since March 2012, new legislation requires all new users of micro-blogging sites to register using their own name and telephone number.

Skype, one of the world's most popular Internet telephone platforms, is closely monitored. Skype services in China are available through a local partner, the TOM media group. The Chinese-language version of Skype, known as TOM-Skype, is slightly different from the downloadable versions in other countries. A report by OpenNet Initiative Asia says everyday conversations are captured on servers. Interception and storage of a conversation may be triggered by a sender's or recipient's name or by keywords that occur in the conversation.

On 30 January, the *New York Times* reported that it had been the target of attacks by the Chinese government. The first breach took place on 13 September 2012 when the newspaper was preparing to publish an article about the fortune amassed by the family of outgoing Prime Minister Wen Jia-bao. The newspaper said the purpose of attacks was to identify the sources that supplied the newspaper with information about corruption among the prime minister's entourage. The *Wall Street Journal* and *CNN* also said they had been the targets of cyber attacks from China. In February, Twitter disclosed that the accounts of some 250,000 subscribers had been the victims of attacks from China similar to those carried out on the *New York Times*. Mandiant, the company engaged by the NYT to secure its network, identified the source of the attacks as a group of hackers it called Advanced Persistent Threat 1, a unit of the People's Liberation Army operating from a 12-storey building in the suburbs of Shanghai that had hundreds, possibly thousands, of staff and the direct support of the Chinese government.

East Germany

Before the Digital Revolution, one of the world's biggest mass surveillance operations was carried out by the Stasi, the secret police of the former East Germany. By the time the state collapsed in 1989, the Stasi had built up an estimated civilian network of 300,000 informants (approximately one in fifty of the population), who monitored even minute hints of political dissent among other citizens. Many West Germans visiting friends and family in East Germany were also subject to Stasi spying, as well as many high-ranking West German politicians and persons in the public eye.

Most East German citizens were well aware that their government was spying on them, which led to a culture of mistrust: touchy political issues were only discussed in the comfort of their own four walls and only with the closest of friends and family members, while widely maintaining a façade of unquestioning followership in public.

European Union

The right to privacy is a highly developed area of law in Europe. The Data Protection Directive regulates the processing of personal data within the European Union. For comparison, the US has no data protection law that is comparable to this; instead, the US regulates data protection on a sectoral basis.

Since early 2012, the European Union has been working on a General Data Protection Regulation to replace the Data Protection Directive and harmonise data protection and privacy law. On 20 October 2013, a committee at the European Parliament backed the measure, which, if it is enacted, could require American companies to seek clearance from European officials before complying with United States warrants seeking private data. The vote is part of efforts in Europe to shield citizens from on-line surveillance in the wake of revelations about a far-reaching spying program by the U.S. National Security Agency. European Union justice and rights commissioner Viviane Reding said "The question has arisen whether the large-scale collection and processing of personal information under US surveillance programmes is necessary and proportionate to meet the interests of national security." The EU is also asking the US for changes to US legislation to match the legal redress offered in Europe; American citizens in Europe can go to the courts if they feel their rights are infringed but Europeans without right of residence in America cannot. When the EU / US arrangement to implement International Safe Harbor Privacy Principles were struck down by the European Court of Justice, a new framework for transatlantic data flows, called the "EU-US Privacy Shield", was adopted in July 2016.

In April 2014, the European Court of Justice declared invalid the EU Data Retention Directive. The Court said it violates two basic rights - respect for private life and protection of personal data. The legislative body of the European Union passed the Data Retention Directive on 15 December 2005. It requires that telecommunication operators retain metadata for telephone, Internet, and other telecommunication services for periods of not less than six months and not more than two years from the date of the communication as determined by each EU member state and, upon request, to make the data available to various governmental bodies. Access to this information is not limited to investigation of serious crimes, nor is a warrant required for access.

Undertaken under the *Seventh Framework Programme for research and technological development* (FP7 - Science in Society) some multidisciplinary and mission oriented mass surveillance activities (for example INDECT and HIDE) were funded by the European Commission in association with industrial partners.

The INDECT Project ("Intelligent information system supporting observation, searching and detection for security of citizens in urban environment") develops an intelligent urban environment observation system to register and exchange operational data for the automatic detection, recognition and intelligent processing of all information of abnormal behaviour or violence.

The main expected results of the INDECT project are:

- Trial of intelligent analysis of video and audio data for threat detection in urban environments,

- Creation of tools and technology for privacy and data protection during storage and transmission of information using quantum cryptography and new methods of digital watermarking,

- Performing computer-aided detection of threats and targeted crimes in Internet resources with privacy-protecting solutions,

- Construction of a search engine for rapid semantic search based on watermarking of content related to child pornography and human organ trafficking,

- Implementation of a distributed computer system that is capable of effective intelligent processing.

HIDE ("Homeland Security, Biometric Identification & Personal Detection Ethics") was a research project funded by the European Commission within the scope of the Seventh RTD Framework Programme (FP7). The consortium, coordinated by Emilio Mordini, explored the ethical and privacy implications of biometrics and personal detection technologies, focusing on the continuum between personal detection, authentication, identification and mass surveillance.

Germany

In 2002 German citizens were tipped off about wiretapping, when a software error led to a phone number allocated to the German Secret Service being listed on mobile telephone bills.

India

The Indian parliament passed the Information Technology Act of 2008 with no debate, giving the government fiat power to tap all communications without a court order or a warrant. Section 69 of the act states "Section 69 empowers the Central Government/State Government/ its authorized agency to intercept, monitor or decrypt any information generated, transmitted, received or stored in any computer resource if it is necessary or expedient so to do in the interest of the sovereignty or integrity of India, defence of India, security of the State, friendly relations with foreign States or public order or for preventing incitement to the commission of any cognizable offence or for investigation of any offence."

India is setting up a national intelligence grid called NATGRID, which would be fully set up by May 2011 where each individual's data ranging from land records, Internet logs, air and rail PNR, phone records, gun records, driving license, property records, insurance, and income tax records would be available in real time and with no oversight. With a UID from the Unique Identification Authority of India being given to every Indian from February 2011, the government would be able track people in real time. A national population registry of all citizens will be established by the 2011 census, during which fingerprints and iris scans would be taken along with GPS records of each household.

As per the initial plan, access to the combined data will be given to 11 agencies, including the Research and Analysis Wing, the Intelligence Bureau, the Enforcement Directorate, the National Investigation Agency, the Central Bureau of Investigation, the Directorate of Revenue Intelligence and the Narcotics Control Bureau.

Iran

Iran is one of the five countries on Reporters Without Borders' March 2013 list of "State Enemies of the Internet", countries whose governments are involved in naturally active efforts to news providers. The government runs or controls almost all of the country's institutions for regulating, managing or legislating on telecommunications. The Supreme Council for Cyberspace, which was headed by President Ahmadinejad, was established in March 2012 and now determines digital policy. The construction of a parallel "Iranian Internet", with a high connection speed but fully monitored and censored, is almost complete.

The tools used by the Iranian authorities to monitor and control the Internet include data interception tools capable of Deep Packet Inspection. Interception products from leading Chinese companies such as ZTE and Huawei are in use. The products provided by Huawei to Mobin Net, the leading national provider of mobile broadband, can be used to analyze email content, track browsing history and block access to sites. The products that ZTA sold to the Telecommunication Company of Iran (TCI) offer similar services plus the possibility of monitoring the mobile network. European companies are the source of other spying and data analysis tools. Products designed by Ericsson and Nokia Siemens Networks (later Trovicor) are in use. These companies sold SMS interception and user location products to Mobile Communication Company of Iran and Irancell, Iran's two biggest mobile phone companies, in 2009 and they were used to identify Iranian citizens during the post-election uprising in 2009. The use of Israeli surveillance devices has also been detected in Iran. The network traffic management and surveillance device NetEnforcer was provided by Israel to Denmark and then resold to Iran. Similarly, US equipment has found its way to Iran via the Chinese company ZTE.

Netherlands

According to a 2004 report, the government of the Netherlands carries out more clandestine wiretaps and intercepts than any country, per capita, in the world. The Dutch military intelligence service MIVD operates a satellite ground station to intercept foreign satellite links and also a facility to eavesdrop on foreign high-frequency radio traffic.

Russia

The SORM (and SORM-2) laws enable complete monitoring of any communication, electronic or traditional, by eight state agencies, without warrant. These laws seem to be in conflict with Article 23 of the Constitution of Russia which states:

1. Everyone shall have the right to the inviolability of private life, personal and family secrets, the protection of honour and good name.

2. Everyone shall have the right to privacy of correspondence, of telephone conversations, postal, telegraph and other messages. Limitations of this right shall be allowed only by court decision.

In 2015, the European Court for Human Rights ruled that the legislation violated Article 8 of the European Convention on Human Rights (*Zakharov v. Russia*).

Yarovaya Law required storage and unconditional access to private communication data for law enforcement.

Sweden

Prior to 2009, the National Defence Radio Establishment (FRA) was limited to wireless signals intelligence (SIGINT), although it was left largely unregulated. In December 2009, new legislation went into effect, allowing the FRA to monitor cable bound signals passing the Swedish border. Communications service providers are legally required, under confidentiality, to transfer cable communications crossing Swedish borders to specific "interaction points", where data may be accessed after a court order. The number of companies affected by the legislation was estimated as "being limited (approximately ten)".

The FRA has been contested since the change in its legislation, mainly because of the public perception the change would enable mass surveillance. The FRA categorically deny this allegation, as they are not allowed to initialize any surveillance on their own, and has no direct access to communication lines. All SIGINT has to be authorized by a special court and meet a set of narrow requirements, something Minister for Defence Sten Tolgfors have been quoted as saying, "should render the debate on mass surveillance invalid." Due to the architecture of Internet backbones in the Nordic area, a large portion of Norwegian and Finnish traffic will also be affected by the Swedish wiretapping.

Syria

Syria is one of the five countries on Reporters Without Borders' March 2013 list of "State Enemies of the Internet", countries whose governments are involved in active, intrusive surveillance of news providers, resulting in grave violations of freedom of information and human rights. Syria has stepped up its web censorship and cyber-monitoring as the country's civil war has intensified. At least 13 Blue Coat proxy servers are in use, Skype calls are intercepted, and social engineering techniques, phishing, and malware attacks are all in use.

United Kingdom

State surveillance in the United Kingdom has formed part of the public consciousness since the 19th century. The postal espionage crisis of 1844 sparked the first panic over the privacy of citizens. However, in the 20th century, electronic surveillance capabilities grew out of wartime signal intelligence and pioneering code breaking. In 1946, the Government Communications Headquarters (GCHQ) was formed. The United Kingdom and the United States signed the bilateral UKUSA Agreement in 1948. It was later broadened to include Canada, Australia and New Zealand, as well as cooperation with several "third-party" nations. This became the cornerstone of Western intelligence gathering and the "Special Relationship" between the UK and the USA.

After the growth of the Internet and development of the World Wide Web, a series of media reports in 2013 revealed more recent programs and techniques involving GCHQ, such as Tempora.

The use of these capabilities is controlled by laws made in the UK Parliament. In particular, access to the content of private messages (that is, interception of a communication) must be authorized by a warrant signed by a Secretary of State. In addition European Union data privacy law applies in UK law. The UK exhibits governance and safeguards as well as use of electronic surveillance.

The Investigatory Powers Tribunal, a judicial oversight body for the intelligence agencies, ruled in December 2014 that the legislative framework in the United Kingdom does not breach the European Convention on Human Rights. However, the Tribunal stated in February 2015 that one particular aspect, the data-sharing arrangement that allowed UK Intelligence services to request data from the US surveillance programs Prism and Upstream, had been in contravention of human rights law prior to this until two paragraphs of additional information, providing details about the procedures and safeguards, were disclosed to the public in December 2014.

In its December 2014 ruling, the Investigatory Powers Tribunal found that the legislative framework in the United Kingdom does not permit mass surveillance and that while GCHQ collects and analyses data in bulk, it does not practice mass surveillance. A report on Privacy and Security published by the Intelligence and Security Committee of Parliament also came to this view, although it found past shortcomings in oversight and said the legal framework should be simplified to improve transparency. This view is supported by independent reports from the Interception of Communications Commissioner. However, notable civil liberties groups continue to express strong views to the contrary and plan to appeal the ruling to the European Court of Human Rights, while others have criticised these viewpoints in turn.

RAF Menwith Hill, a large site in the United Kingdom, part of ECHELON and the UKUSA Agreement.

The Regulation of Investigatory Powers Act 2000 (RIP or RIPA) is a significant piece of legislation that granted and regulated the powers of public bodies to carry out surveillance and investigation. In 2002 the UK government announced plans to extend the Regulation of Investigatory Powers Act so that at least 28 government departments would be given powers to access metadata about citizens' web, e-mail, telephone and fax records, without a warrant and without a subject's knowledge.

The Protection of Freedoms Act 2012 includes several provisions related to controlling and restricting the collection, storage, retention, and use of information in government databases.

Supported by all three major political parties, the UK Parliament passed the Data Retention and Investigatory Powers Act in July 2014 to ensure police and security services retain existing powers to access phone and Internet records. The Investigatory Powers Bill published in November 2015 for scrutiny by Parliament would require Internet service providers and mobile phone companies to maintain records of (but not the content of) customers' Internet connections for 12 months. In addition, it would create a requirement for judges to review the warrants authorised by a Secretary of State before they come into force.

Many advanced nation-states have implemented laws that partially protect citizens from unwarranted intrusion, such as the Human Rights Act 1998 and Data Protection Act 1998 in the United Kingdom, and laws that require a formal warrant before private data may be gathered by a government.

The UK is a member of the European Union, participates in its programs, and is subject to EU policies and directives on surveillance.

The vast majority of video surveillance cameras in the UK are not operated by government bodies, but by private individuals or companies, especially to monitor the interiors of shops and businesses. According to 2011 Freedom of Information Act requests, the total number of local government operated CCTV cameras was around 52,000 over the entirety of the UK. The prevalence of video surveillance in the UK is often overstated due to unreliable estimates being requoted; for example one report in 2002 extrapolated from a very small sample to estimate the number of cameras in the UK at 4.2 million (of which 500,000 in London). More reliable estimates put the number of private and local government operated cameras in the United Kingdom at around 1.85 million in 2011.

United States

Historically, mass surveillance was used as part of wartime censorship to control communications that could damage the war effort and aid the enemy. For example, during the world wars, every international telegram from or to the United States sent through companies such as Western Union was reviewed by the US military. After the wars were over, surveillance continued in programs such as the Black Chamber following World War I and project Shamrock following World War II. COINTELPRO projects conducted by the U.S. Federal Bureau of Investigation (FBI) between 1956 and 1971 targeted various "subversive" organizations, including peaceful anti-war and racial equality activists such as Albert Einstein and Martin Luther King Jr.

Billions of dollars per year are spent, by agencies such as the National Security Agency (NSA) and the Federal Bureau of Investigation (FBI), to develop, purchase, implement, and operate systems such as Carnivore, ECHELON, and NarusInsight to intercept and analyze the immense amount of data that traverses the Internet and telephone system every day.

Since the September 11, 2001, terrorist attacks, a vast domestic intelligence apparatus has been built to collect information using the NSA, FBI, local police, state homeland security offices and military criminal investigators. The intelligence apparatus collects, analyzes and stores information about millions of (if not all) American citizens, many of whom have not been accused of any wrongdoing.

Under the Mail Isolation Control and Tracking program, the U.S. Postal Service photographs the exterior of every piece of paper mail that is processed in the United States — about 160 billion pieces in 2012. The U.S. Postmaster General stated that the system is primarily used for mail sorting, but the images are available for possible use by law enforcement agencies. Created in 2001 following the anthrax attacks that killed five people, it is a sweeping expansion of a 100-year-old program called "mail cover" which targets people suspected of crimes.

The FBI developed the computer programs "Magic Lantern" and CIPAV, which they can remotely install on a computer system, in order to monitor a person's computer activity.

The NSA has been gathering information on financial records, Internet surfing habits, and monitoring e-mails. They have also performed extensive analysis of social networks such as Myspace.

The PRISM special source operation system legally immunized private companies that cooperate voluntarily with U.S. intelligence collection. According to *The Register*, the FISA Amendments Act of 2008 "specifically authorizes intelligence agencies to monitor the phone, email, and other communications of U.S. citizens for up to a week without obtaining a warrant" when one of the parties is outside the U.S. PRISM was first publicly revealed on 6 June 2013, after classified documents about the program were leaked to *The Washington Post* and *The Guardian* by American Edward Snowden.

The Communications Assistance for Law Enforcement Act (CALEA) requires that all U.S. telecommunications and Internet service providers modify their networks to allow easy wiretapping of telephone, VoIP, and broadband Internet traffic.

In early 2006, *USA Today* reported that several major telephone companies were providing the telephone call records of U.S. citizens to the National Security Agency (NSA), which is storing them in a large database known as the NSA call database. This report came on the heels of allegations that the U.S. government had been conducting electronic surveillance of domestic telephone calls without warrants. In 2013, the existence of the Hemisphere Project, through which AT&T provides telephone call data to federal agencies, became publicly known.

Traffic cameras, which were meant to help enforce traffic laws at intersections, may be used by law enforcement agencies for purposes unrelated to traffic violations. Some cameras allow for the identification of individuals inside a vehicle and license plate data to be collected and time stamped for cross reference with other data used by police. The Department of Homeland Security is funding networks of surveillance cameras in cities and towns as part of its efforts to combat terrorism.

The New York City Police Department infiltrated and compiled dossiers on protest groups before the 2004 Republican National Convention, leading to over 1,800 arrests.

Vietnam

Vietnam is one of the five countries on Reporters Without Borders' March 2013 list of "State Enemies of the Internet", countries whose governments are involved in active, intrusive surveillance of news providers, resulting in grave violations of freedom of information and human rights. Most of the country's 16 service providers are directly or indirectly controlled by the Vietnamese Communist Party. The industry leader, Vietnam Posts and Telecommunications Group, which controls 74 per cent of the market, is state-owned. So is Viettel, an enterprise of the Vietnamese armed forces. FPT Telecom is a private firm, but is accountable to the Party and depends on the market leaders for bandwidth.

Service providers are the major instruments of control and surveillance. Bloggers monitored by the government frequently undergo man-in-the-middle attacks. These are designed to intercept data meant to be sent to secure (https) sites, allowing passwords and other communication to be intercepted. According to a July 2012 Freedom House report, 91 percent of survey respondents connected to the Internet on their mobile devices and the government monitors conversations and tracks the calls of "activists" or "reactionaries."

Commercial Mass Surveillance

As a result of the digital revolution, many aspects of life are now captured and stored in digital form. Concern has been expressed that governments may use this information to conduct mass surveillance on their populations. Commercial mass surveillance often makes use of copyright laws and "user agreements" to obtain (typically uninformed) 'consent' to surveillance from consumers who use their software or other related materials. This allows gathering of information which would be technically illegal if performed by government agencies. This data is then often shared with government agencies - thereby - in practice - defeating the purpose of such privacy protections.

One of the most common forms of mass surveillance is carried out by commercial organizations. Many people are willing to join supermarket and grocery loyalty card programs, trading their personal information and surveillance of their shopping habits in exchange for a discount on their groceries, although base prices might be increased to encourage participation in the program. Since a significant proportion of purchases are carried out by credit or debit cards, which can also be easily tracked, it is questionable whether loyalty cards provide any significant additional privacy threat.

Through programs like Google's AdSense, OpenSocial and their increasing pool of so-called "web gadgets", "social gadgets" and other Google-hosted services many web sites on the Internet are effectively feeding user information about sites visited by the users, and now also their social connections, to Google. Facebook also keep this information, although its acquisition is limited to page views within Facebook. This data is valuable for authorities, advertisers and others interested in profiling users, trends and web site marketing performance. Google, Facebook and others are increasingly becoming more guarded about this data as their reach increases and the data becomes more all inclusive, making it more valuable.

New features like geolocation give an even increased admission of monitoring capabilities to large service providers like Google, where they also are enabled to track one's physical movements while users are using mobile devices, especially those which are syncing without any user interaction. Google's Gmail service is increasingly employing features to work as a stand-alone application which also might activate while a web browser is not even active for synchronizing; a feature mentioned on the Google I/O 2009 developer conference while showing the upcoming HTML5 features which Google and others are actively defining and promoting.

In 2008 at the World Economic Forum in Davos, Google CEO Eric Schmidt, said: "The arrival of a truly mobile Web, offering a new generation of location-based advertising, is set to unleash a 'huge revolution'". At the Mobile World Congress in Barcelona on 16 February 2010, Google presented their vision of a new business model for mobile operators and trying to convince mobile operators to embrace location-based services and advertising. With Google as the advertising provider, it would mean that every mobile operator using their location-based advertising service would be revealing the location of their mobile customers to Google.

> "Google will also know more about the customer - because it benefits the customer to tell Google more about them. The more we know about the customer, the better the quality of searches, the better the quality of the apps. The operator one is

"required", if you will, and the Google one will be optional. And today I would say, a minority choose to do that, but I think over time a majority will... because of the stored values in the servers and so forth and so on...."

—2010 Mobile World Congress keynote speech, Google CEO Eric Schmidt

Organizations like the Electronic Frontier Foundation are constantly informing users on the importance of privacy, and considerations about technologies like geolocation.

Computer company Microsoft patented in 2011 a product distribution system with a camera or capture device that monitors the viewers that consume the product, allowing the provider to take "remedial action" if the actual viewers do not match the distribution license.

Reporters Without Borders' March 2013 *Special report on Internet Surveillance* contained a list of "Corporate Enemies of the Internet", companies that sell products that are liable to be used by governments to violate human rights and freedom of information. The five companies on the initial list were: Amesys (France), Blue Coat Systems (U.S.), Gamma (UK and Germany), Hacking Team (Italy), and Trovicor (Germany), but the list was not exhaustive and is likely to be expanded in the future.

Surveillance State

A surveillance state is a country where the government engages in pervasive surveillance of large numbers of its citizens and visitors. Such widespread surveillance is usually justified as being necessary to prevent crime or acts of terrorism, but may also be used to stifle criticism of and opposition to the government.

Germans protesting against the NSA surveillance program PRISM at Checkpoint Charlie in Berlin.

Examples of early surveillance states include the former Soviet Union and the former East Germany, which had a large network of informers and an advanced technology base in computing and spy-camera technology. But these states did not have today's technologies for mass surveillance, such as the use of databases and pattern recognition software to cross-correlate information obtained by wire tapping, including speech recognition and telecommunications traffic analysis, monitoring of financial transactions, automatic number plate recognition, the tracking of the position of mobile telephones, and facial recognition systems and the like which recognize people by their appearance, gait, DNA profiling, etc.

Smart Cities

The development of smart cities has seen the increased adoption of surveillance technologies by governments, although the primary purpose of surveillance in such cities is to use information and communication technologies to improve the urban environment. The implementation of such technology by a number of cities has resulted in increased efficiencies in urban infrastructure as well as improved community participation.

The development of smart city technology has also led to increased potential for unwarranted intrusions into privacy and restrictions upon autonomy. The widespread incorporation of information and communication technologies within the daily life of urban residents results in increases in the surveillance capacity of states - to the extent that individuals may be unaware of what information is being accessed, when the access occurs and for what purpose. It is possible that such conditions could give rise to the development of an electronic police state.

Electronic Police State

Banner in Bangkok, observed on 30 June 2014 during the 2014 Thai coup d'état, informing the Thai public that 'like' or 'share' activity on social media could land them in prison.

An electronic police state is a state in which the government aggressively uses electronic technologies to record, collect, store, organize, analyze, search, and distribute information about its citizens. Electronic police states also engage in mass government surveillance of landline and cellular telephone traffic, mail, email, web surfing, Internet searches, radio, and other forms of electronic communication as well as widespread use of video surveillance. The information is usually collected in secret.

The crucial elements are not politically based, so long as the government can afford the technology and the populace will permit it to be used, an electronic police state can form. The continual use of electronic mass surveillance can result in constant low-level fear within the population, which can lead to self-censorship and exerts a powerful coercive force upon the populace.

Seventeen factors for judging the development of an electronic police state were suggested in *The Electronic Police State: 2008 National Rankings*:

- Daily documents: Requirement for the use and tracking of state-issued identity documents and registration.

- Border and travel control: Inspections at borders, searching computers and cell phones, demanding decryption of data, and tracking travel within as well as to and from a country.

- Financial tracking: A state's ability to record and search financial transactions: checks, credit cards, wires, etc.

- Gag orders: Restrictions on and criminal penalties for the disclosure of the existence of state surveillance programs.

- Anti-crypto laws: Outlawing or restricting cryptography and/or privacy enhancing technologies.

- Lack of constitutional protections: A lack of constitutional privacy protections or the routine overriding of such protections.

- Data storage: The ability of the state to store the data gathered.

- Data search: The ability to organize and search the data gathered.

- Data retention requirements: Laws that require Internet and other service providers to save detailed records of their customers' Internet usage for a minimum period of time.

  o Telephone data retention requirements: Laws that require telephone companies to record and save records of their customers' telephone usage.

  o Cell phone data retention requirements: Laws that require cellular telephone companies to record and save records of their customers' usage and location.

- Medical records: Government access to the records of medical service providers.

- Enforcement: The state's ability to use force to seize anyone they want, whenever they want.

- Lack of *habeas corpus*: Lack of a right for a person under arrest to be brought before a judge or into court in a timely fashion or the overriding of such rights.

- Lack of a police-intel barrier: The lack of a barrier between police organizations and intelligence organizations, or the overriding of such barriers.

- Covert hacking: State operatives collecting, removing, or adding digital evidence to/from private computers without permission or the knowledge of the computers' owners.

- Loose or no warrants: Arrests or searches made without warrants or without careful examination and review of police statements and justifications by a truly independent judge or other third-party.

The list includes factors that apply to other forms of police states, such as the use of identity documents and police enforcement, but go considerably beyond them and emphasize the use of technology to gather and process the information collected.

In Popular Culture

Mass surveillance has been prominently featured in a wide array of books, films, and other media. Perhaps the most iconic example of fictional mass surveillance is George Orwell's 1949 novel *Nineteen Eighty-Four*, which depicts a dystopian surveillance state. Other media featuring mass surveillance systems include *Person of Interest* and other TV shows and other media types.

References

- Irina D. Manta Spring 2011 The Puzzle of Criminal Sanctions for Intellectual Property Infringement Harvard Journal of Law & Technology 24(2):469–518

- Winkler, Ira. Spies Among Us: How to Stop the Spies, Terrorists, Hackers, and Criminals You Don't Even Know You Encounter Every Day. John Wiley & Sons. 2005. pg. 92. ISBN 9780764589904

- Fried, Ina (June 15, 2005). "Blue Hat summit meant to reveal ways of the other side". Microsoft meets the hackers. CNET News. Retrieved May 31, 2010

- Miriam Bitton (2012) Rethinking the Anti-Counterfeiting Trade Agreement's Criminal Copyright Enforcement Measures The Journal Of Criminal Law & Criminology 102(1):67–117

- Moore, Robert (2005). Cybercrime: Investigating High Technology Computer Crime. Matthew Bender & Company. p. 258. ISBN 1-59345-303-5. Robert Moore

- Matt Eaton (17 April 2014). "Tribeca Film Festival programmer urges film industry to forget piracy and embrace internet". ABC News. Retrieved 21 April 2014

- Quayle, Ethel (September 2008). "The COPINE Project". Irish Probation Journal. Probation Board for Northern Ireland. 5. ISSN 1649-6396

- Moore, Robert (2006). Cybercrime: Investigating High-Technology Computer Crime (1st ed.). Cincinnati, Ohio: Anderson Publishing. ISBN 978-1-59345-303-9

- Samuel Gibbs (6 May 2014). "Piracy study shows illegal downloaders more likely to pay for films than music". The Guardian. Retrieved 12 May 2014

- Janis Wolak; David Finkelhor; Kimberly Mitchell (2011). "Child Pornography Possessors: Trends in Offender and Case Characteristics". Sexual Abuse: A Journal of Research and Treatment. 23 (22). doi:10.1177/1079063210372143

- Correa, Carlos Maria; Li, Xuan (2009). Intellectual property enforcement: international perspectives. Edward Elgar Publishing. p. 211. ISBN 978-1-84844-663-2

- "Shadow Market – In Brief" (PDF). 2011 BSA Global Software Piracy Study. Business Software Alliance (BSA). 2011. Retrieved 21 April 2014

- Taylor, M.; Quayle, E.; Holland, G. (2001). "Child Pornography, the Internet and Offending". The Canadian Journal of Policy Research. ISUMA. 2 (2): 94–100

- Virginia Crisp, Gabriel Menotti Gonring (2015). Besides the Screen: Moving Images through Distribution, Promotion and Curation. Palgrave Macmillan. ISBN 9781137471031

- "Fifth Annual BSA and IDC Global Software Piracy Study" (PDF). Fifth Annual BSA and IDC Global Software Piracy Study. Business Software Alliance (BSA). 2007. Retrieved 21 April 2014

2

Classification of Cybercrime

An Internet fraud is a scam which takes place by using the Internet. It usually occurs via the email, message boards or through websites. Some of the topics explained are cyberterrorism, cyberwarfare, international cybercrime and malware. The major components of cybercrime are discussed in this chapter.

Internet Fraud

An Internet fraud (online scam) is the use of Internet services or software with Internet access to defraud victims or to otherwise take advantage of them; for example, by stealing personal information, which can even lead to identity theft. Internet services can be used to present fraudulent solicitations to prospective victims, to conduct fraudulent transactions, or to transmit the proceeds of fraud to financial institutions or to others connected with the scheme. Research suggests that online scams can happen through social engineering and social influence. It can occur in chat rooms, social media, email, message boards, or on websites.

Counterfeit Postal Money Orders

According to the FBI, on April 26, 2005 Tom Zeller Jr. wrote an article in *The New York Times* regarding a surge in the quantity and quality of the forging of U.S. postal money orders, and its use to commit online fraud.

In the United States of America, the penalty for making or using counterfeit postal money orders is up to ten years in jail and/or a $25,000 fine.

Online Automotive Fraud

A fraudster posts a nonexistent vehicle for sale to a website, typically a luxury or sports car, advertised for well below its market value. The details of the vehicle, including photos and description, are typically lifted from sites such as Craigslist, AutoTrader.com and Cars.com. An interested buyer, hopeful for a bargain, emails the fraudster, who responds saying the car is still available but is located overseas. Or, the scammer will say that he is out of the country but the car is with a shipping company. The scam artist then instructs the victim to send a deposit or full payment via wire transfer to initiate the "shipping" process. To make the transaction seem more legitimate, the fraudster will ask the buyer to send money to a fake agent of a third party that claims to provide purchase protection. The unwitting victims wire the funds, and subsequently discover they have been scammed. In response, auto sales websites often post warnings to buyers, for example, those on Craigslist which warn not to accept offers in which vehicles are shipped, where funds are paid using Western Union or wire, etcetera, requesting those postings to be flagged as abuse.

Dating Fraud

With dating fraud, often the con artist develops a relationship with their victim through an online dating site and convinces the victim to send money to the fraudster. The requests for money can be a one-time event, or repeated over an extended period of time.

Although online dating has its dangers, three major dating services, eHarmony; Match.com and Spark Networks, have all agreed to take steps to keep their members safe from common online dating dangers. These steps include: checking registered members against the national sex offender data base, including ongoing tips and guides on how to meet that special someone in person in a safe way, ongoing tips and guides on how to safely interact with other members so as to avoid fraud and rapid abuse reporting systems so members can report abuse or suspected fraud as it happens, allowing the companies to take swifter action.

A new term in dating fraud is "catfish", referring to "a person who creates a false online identity in the hopes of luring people into romantic relationships."

Charity Fraud

The scammer poses as a charitable organization soliciting donations to help the victims of a natural disaster, terrorist attack (such as the Sept. 11 World Trade Center attack), regional conflict, or epidemic. Hurricane Katrina and the 2004 tsunami were popular targets of scammers perpetrating charity scams; other more timeless scam charities purport to be raising money for cancer, AIDS or Ebola virus research, children's orphanages (the scammer pretends to work for the orphanage or a non-profit associated with it), or impersonates charities such as the Red Cross or United Way. The scammer asks for donations, often linking to online news articles to strengthen their story of a funds drive. The scammer's victims are charitable people who believe they are helping a worthy cause and expect nothing in return. Once sent, the money is gone and the scammer often disappears, though many attempt to keep the scam going by asking for a series of payments. The victim may sometimes find themselves in legal trouble after deducting their supposed donations from their income taxes. United States tax law states that charitable donations are only deductible if made to a qualified non-profit organization. The scammer may tell the victim their donation is deductible and provide all necessary proof of donation, but the information provided by the scammer is fictional, and if audited, the victim faces stiff penalties as a result of the fraud. Though these scams have some of the highest success rates especially following a major disaster, and are employed by scammers all over the world, the average loss per victim is less than other fraud schemes. This is because, unlike scams involving a large expected payoff, the victim is far less likely to borrow money to donate or donate more than they can spare.

Internet Ticket Fraud

A variation of Internet marketing fraud offers tickets to sought-after events such as concerts, shows, and sports events. The tickets are fake, or are never delivered. The proliferation of online ticket agencies, and the existence of experienced and dishonest ticket resellers, has fueled this kind of fraud. Many such scams are run by British ticket touts, though they may base their operations in other countries.

A prime example was the global 2008 Beijing Olympic Games ticket fraud run by US-registered Xclusive Leisure and Hospitality, sold through a professionally designed website, www.beijing-ticketing.com, with the name "Beijing 2008 Ticketing". On 4 August it was reported that more than A$50 million worth of fake tickets had been sold through the website. On 6 August it was reported that the person behind the scam, which was wholly based outside China, was a British ticket tout, Terance Shepherd.

Click Fraud

Click fraud occurs when websites that are affiliates of advertising networks that pay per view or per click use spyware to force views or clicks to ads on their own websites. The affiliate is then paid a commission on the cost-per-click that was artificially generated. Affiliate programs such as Google's AdSense pay high commissions that drive the generation of bogus clicks. With paid clicks costing as much as US$100 and an online advertising industry worth more than US$10 billion, this form of Internet fraud is on the increase.

Internet "System" Fraud

When reached by telephone, you are asked if you are (first name, then family name) and expected to reply as if it were anyone asking. What follows is designed to project an "authoritative message." It has been reported the caller says, "We are calling from Microsoft® Division 35." (or similar pronouncement).

"This serves as official notification that your computer has been spreading a virus which must be stopped. It has caused corruption up-and-down the Internet damaging servers; thus coming to the attention of Microsoft® engineers, in this corrective and disciplinary department. Failure to comply carries stiff monetary damages and punitive legal measures." This is followed with a vigorous message that you may employ the caller to take the necessary corrective action for you at a cost. Needless to say your money will be lost; also you risk losing your identity and other assets which can be attacked.

Variations of the message has been heard; assuredly it is all quite false. Microsoft® does not call "anyone" about the Internet. It is not even within their purview. If such happened indeed, it would likely be Cisco® Systems and they would send officials personally. Moreover, such things do not occur as stated.

If you recognize language dialects they are identifiable as being the "Indian Continent" dialect. To avoid repetitive calls, just hang up. Hearing lengths of the message is reported by one recipient as occurring monthly for over a year.

Email Spoofing

Sender data shown in emails can be "spoofed", displaying a fake return address on outgoing email to hide the true origin of the message, therefore protecting it from being traced. The Sender Policy Framework protocol helps to combat email spoofing.

Short-selling or "Scalping" Schemes

A short-selling scheme is similar to the "pump-and-dump" scheme. The swindler disseminates false or fraudulent information through the same methods, but this time with the purpose of causing dramatic price *decreases* in a specific company's stock. Once the stock price falls to the desired level, the fraudster buys the stock (or options on the stock), and then reverses the false information—or just waits for the effects of the fraudulent information to wear off with time, or be disproved by the company or the media. Once the stock goes back to its normal level, the criminal sells the stock or option at a profit.

Identity Theft

I handed Flavia down the broad marble steps.

The Prisoner of Zenda (1894), with a "theft of identity" of the king.

Identity theft is the deliberate use of someone else's identity, usually as a method to gain a financial advantage or obtain credit and other benefits in the other person's name, and perhaps to the other person's disadvantage or loss. The person whose identity has been assumed may suffer adverse consequences if they are held responsible for the perpetrator's actions. Identity theft occurs when someone uses another's personally identifying information, like their name, identifying number, or credit card number, without their permission, to commit fraud or other crimes. The term *identity theft* was coined in 1964.

"Determining the link between data breaches and identity theft is challenging, primarily because identity theft victims often do not know how their personal information was obtained," and identity theft is not always detectable by the individual victims, according to a report done for the FTC. Identity fraud is often but not necessarily the consequence of identity theft. Someone can steal or misappropriate personal information without then committing identity theft using the information about every person, such as when a major data breach occurs. A US Government Accountability Office study determined that "most breaches have not resulted in detected incidents of identity theft". The report also warned that "the full extent is unknown". A later unpublished study by Carnegie Mellon University noted that "Most often, the causes of identity theft is not known," but reported that someone else concluded that "the probability of becoming a victim to identity theft as a result of a data breach is … around only 2%". More recently, an association of consumer data companies noted that one of the largest data breaches ever, accounting for over four million records, resulted in only about 1,800 instances of identity theft, according to the company whose systems were breached.

An October 2010 article entitled "Cyber Crime Made Easy" explained the level to which hackers are using malicious software. As one security specialist named Gunter Ollmann said, "Interested in credit card theft? There's an app for that." This statement summed up the ease with which these hackers are accessing all kinds of information online. The new program for infecting users' computers is called Zeus; and the program is so hacker friendly that even an inexperienced hacker can operate it. Although the hacking program is easy to use, that fact does not diminish the devastating effects that Zeus (or other software like Zeus) can do to a computer and the user. For example, the article stated that programs like Zeus can steal credit card information, important documents, and even documents necessary for homeland security. If the hacker were to gain this information, it would mean identity theft or even a possible terrorist attack. The ITAC says that about 15 milion Americans are having their identity stolen, in 2012.

Types

Sources such as the non-profit Identity Theft Resource Center sub-divide identity theft into five categories:

- Criminal identity theft (posing as another person when apprehended for a crime)

- Financial identity theft (using another's identity to obtain credit, goods and services)

- Identity cloning (using another's information to assume his or her identity in daily life)

- Medical identity theft (using another's identity to obtain medical care or drugs)

- Child identity theft.

Identity theft may be used to facilitate or fund other crimes including illegal immigration, terrorism, phishing and espionage. There are cases of identity cloning to attack payment systems, including online credit card processing and medical insurance.

Identity Cloning and Concealment

In this situation, the identity thief impersonates someone else in order to conceal their own true identity. Examples might be illegal immigrants, people hiding from creditors or other individuals, or those who simply want to become "anonymous" for personal reasons. Another example are *posers*, a label given to people who use somebody else's photos and information through social networking sites. Mostly, posers create believable stories involving friends of the real person they are imitating. Unlike identity theft used to obtain credit which usually comes to light when the debts mount, concealment may continue indefinitely without being detected, particularly if the identity thief is able to obtain false credentials in order to pass various authentication tests in everyday life.

Criminal Identity Theft

When a criminal fraudulently identifies himself to police as another individual at the point of arrest, it is sometimes referred to as "Criminal Identity Theft." In some cases criminals have previously obtained state-issued identity documents using credentials stolen from others, or have simply presented fake ID. Provided the subterfuge works, charges may be placed under the victim's name, letting the criminal off the hook. Victims might only learn of such incidents by chance, for example by receiving court summons, discovering their drivers licenses are suspended when stopped for minor traffic violations, or through background checks performed for employment purposes.

It can be difficult for the victim of a criminal identity theft to clear their record. The steps required to clear the victim's incorrect criminal record depend in which jurisdiction the crime occurred and whether the true identity of the criminal can be determined. The victim might need to locate the original arresting officers and prove their own identity by some reliable means such as fingerprinting or DNA testing, and may need to go to a court hearing to be cleared of the charges. Obtaining an expungement of court records may also be required. Authorities might permanently maintain the victim's name as an alias for the criminal's true identity in their criminal records databases. One problem that victims of criminal identity theft may encounter is that various data aggregators might still have the incorrect criminal records in their databases even after court and police records are corrected. Thus it is possible that a future background check will return the incorrect criminal records. This is just one example of the kinds of impact that may continue to affect the victims of identity theft for some months or even years after the crime, aside from the psychological trauma that being 'cloned' typically engenders.

Synthetic Identity Theft

A variation of identity theft which has recently become more common is *synthetic identity theft*, in which identities are completely or partially fabricated. The most common technique involves combining a real social security number with a name and birthdate other than the ones associated with the number. Synthetic identity theft is more difficult to track as it doesn't show on either person's credit report directly, but may appear as an entirely new file in the credit bureau or as a subfile on one of the victim's credit reports. Synthetic identity theft primarily harms the creditors who unwittingly grant the fraudsters credit. Individual victims can be affected if their names become confused with the synthetic identities, or if negative information in their subfiles impacts their credit ratings.

Medical Identity Theft

Privacy researcher Pam Dixon, founder of the World Privacy Forum, coined the term medical identity theft and released the first major report about this issue in 2006. In the report, she defined the crime for the first time and made the plight of victims public. The report's definition of the crime is that medical identity theft occurs when someone seeks medical care under the identity of another person. Insurance theft is also very common, if a thief has your insurance information and or your insurance card, they can seek medical attention posing as yourself. In addition to risks of financial harm common to all forms of identity theft, the thief's medical history may be added to the victim's medical records. Inaccurate information in the victim's records is difficult to correct and may affect future insurability or cause doctors relying on the misinformation to deliver inappropriate medical care. After the publication of the report, which contained a recommendation that consumers receive notifications of medical data breach incidents, California passed a law requiring this, and then finally HIPAA was expanded to also require medical breach notification when breaches affect 500 or more people. Data collected and stored by hospitals and other organisations such as medical aid schemes is up to 10 times more valuable to cybercriminals than credit card information.

Child Identity Theft

Child identity theft occurs when a minor's identity is used by another person for the impostor's personal gain. The impostor can be a family member, a friend, or even a stranger who targets children. The Social Security numbers of children are valued because they do not have any information associated with them. Thieves can establish lines of credit, obtain driver's licenses, or even buy a house using a child's identity. This fraud can go undetected for years, as most children do not discover the problem until years later. Child identity theft is fairly common, and studies have shown that the problem is growing. The largest study on child identity theft, as reported by Richard Power of the Carnegie Mellon Cylab with data supplied by AllClear ID, found that of 40,000 children, 10.2% were victims of identity theft.

Financial Identity Theft

The most common type is financial identity theft, where someone wants to gain economical benefits in someone else's name. This includes getting credits, loans, goods and services, claiming to be someone else.

Techniques for Obtaining and Exploiting Personal Information for Identity theft

Identity thieves typically obtain and exploit personally identifiable information about individuals, or various credentials they use to authenticate themselves, in order to impersonate them. Examples include:

- Rummaging through rubbish for personal information (dumpster diving)

- Retrieving personal data from redundant IT equipment and storage media including PCs, servers, PDAs, mobile phones, USB memory sticks and hard drives that have been disposed of carelessly at public dump sites, given away or sold on without having been properly sanitized

- Using public records about individual citizens, published in official registers such as electoral rolls

- Stealing bank or credit cards, identification cards, passports, authentication tokens ... typically by pickpocketing, housebreaking or mail theft

- Common-knowledge questioning schemes that offer account verification and compromise: "What's your mother's maiden name?", "what was your first car model?", or "What was your first pet's name?", etc.

- Skimming information from bank or credit cards using compromised or hand-held card readers, and creating clone cards

- Using 'contactless' credit card readers to acquire data wirelessly from RFID-enabled passports

- Shoulder-Surfing, involves an individual who discreetly watches or hears others providing valuable personal information. This is particularly done in crowded places because it is relatively easy to observe someone as they fill out forms, enter PIN numbers on ATM's or even type passwords on smartphones.

- Stealing personal information from computers using breaches in browser security or malware such as Trojan horse keystroke logging programs or other forms of spyware

- Hacking computer networks, systems and databases to obtain personal data, often in large quantities

- Exploiting breaches that result in the publication or more limited disclosure of personal information such as names, addresses, Social Security number or credit card numbers

- Advertising bogus job offers in order to accumulate resumes and applications typically disclosing applicants' names, home and email addresses, telephone numbers and sometimes their banking details

- Exploiting insider access and abusing the rights of privileged IT users to access personal data on their employers' systems

- Infiltrating organizations that store and process large amounts or particularly valuable personal information

- Impersonating trusted organizations in emails, SMS text messages, phone calls or other forms of communication in order to dupe victims into disclosing their personal information or login credentials, typically on a fake corporate website or data collection form (phishing)

- Brute-force attacking weak passwords and using inspired guesswork to compromise weak password reset questions

- Obtaining castings of fingers for falsifying fingerprint identification.

- Browsing social networking websites for personal details published by users, often using this information to appear more credible in subsequent social engineering activities

- Diverting victims' email or post in order to obtain personal information and credentials such as credit cards, billing and bank/credit card statements, or to delay the discovery of new accounts and credit agreements opened by the identity thieves in the victims' names

- Using false pretenses to trick individuals, customer service representatives and help desk workers into disclosing personal information and login details or changing user passwords/access rights (pretexting)

- Stealing cheques (checks) to acquire banking information, including account numbers and bank routing numbers or sort code

- Guessing Social Security numbers by using information found on Internet social networks such as Facebook and MySpace

- Low security/privacy protection on photos that are easily clickable and downloaded on social networking sites.

- Befriending strangers on social networks and taking advantage of their trust until private information is given.

Indicators that you may be a Victim of Identity Theft

The majority of identity theft victims do not realize that they are a victim until it has negatively impacted their lives. Many people do not find out that their identities have been stolen until they are contacted by financial institutions or discover suspicious activities on their bank accounts. According to an article by Herb Weisbaum, everyone in the US should assume that their personal information has been compromised at one point. It is therefore of great importance to watch out for warning signs that your identity has been compromised. The following are ten indicators that someone else might be using your identity.

1. Credit or debit card charges for goods or services you are not aware of, including unauthorized withdrawals from your account

2. Receiving calls from credit or debit card fraud control department warning of possible suspicious activity on your credit card account

3. Receiving credit cards that you did not apply for

4. Receiving information that a credit scoring investigation was done. They are often done when a loan or phone subscription was applied for.

5. Checks bouncing for lack of enough money in your account to cover the amount. This might be as a result of unauthorized withdrawals from your account

6. Identity theft criminals may commit crimes with your personal information. You may not realize this until you see the police on your door arresting you for crimes that you did not commit

7. Sudden changes to your credit score may indicate that someone else is using your credit cards

8. Bills for services like gas, water, electricity not arriving in time. This can be an indication that your mail was stolen or redirected

9. Being not approved for loans because your credit report indicates that you are not credit worthy

10. Receiving notification from your post office informing you that your mails are being forwarded to another unknown address

11. Your yearly tax returns indicating that you have earned more than you have actually earned. This might indicate that someone is using your national identification number e.g. SSN to report their earnings to the tax authorities

Individual Identity Protection

The acquisition of personal identifiers is made possible through serious breaches of privacy. For consumers, this is usually a result of them naively providing their personal information or login credentials to the identity thieves as a result of being duped but identity-related documents such as credit cards, bank statements, utility bills, checkbooks etc. may also be physically stolen from vehicles, homes, offices, and not the least letter boxes, or directly from victims by pickpockets and bag snatchers. Guardianship of personal identifiers by consumers is the most common intervention strategy recommended by the US Federal Trade Commission, Canadian Phone Busters and most sites that address identity theft. Such organizations offer recommendations on how individuals can prevent their information falling into the wrong hands.

Identity theft can be partially mitigated by *not* identifying oneself unnecessarily (a form of information security control known as risk avoidance). This implies that organizations, IT systems and procedures should not demand excessive amounts of personal information or credentials for identification and authentication. Requiring, storing and processing personal identifiers (such as Social Security number, national identification number, driver's license number, credit card number, etc.) increases the risks of identity theft unless this valuable personal information is adequately secured at all times. Committing personal identifiers to memory is a sound practice that can reduce the risks of a would-be identity thief from obtaining these records. To help in remembering numbers such as social security numbers and credit card numbers, it is helpful to consider using mnemonic techniques or memory aids such as the mnemonic Major System.

Identity thieves sometimes impersonate dead people, using personal information obtained from death notices, gravestones and other sources to exploit delays between the death and the closure of the person's accounts, the inattentiveness of grieving families and weaknesses in the processes for credit-checking. Such crimes may continue for some time until the deceased's families or the authorities notice and react to anomalies.

In recent years, commercial identity theft protection/insurance services have become available in many countries. These services purport to help protect the individual from identity theft or help detect that identity theft has occurred in exchange for a monthly or annual membership fee or premium. The services typically work either by setting fraud alerts on the individual's credit files with the three major credit bureaus or by setting up credit report monitoring with the credit bureaux. While identity theft protection/insurance services have been heavily marketed, their value has been called into question.

Identity Protection by organizations

In their May 1998 testimony before the United States Senate, the Federal Trade Commission (FTC) discussed the sale of Social Security numbers and other personal identifiers by credit-raters and data miners. The FTC agreed to the industry's self-regulating principles restricting access to information on credit reports. According to the industry, the restrictions vary according to the category of customer. Credit reporting agencies gather and disclose personal and credit information to a wide business client base.

Poor stewardship of personal data by organizations, resulting in unauthorized access to sensitive data, can expose individuals to the risk of identity theft. The Privacy Rights Clearinghouse has documented over 900 individual data breaches by US companies and government agencies since January 2005, which together have involved over 200 million total records containing sensitive personal information, many containing social security numbers. Poor corporate diligence standards which can result in data breaches include:

- failure to shred confidential information before throwing it into dumpsters

- failure to ensure adequate network security

- credit card numbers stolen by call center agents and people with access to call recordings

- the theft of laptop computers or portable media being carried off-site containing vast amounts of personal information. The use of strong encryption on these devices can reduce the chance of data being misused should a criminal obtain them.

- the brokerage of personal information to other businesses without ensuring that the purchaser maintains adequate security controls

- Failure of governments, when registering sole proprietorships, partnerships, and corporations, to determine if the officers listed in the Articles of Incorporation are who they say they are. This potentially allows criminals access to personal information through credit rating and data mining services.

The failure of corporate or government organizations to protect consumer privacy, client confidentiality and political privacy has been criticized for facilitating the acquisition of personal identifiers by criminals.

Using various types of biometric information, such as fingerprints, for identification and authentication has been cited as a way to thwart identity thieves, however there are technological limitations and privacy concerns associated with these methods as well.

Legal Responses

International

In March 2014, after it was learned two passengers with stolen passports were on board Malaysia Airlines Flight 370 which went missing on March 8, 2014, it came to light that Interpol maintains a database of 40 million lost and stolen travel documents from 157 countries which it makes available to governments and the public, including airlines and hotels. The Stolen and Lost Travel Documents (SLTD) database however is little used. *Big News Network* which is based in the UAE, observed that Interpol Secretary General Ronald K. Noble told a forum in Abu Dhabi the previous month this was the case. "The bad news is that, despite being incredibly cost effective and deployable to virtually anywhere in the world, only a handful of countries are systematically using SLTD to screen travelers. The result is a major gap in our global security apparatus that is left vulnerable to exploitation by criminals and terrorists," Noble is quoted as saying.

Australia

In Australia, each state has enacted laws that deal with different aspects of identity or fraud issues. Some states have now amended relevant criminal laws to reflect crimes of identity theft, such as the Criminal Law Consolidation Act 1935 (SA), Crimes Amendment (Fraud, Identity and Forgery Offences) Act 2009 and also in Queensland under the Criminal Code 1899 (QLD). Other states and territories are in states of development in respect of regulatory frameworks relating to identity theft such as Western Australia in respect of Criminal Code Amendment (Identity Crime) Bill 2009.

On the Commonwealth level, under the *Criminal Code Amendment (Theft, Fraud, Bribery & Related Offences) Act 2000* which amended certain provisions within the *Criminal Code Act 1995*,

135.1 General Dishonesty

> (3) A person is guilty of an offence if a) the person does anything with the intention of dishonestly *causing a loss to another person*; and b) the other person is a Commonwealth entity. Penalty: *Imprisonment for 5 years.*

Likewise, each state has enacted their own privacy laws to prevent misuse of personal information and data. The Commonwealth *Privacy Act* is applicable only to Commonwealth and territory agencies, and to certain private sector bodies (where for example they deal with sensitive records, such as medical records, or they have more than $3 million turnover PA).

Canada

Under section 402.2 of the *Criminal Code,*

Everyone commits an offence who knowingly obtains or possesses another person's identity information in circumstances giving rise to a reasonable inference that the information is intended to be used to commit an indictable offence that includes fraud, deceit or falsehood as an element of the offence.

is guilty of an indictable offence and liable to imprisonment for a term of not more than five years; or is guilty of an offence punishable on summary conviction.

Under section 403 of the *Criminal Code,*

(1) Everyone commits an offence who fraudulently personates another person, living or dead,

(a) with intent to gain advantage for themselves or another person; (b) with intent to obtain any property or an interest in any property; (c) with intent to cause disadvantage to the person being personated or another person; or (d) with intent to avoid arrest or prosecution or to obstruct, pervert or defeat the course of justice. is guilty of an indictable offence and liable to imprisonment for a term of not more than 10 years; or guilty of an offence punishable on summary conviction.

In Canada, *Privacy Act* (federal legislation) covers only federal government, agencies and crown corporations. Each province and territory has its own privacy law and privacy commissioners to limit the storage and use of personal data. For the private sector, the purpose of the Personal Information Protection and Electronic Documents Act (2000, c. 5) (known as PIPEDA) is to establish rules to govern the collection, use and disclosure of personal information; except for the provinces of Quebec, Ontario, Alberta and British Columbia where provincial laws have been deemed substantially similar.

France

In France, a person convicted of identity theft can be sentenced up to five years in prison and fined up to €75,000.

Hong Kong

Under HK Laws. Chap 210 *Theft Ordinance*, sec. 16A Fraud

(1)   If any person by any deceit (whether or not the deceit is the sole or main inducement) and with intent to defraud induces another person to commit an act or make an omission, which results either-

    (a) in benefit to any person other than the second-mentioned person; or (b) in prejudice or a substantial risk of prejudice to any person other than the first-mentioned person, the first-mentioned person commits the offense of fraud and is liable on conviction upon indictment to imprisonment for 14 years.

Under the *Personal Data (Privacy) Ordinance*, it established the post of Privacy Commissioner for Personal Data and mandate how much personal information one can collect, retain and destruction. This legislation also provides citizens the right to request information held by businesses and government to the extent provided by this law.

India

Under the Information Technology Act 2000 Chapter IX Sec 66C

SECTION 66C

PUNISHMENT FOR IDENTITY THEFT Whoever, fraudulently or dishonestly makes use of the electronic signature, password or any other unique identification feature of any other person, shall be punished with imprisonment of either description for a term which may extend to three years and shall also be liable to fine which may extend to rupees one lakh.

Philippines

Social networking sites are one of the most famous spreader of *posers* in the online community, giving the users freedom to place any information they want without any verification that the account is being used by the real person.

Philippines, which ranks eighth in the numbers of users of Facebook and other social networking sites such as Twitter, Multiply and Tumblr, has been known as source of various identity theft problems. Identities of those people who carelessly put personal information on their profiles can easily be stolen just by simple browsing. There are people who meet online, get to know each other through the free Facebook chat and exchange of messages that then leads to sharing of private information. Others get romantically involved with their online friends that they tend to give too much information such as their social security number, bank account and even personal basic information such as home address and company address.

This phenomena lead to the creation of Senate Bill 52: Cybercrime Prevention Act of 2010. Section 2 of this bill states that it recognizes the importance of communication and multimedia for the development, exploitation and dissemination of information but violators will be punished by the law through imprisonment or a fine upwards of Php200,000, but not exceeding 1 million, or depending on the damage caused, or both (Section 7).

Sweden

Sweden has had relatively few problems with identity theft. This is because only Swedish identity documents have been accepted for identity verification. Stolen documents are traceable by banks and some other institutions. The banks have the duty to check the identity of people withdrawing money or getting loans. If a bank gives money to someone using an identity document reported as stolen, the bank must take the loss. Since 2008, any EU passport is valid in Sweden for identity check, and Swedish passports are valid all over the EU. This makes it harder to detect stolen documents, but still banks in Sweden must ensure that stolen documents are not accepted.

Other types of identity theft have become more common in Sweden. One common example is ordering a credit card to someone who has an unlocked letterbox and is not home in the daytime. The thief steals the letter with the credit card and then the letter with the code which typically arrives a few days later. Usage of a stolen credit card is hard in Sweden, since an identity document or a PIN code it is normally demanded. If the shop does not demand that, it must take the loss from stolen credit cards. The method of observing someone using the credit card PIN code, stealing the card or skimming it, and then using the card, has become more common.

Legally, Sweden is an open society. The Principle of Public Access says that all information kept by public authorities must be available for anyone except in certain cases. Specifically, anyone's address, income, taxes etc. are available to anyone. This makes fraud easier (the address is restricted only for people who needs to hide).

There was until 2016 no legal ban specifically against using someone's identity, only on the indirect damage caused. To impersonate someone else for financial gain is a kind of fraud, which is described in the Criminal Code (Swedish: *brottsbalken*). To impersonate someone else to discredit someone by breaking into social media accounts and provoke, is libel, but that is hard to sentence someone for. A new law was introduced late 2016 which partially banned unpermitted identity usage.

United Kingdom

In the United Kingdom personal data is protected by the Data Protection Act 1998. The Act covers all personal data which an organization may hold, including names, birthday and anniversary dates, addresses, telephone numbers, etc.

Under English law (which extends to Wales but not to Northern Ireland or Scotland), the deception offences under the Theft Act 1968 increasingly contend with identity theft situations. In *R v Seward* (2005) EWCA Crim 1941 the defendant was acting as the "front man" in the use of stolen credit cards and other documents to obtain goods. He obtained goods to the value of £10,000 for others who are unlikely ever to be identified. The Court of Appeal considered sentencing policy for deception offenses involving "identity theft" and concluded that a prison sentence was required. Henriques J. said at para 14:"Identity fraud is a particularly pernicious and prevalent form of dishonesty calling for, in our judgment, deterrent sentences."

Statistics released by CIFAS - The UK's Fraud Prevention Service show that there were 89,000 victims of identity theft in the UK 2010. This compared with 2009 where there were 85,000 victims.

Men in their 30s and 40s are the most common UK victims and identity fraud now accounts for nearly half of all frauds recorded.

United States

The increase in crimes of identity theft led to the drafting of the Identity Theft and Assumption Deterrence Act. In 1998, The Federal Trade Commission appeared before the United States Senate. The FTC discussed crimes which exploit consumer credit to commit loan fraud, mortgage fraud, lines-of-credit fraud, credit card fraud, commodities and services frauds. The Identity Theft Deterrence Act (2003)[ITADA] amended U.S. Code Title 18, 1028 ("Fraud related to activity in connection with identification documents, authentication features, and information"). The statute now makes the possession of any "means of identification" to "knowingly transfer, possess, or use without lawful authority" a federal crime, alongside unlawful possession of identification documents. However, for federal jurisdiction to prosecute, the crime must include an "identification document" that either: (a) is purportedly issued by the United States, (b) is used or intended to defraud the United States, (c) is sent through the mail, or (d) is used in a manner that affects interstate or foreign commerce. Punishment can be up to 5, 15, 20, or 30 years in federal prison, plus fines, depending on the underlying crime per 18 U.S.C. 1028(b). In addition, punishments for the unlawful use of a "means of identification" were strengthened in 1028A ("Aggravated Identity Theft"), allowing for a consecutive sentence under specific enumerated felony violations as defined in 1028A(c)(1) through (11).

The Act also provides the Federal Trade Commission with authority to track the number of incidents and the dollar value of losses. Their figures relate mainly to consumer financial crimes and not the broader range of all identification-based crimes.

If charges are brought by state or local law enforcement agencies, different penalties apply depending on the state.

Six Federal agencies conducted a joint task force to increase the ability to detect identity theft. Their joint recommendation on "red flag" guidelines is a set of requirements on financial institutions and other entities which furnish credit data to credit reporting services to develop written plans for detecting identity theft. The FTC has determined that most medical practices are considered creditors and are subject to requirements to develop a plan to prevent and respond to patient identity theft. These plans must be adopted by each organization's Board of Directors and monitored by senior executives.

Identity theft complaints as a percentage of all fraud complaints decreased from 2004-2006. The Federal Trade Commission reported that fraud complaints in general were growing faster than ID theft complaints. The findings were similar in two other FTC studies done in 2003 and 2005. In 2003, 4.6 percent of the US population said they were a victim of ID theft. In 2005, that number had dropped to 3.7 percent of the population. The Commission's 2003 estimate was that identity theft accounted for some $52.6 billion of losses in the preceding year alone and affected more than 9.91 million Americans; the figure comprises $47.6 billion lost by businesses and $5 billion lost by consumers.

According to the U.S. Bureau of Justice Statistics, in 2010, 7% of US households experienced identity theft - up from 5.5% in 2005 when the figures were first assembled, but broadly flat since 2007. In 2012, approximately 16.6 million persons, or 7% of all U.S. residents age 16 or older, reported being victims of one or more incidents of identity theft.

Two states, California and Wisconsin have created an Office of Privacy Protection to assist their citizens in avoiding and recovering from identity theft.

In 2009, Indiana created an Identity Theft Unit within their Office of Attorney General to educate and assist consumers in avoiding and recovering from identity theft as well as assist law enforcement in investigating and prosecuting identity theft crimes.

In Massachusetts in 2009-2010, Governor Deval Patrick made a commitment to balance consumer protection with the needs of small business owners. His Office of Consumer Affairs and Business Regulation announced certain adjustments to Massachusetts' identity theft regulations that maintain protections and also allows flexibility in compliance. These updated regulations went into effect on March 1, 2010. The regulations are clear that their approach to data security is a risk-based approach important to small businesses and might not handle a lot of personal information about customers.

The IRS has created the IRS Identity Protection Specialized Unit to help taxpayers' who are victims of federal tax-related identity theft. Generally, the identity thief will use a stolen SSN to file a forged tax return and attempt to get a fraudulent refund early in the filing season. A taxpayer will need to fill out Form 14039, *Identity Theft Affidavit*.

Most states followed California's lead and enacted mandatory data breach notification laws. As a result, companies that report a data breach typically report it to all their customers.

Spread and Impact

Surveys in the USA from 2003 to 2006 showed a decrease in the total number of victims and a decrease in the total value of identity fraud from US$47.6 billion in 2003 to $15.6 billion in 2006. The average fraud per person decreased from $4,789 in 2003 to $1,882 in 2006. A Microsoft report shows that this drop is due to statistical problems with the methodology, that such survey-based estimates are "hopelessly flawed" and exaggerate the true losses by orders of magnitude.

The 2003 survey from the Identity Theft Resource Center found that:

- Only 15% of victims find out about the theft through proactive action taken by a business

- The average time spent by victims resolving the problem is about 330 hours

- 73% of respondents indicated the crime involved the thief acquiring a credit card

In a widely publicized account, Michelle Brown, a victim of identity fraud, testified before a U.S. Senate Committee Hearing on Identity Theft. Ms. Brown testified that: "over a year and a half from January 1998 through July 1999, one individual impersonated me to procure over $50,000 in goods and services. Not only did she damage my credit, but she escalated her crimes to a level that I never truly expected: she engaged in drug trafficking. The crime resulted in my erroneous arrest record, a warrant out for my arrest, and eventually, a prison record when she was booked under my name as an inmate in the Chicago Federal Prison."

In Australia, identity theft was estimated to be worth between A$1billion and A$4 billion per annum in 2001.

In the United Kingdom, the Home Office reported that identity fraud costs the UK economy £1.2 billion annually (experts believe that the real figure could be much higher) although privacy groups object to the validity of these numbers, arguing that they are being used by the government to push for introduction of national ID cards. Confusion over exactly what constitutes identity theft has led to claims that statistics may be exaggerated. An extensively reported study from Microsoft Research in 2011 finds that estimates of identity theft losses contain enormous exaggerations, writing that surveys "are so compromised and biased that no faith whatever can be placed in their findings."

Email Spoofing

Email spoofing is the creation of email messages with a forged sender address.

Because the core email protocols do not have any mechanism for authentication, it is common for spam and phishing emails to use such spoofing to mislead the recipient about the origin of the message.

Technical Detail

When an SMTP email is sent, the initial connection provides two pieces of address information:

- MAIL FROM: - generally presented to the recipient as the *Return-path:* header but not normally visible to the end user, and by default *no checks* are done that the sending system is authorized to send on behalf of that address.

- RCPT TO: - specifies which email address the email is delivered to, is not normally visible to the end user but *may* be present in the headers as part of the "Received:" header.

Together these are sometimes referred to as the "envelope" addressing, by analogy with a traditional paper envelope, and unless the receiving mail server signals that it has problems with either of these items, the sending system sends the "DATA" command, and typically sends several header items, including:

- From: Joe Q Doe <joeqdoe@example.com> - the address visible to the recipient; but again, by default no checks are done that the sending system is authorized to send on behalf of that address.

- Reply-to: Jane Roe <Jane.Roe@example.mil> - similarly not checked

and sometimes:

- Sender: Jin Jo <jin.jo@example.jp> - also not checked

The result is that the email recipient sees the email as having come from the address in the *From:* header; they may sometimes be able to find the *MAIL FROM* address; and if they reply to the email it will go to either the address presented in the *From:* or *Reply-to:* header - but none of these addresses are typically reliable, so automated bounce messages may generate backscatter.

Use by Spam and Worms

Malware such as Klez and Sober and many more modern examples often search for email addresses within the computer they have infected, and use those addresses both as targets for email, but also to create credible forged *From* fields in the emails that they send, so that these emails are more likely to be opened. For example:

- Alice is sent an infected email which she opens, running the worm code.

- The worm code searches Alice's email address book and finds the addresses of Bob and Charlie.

- From Alice's computer, the worm sends an infected email to Bob, but forged to appear to have been sent by Charlie.

In this case, even if Bob's system detects the incoming mail as containing malware, he sees the source as being Charlie, even though it really came from Alice's computer; meanwhile Alice may remain unaware that her computer has been infected.

Fooling Media

It has happened that the media printed false stories based on spoofed e-mails.

- In October 2013, an e-mail which looked like it was from the Swedish company Fingerprint Cards was sent to a news agency, saying that Samsung offered to purchase the company. The news spread and the stock exchange rate surged by 50%. It was later discovered the e-mail was a fake.

Legitimate use

In the early Internet, "legitimately spoofed" email was common. For example, a visiting user might use the local organization's SMTP server to send email from the user's foreign address. Since most servers were configured as "open relays", this was a common practice. As spam email became an annoying problem, these sorts of "legitimate" uses fell out of favor.

When multiple software systems communicate with each other via email, spoofing may be required in order to facilitate such communication. In any scenario where an email address is set up to automatically forward incoming emails to a system which only accepts emails from the email forwarder, spoofing is required in order to facilitate this behavior. This is common between ticketing systems which communicate with other ticketing systems.

The Effect on Mailservers

Traditionally, mail servers could accept a mail item, then later send a Non-Delivery Report or "bounce" message if it couldn't be delivered or had been quarantined for any reason. These would be sent to the "MAIL FROM:" aka "Return Path" address. With the massive rise in forged addresses, Best Practice is now to *not* generate NDRs for detected spam, viruses etc. but to reject the email during the SMTP transaction. When mail administrators fail to take this approach, their systems are guilty of sending "backscatter" emails to innocent parties - in itself a form of spam - or being used to perform "Joe job" attacks.

Identifying the Source of the Email

Although email spoofing is effective in forging the email address, the IP address of the computer sending the mail can generally be identified from the "Received:" lines in the email header. In many cases this is likely to be an innocent third party infected by malware that is sending the email without the owner's knowledge.

Countermeasures

The SSL/TLS system used to encrypt server-to-server email traffic can also be used to enforce authentication, but in practice it is seldom used, and a range of other potential solutions have also failed to gain traction.

However a number of effective systems are now widely used, including:

- SPF

- Sender ID

- DKIM

- DMARC

Although their use is increasing, estimates vary widely as to what percentage of emails have no form of domain authentication: from 8.6% to "almost half". To effectively stop forged email being delivered, the sending domains, their mail servers, and the receiving system all need to be configured correctly for these higher standards of authentication.

Phishing

Dear valued customer of TrustedBank,

We have recieved notice that you have recently attempted to withdraw the following amount from your checking account while in another country: $135.25.

If this information is not correct, someone unknown may have access to your account. As a safety measure, please visit our website via the link below to verify your personal information:

http://www.trustedbank.com/general/custverifyinfo.asp

Once you have done this, our fraud department will work to resolve this discrepency. We are happy you have chosen us to do business with.

Thank you,
TrustedBank

Member FDIC © 2005 TrustedBank, Inc.

An example of a phishing email, disguised as an official email from a (fictional) bank. The sender is attempting to trick the recipient into revealing confidential information by "confirming" it at the phisher's website. Note the misspelling of the words *received* and *discrepancy* as *recieved* and *discrepency*. Also note that although the URL of the bank's webpage appears to be legitimate, the hyperlink would actually be pointed at the phisher's webpage.

Phishing is the attempt to obtain sensitive information such as usernames, passwords, and credit card details (and, indirectly, money), often for malicious reasons, by disguising as a trustworthy entity in an electronic communication. The word is a neologism created as a homophone of *fishing* due to the similarity of using a bait in an attempt to catch a victim. According to the 2013 Microsoft Computing Safety Index, released in February 2014, the annual worldwide impact of phishing could be as high as US$5 billion.

Phishing is typically carried out by email spoofing or instant messaging, and it often directs users to enter personal information at a fake website, the look and feel of which are almost identical to the legitimate one. Communications purporting to be from social web sites, auction sites, banks, online payment processors or IT administrators are often used to lure victims. Phishing emails may contain links to websites that are infected with malware.

Phishing is an example of social engineering techniques used to deceive users, and exploits weaknesses in current web security. Attempts to deal with the growing number of reported phishing incidents include legislation, user training, public awareness, and technical security measures.

Phishing Types

Spear Phishing

Phishing attempts directed at specific individuals or companies have been termed spear phishing. Attackers may gather personal information about their target to increase their probability of success. This technique is by far the most successful on the internet today, accounting for 91% of attacks.

Clone Phishing

Clone phishing is a type of phishing attack whereby a legitimate, and previously delivered, email containing an attachment or link has had its content and recipient address(es) taken and used to create an almost identical or cloned email. The attachment or link within the email is replaced with a malicious version and then sent from an email address spoofed to appear to come from the original sender. It may claim to be a resend of the original or an updated version to the original. This technique could be used to pivot (indirectly) from a previously infected machine and gain a foothold on another machine, by exploiting the social trust associated with the inferred connection due to both parties receiving the original email.

Whaling

Several phishing attacks have been directed specifically at senior executives and other high-profile targets within businesses, and the term whaling has been coined for these kinds of attacks. In the case of whaling, the masquerading web page/email will take a more serious executive-level form. The content will be crafted to target an upper manager and the person's role in the company. The content of a whaling attack email is often written as a legal subpoena, customer complaint, or executive issue. Whaling scam emails are designed to masquerade as a critical business email, sent from a legitimate business authority. The content is meant to be tailored for upper management, and usually involves some kind of falsified company-wide concern. Whaling phishers have also forged official-looking FBI subpoena emails, and claimed that the manager needs to click a link and install special software to view the subpoena.

Link Manipulation

Most methods of phishing use some form of technical deception designed to make a link in an email (and the spoofed website it leads to) appear to belong to the spoofed organization. Misspelled URLs or the use of subdomains are common tricks used by phishers. In the following example URL, `http://www.yourbank.example.com/`, it appears as though the URL will take you to the *example* section of the *yourbank* website; actually this URL points to the "*yourbank*" (i.e. phishing) section of the *example* website. Another common trick is to make the displayed text for a link (the text between the <A> tags) suggest a reliable destination, when the link actually goes to the phishers' site. Many desktop email clients and web browsers will show a link's target URL in the status bar while hovering the mouse over it. This behavior, however, may in some circumstances be overridden by the phisher. Equivalent mobile apps generally do not have this preview feature.

A further problem with URLs has been found in the handling of internationalized domain names (IDN) in web browsers, that might allow visually identical web addresses to lead to different, possibly malicious, websites. Despite the publicity surrounding the flaw, known as IDN spoofing or homograph attack, phishers have taken advantage of a similar risk, using open URL redirectors on the websites of trusted organizations to disguise malicious URLs with a trusted domain. Even digital certificates do not solve this problem because it is quite possible for a phisher to purchase a valid certificate and subsequently change content to spoof a genuine website, or, to host the phish site without SSL at all.

Filter Evasion

Phishers have even started using images instead of text to make it harder for anti-phishing filters to detect text commonly used in phishing emails. However, this has led to the evolution of more sophisticated anti-phishing filters that are able to recover hidden text in images. These filters use OCR (optical character recognition) to optically scan the image and filter it.

Some anti-phishing filters have even used IWR (intelligent word recognition), which is not meant to completely replace OCR, but these filters can even detect cursive, hand-written, rotated (including upside-down text), or distorted (such as made wavy, stretched vertically or laterally, or in different directions) text, as well as text on colored backgrounds.

Website Forgery

Once a victim visits the phishing website, the deception is not over. Some phishing scams use JavaScript commands in order to alter the address bar. This is done either by placing a picture of a legitimate URL over the address bar, or by closing the original bar and opening up a new one with the legitimate URL.

An attacker can even use flaws in a trusted website's own scripts against the victim. These types of attacks (known as cross-site scripting) are particularly problematic, because they direct the user to sign in at their bank or service's own web page, where everything from the web address to the security certificates appears correct. In reality, the link to the website is crafted to carry out the attack, making it very difficult to spot without specialist knowledge. Just such a flaw was used in 2006 against PayPal.

A Universal Man-in-the-middle (MITM) Phishing Kit, discovered in 2007, provides a simple-to-use interface that allows a phisher to convincingly reproduce websites and capture log-in details entered at the fake site.

To avoid anti-phishing techniques that scan websites for phishing-related text, phishers have begun to use Flash-based websites (a technique known as phlashing). These look much like the real website, but hide the text in a multimedia object.

Covert Redirect

Covert redirect is a subtle method to perform phishing attacks that makes links appear legitimate, but actually redirect a victim to an attacker's website. The flaw is usually masqueraded under a log-in popup based on an affected site's domain. It can affect OAuth 2.0 and OpenID based on well-known exploit parameters as well. This often makes use of open redirect and XSS vulnerabilities in the third-party application websites.

Normal phishing attempts can be easy to spot because the malicious page's URL will usually be different from the real site link. For covert redirect, an attacker could use a real website instead by corrupting the site with a malicious login popup dialogue box. This makes covert redirect different from others.

For example, suppose a victim clicks a malicious phishing link beginning with Facebook. A popup window from Facebook will ask whether the victim would like to authorize the app. If the victim chooses to authorize the app, a "token" will be sent to the attacker and the victim's personal sensitive information could be exposed. These information may include the email address, birth date, contacts, and work history. In case the "token" has greater privilege, the attacker could obtain more sensitive information including the mailbox, online presence, and friends list. Worse still, the attacker may possibly control and operate the user's account. Even if the victim does not choose to authorize the app, he or she will still get redirected to a website controlled by the attacker. This could potentially further compromise the victim.

This vulnerability was discovered by Wang Jing, a Mathematics Ph.D. student at School of Physical and Mathematical Sciences in Nanyang Technological University in Singapore. Covert redirect is a notable security flaw, though it is not a threat to the Internet worth significant attention.

Social Engineering

Users can be incentivised to click on various kinds of unexpected content for a variety of technical and social reasons. For example, a malicious attachment might masquerade as a benign linked Google doc.

Alternatively users might be outraged by a fake news story, click a link and become infected.

Phone Phishing

Not all phishing attacks require a fake website. Messages that claimed to be from a bank told users to dial a phone number regarding problems with their bank accounts. Once the phone number (owned by the phisher, and provided by a voice over IP service) was dialed, prompts told users to enter their account numbers and PIN. Vishing (voice phishing) sometimes uses fake caller-ID data to give the appearance that calls come from a trusted organisation. SMS phishing uses cell phone text messages to induce people to divulge their personal information.

Other Techniques

- Another attack used successfully is to forward the client to a bank's legitimate website, then to place a popup window requesting credentials on top of the page in a way that makes many users think the bank is requesting this sensitive information.

- Tabnabbing takes advantage of tabbed browsing, with multiple open tabs. This method silently redirects the user to the affected site. This technique operates in reverse to most phishing techniques in that it doesn't directly take the user to the fraudulent site, but instead loads the fake page in one of the browser's open tabs.

- Evil twin is a phishing technique that is hard to detect. A phisher creates a fake wireless network that looks similar to a legitimate public network that may be found in public places such as airports, hotels or coffee shops. Whenever someone logs on to the bogus network, fraudsters try to capture their passwords and/or credit card information.

History

1980s

A phishing technique was described in detail in a paper and presentation delivered to the 1987 International HP Users Group, Interex.

1990s

The term 'phishing' is said to have been coined by the well known spammer and hacker in the mid-90s, Khan C Smith. The first recorded mention of the term is found in the hacking tool AOHell (according to its creator), which included a function for attempting to steal the passwords or financial details of America Online users.

Early AOL Phishing

Phishing on AOL was closely associated with the warez community that exchanged unlicensed software and the black hat hacking scene that perpetrated credit card fraud and other online crimes. AOL enforcement would detect words used in AOL chat rooms to suspend the accounts individuals involved in counterfeiting software and trading stolen accounts. The term was used because '<><' is the single most common tag of HTML that was found in all chat transcripts naturally, and as such could not be detected or filtered by AOL staff. The symbol <>< was replaced for any wording that referred to stolen credit cards, accounts, or illegal activity. Since the symbol looked like a fish, and due to the popularity of phreaking it was adapted as 'Phishing'. AOHell, released in early 1995, was a program designed to hack AOL users by allowing the attacker to pose as an AOL staff member, and send an instant message to a potential victim, asking him to reveal his password. In order to lure the victim into giving up sensitive information, the message might include imperatives such as "verify your account" or "confirm billing information". Once the victim had revealed the password, the attacker could access and use the victim's account for fraudulent purposes. Both phishing and warezing on AOL generally required custom-written programs, such as AOHell. Phishing became so prevalent on AOL that they added a line on all instant messages stating: "no one working at AOL will ask for your password or billing information", though even this didn't prevent some people from giving away their passwords and personal information if they read and believed the IM first. A user using both an AIM account and an AOL account from an ISP simultaneously could phish AOL members with relative impunity as internet AIM accounts could be used by non-AOL internet members and could not be actioned (i.e., reported to AOL TOS department for disciplinary action).. In late 1995, AOL crackers resorted to phishing for legitimate accounts after AOL brought in measures in late 1995 to prevent using fake, algorithmically generated credit card numbers to open accounts. Eventually, AOL's policy enforcement forced copyright infringement off AOL servers, and AOL promptly deactivate accounts involved in phishing, often before the victims could respond. The shutting down of the warez scene on AOL caused most phishers to leave the service.

2000s

- 2001

    o The first known direct attempt against a payment system affected E-gold in June 2001, which was followed up by a "post-9/11 id check" shortly after the September 11 attacks on the World Trade Center.

- 2003

    o The first known phishing attack against a retail bank was reported by The Banker in September 2003.

- 2004

    o It is estimated that between May 2004 and May 2005, approximately 1.2 million computer users in the United States suffered losses caused by phishing, totaling approximately US$929 million. United States businesses lose an estimated US$2 billion per year as their clients become victims.

    o Phishing is recognized as a fully organized part of the black market. Specializations emerged on a global scale that provided phishing software for payment (thereby outsourcing risk), which were assembled and implemented into phishing campaigns by organized gangs.

- 2005

    o In the United Kingdom losses from web banking fraud—mostly from phishing—almost doubled to GB£23.2m in 2005, from GB£12.2m in 2004, while 1 in 20 computer users claimed to have lost out to phishing in 2005.

- 2006

    o Almost half of phishing thefts in 2006 were committed by groups operating through the *Russian Business Network* based in St. Petersburg.

    o Banks dispute with customers over phishing losses. The stance adopted by the UK banking body APACS is that "customers must also take sensible precautions ... so that they are not vulnerable to the criminal." Similarly, when the first spate of phishing attacks hit the Irish Republic's banking sector in September 2006, the Bank of Ireland initially refused to cover losses suffered by its customers, although losses to the tune of €113,000 were made good.

o Phishers are targeting the customers of banks and online payment services. Emails, supposedly from the Internal Revenue Service, have been used to glean sensitive data from U.S. taxpayers. While the first such examples were sent indiscriminately in the expectation that some would be received by customers of a given bank or service, recent research has shown that phishers may in principle be able to determine which banks potential victims use, and target bogus emails accordingly.

o Social networking sites are a prime target of phishing, since the personal details in such sites can be used in identity theft; in late 2006 a computer worm took over pages on MySpace and altered links to direct surfers to websites designed to steal login details. Experiments show a success rate of over 70% for phishing attacks on social networks.

- 2007

    o 3.6 million adults lost US$3.2 billion in the 12 months ending in August 2007. Microsoft claims these estimates are grossly exaggerated and puts the annual phishing loss in the US at US$60 million.

    o Attackers who broke into TD Ameritrade's database and took 6.3 million email addresses (though they were not able to obtain social security numbers, account numbers, names, addresses, dates of birth, phone numbers and trading activity) also wanted the account usernames and passwords, so they launched a follow-up spear phishing attack.

- 2008

    o The RapidShare file sharing site has been targeted by phishing to obtain a premium account, which removes speed caps on downloads, auto-removal of uploads, waits on downloads, and cool down times between uploads.

    o Cryptocurrencies such as Bitcoin, introduced in late 2008, facilitate the sale of malicious software, making transactions secure and anonymous.

- 2009

    o In January 2009, a phishing attack resulted in unauthorized wire transfers of US$1.9 million through Experi-Metal's online banking accounts.

    o In the 3rd Quarter of 2009, the Anti-Phishing Working Group reported receiving 115,370 phishing email reports from consumers with US and China hosting more than 25% of the phishing pages each.

2010s

- 2011

    o In March 2011, Internal RSA staff phished successfully, leading to the master keys for all RSA SecureID security tokens being stolen, then subsequently used to break into US defense suppliers.

o   Chinese phishing campaign targeted Gmail accounts of highly ranked officials of the United States and South Korean governments and militaries, as well as Chinese political activists. The Chinese government denied accusations of taking part in cyber-attacks from within its borders, but there is evidence that the People's Liberation Army has assisted in the coding of cyber-attack software.

o   In November 2011, 110 million customer and credit card records were stolen from Target customers, through a phished subcontractor account. CEO and IT security staff subsequently fired.

- 2012

o   According to Ghosh, there were "445,004 attacks in 2012 as compared to 258,461 in 2011 and 187,203 in 2010", showing that phishing has been increasingly threatening individuals.

- 2013

o   In August 2013, advertising service Outbrain suffered a spearphishing attack and SEA placed redirects into the websites of The Washington Post, Time, and CNN.

o   In October 2013, emails purporting to be from American Express were sent to an unknown number of recipients. A simple DNS change could have been made to thwart this spoofed email, but American Express failed to make any changes.

o   By December 2013, Cryptolocker ransomware infected 250,000 personal computers by first targeting businesses using a Zip archive attachment that claimed to be a customer complaint, and later targeting general public using a link in an email regarding a problem clearing a check. The ransomware scrambles and locks files on the computer and requests the owner make a payment in exchange for the key to unlock and decrypt the files. According to Dell SecureWorks, 0.4% or more of those infected likely agreed to the ransom demand.

- 2014

o   In January 2014, the Seculert Research Lab identified a new targeted attack that used Xtreme RAT. This attack used spear phishing emails to target Israeli organizations and deploy the piece of advanced malware. To date, 15 machines have been compromised including ones belonging to the Civil Administration of Judea and Samaria.

o   According to 3rd Microsoft Computing Safer Index Report released in February 2014, the annual worldwide impact of phishing could be as high as $5 billion.

o   In August 2014, iCloud leaks of celebrity photos - During the investigation, it was found that Collins phished by sending e-mails to the victims that looked like they came from Apple or Google, warning the victims that their accounts might be compromised and asking for their account details. The victims would enter their password, and Collins gained access to their accounts, downloading e-mails and iCloud backups.

- o In September 2014, personal and credit card data of 100+million shoppers of all 2200 Home Depot stores posted for sale on hacking web sites.

- o In November 2014, phishing attacks on ICANN. Notably, administrative access to the Centralized Zone Data System was gained, allowing the attacker to get zone files, and data about users in the system, such as their real names, contact information, and salted hashes of their passwords. Access was also gained to ICANN's public Governmental Advisory Committee wiki, blog, and whois information portal.

- 2015

- o Charles H. Eccleston plead guilty to one count of attempted "unauthorized access and intentional damage to a protected computer" in the attempted Spear-Phishing Cyber Attack on January 15, 2015 when he attempted to infect computers of 80 Department of Energy employees.

- o Eliot Higgins and other journalists associated with Bellingcat, a group researching the shoot down of Malaysia Airlines Flight 17 over Ukraine, were targeted by numerous spearphishing emails. The messages were fake Gmail security notices with Bit.ly and TinyCC shortened URLs. According to ThreatConnect, some of the phishing emails had originated from servers that Fancy Bear had used in previous attacks elsewhere. Bellingcat is best known for having accused Russia of being culpable for the shoot down of MH17, and is frequently derided in the Russian media.

- o In August 2015 Cozy Bear was linked to a spear-phishing cyber-attack against the Pentagon email system causing the shut down of the entire Joint Staff unclassified email system and Internet access during the investigation.

- o In August 2015, Fancy Bear used a zero-day exploit of Java, spoofing the Electronic Frontier Foundation and launching attacks on the White House and NATO. The hackers used a spear phishing attack, directing emails to the false url electronicfrontierfoundation.org.

- 2016

- o Fancy Bear carried out spear phishing attacks on email addresses associated with the Democratic National Committee in the first quarter of 2016. On April 15, which in Russia was a holiday in honor of the military's electronic warfare services, the hackers seemed to become inactive for the day. Another sophisticated hacking group attributed to the Russian Federation, nicknamed Cozy Bear, was also present in the DNC's servers at the same time. However the two groups each appeared to be unaware of the other, as each independently stole the same passwords and otherwise duplicated their efforts. Cozy Bear appears to be a different agency, one more interested in traditional long-term espionage.

- o The Wichita Eagle reported "KU employees fall victim to phishing scam, lose paychecks"

- o Fancy Bear is suspected to be behind a spearphishing attack in August 2016 on members of the Bundestag and multiple political parties such as Linken-faction leader Sahra Wagenknecht, Junge Union and the CDU of Saarland. Authorities fear that sensitive information could be gathered by hackers to later manipulate the public ahead of elections such as Germany's next federal election due in September 2017.

o   In August 2016, the World Anti-Doping Agency reported the receipt of phishing emails sent to users of its database claiming to be official WADA communications requesting their login details. After reviewing the two domains provided by WADA, it was found that the websites' registration and hosting information were consistent with the Russian hacking group Fancy Bear. According to WADA, some of the data the hackers released had been forged.

o   Within hours of the 2016 U.S. election results, Russian hackers sent emails containing dirty zip files from spoofed Harvard University email addresses. Russians used techniques similar to phishing to publish fake news targeted at ordinary American voters.

Anti-phishing

There are anti-phishing websites which publish exact messages that have been recently circulating the internet, such as FraudWatch International and Millersmiles. Such sites often provide specific details about the particular messages. To avoid directly dealing with the source code of web pages, hackers are increasingly using a phishing tool called Super Phisher that makes the work easy when compared to manual methods of creating phishing websites.

As recently as 2007, the adoption of anti-phishing strategies by businesses needing to protect personal and financial information was low. Now there are several different techniques to combat phishing, including legislation and technology created specifically to protect against phishing. These techniques include steps that can be taken by individuals, as well as by organizations. Phone, web site, and email phishing can now be reported to authorities, as described below.

Social Responses

Frame of an animation by the U.S. Federal Trade Commission intended to educate citizens about phishing tactics.

One strategy for combating phishing is to train people to recognize phishing attempts, and to deal with them. Education can be effective, especially where training emphasises conceptual knowledge and provides direct feedback. One newer phishing tactic, which uses phishing emails targeted at a specific company, known as *spear phishing*, has been harnessed to train individuals at various locations, including United States Military Academy at West Point, NY. In a June 2004 experiment with spear phishing, 80% of 500 West Point cadets who were sent a fake email from a non-existent Col. Robert Melville at West Point were tricked into clicking on a link that would supposedly take them to a page where they would enter personal information. (The page informed them that they had been lured.)

People can take steps to avoid phishing attempts by slightly modifying their browsing habits. When contacted about an account needing to be "verified" (or any other topic used by phishers), it is a sensible precaution to contact the company from which the email apparently originates to check that the email is legitimate. Alternatively, the address that the individual knows is the company's genuine website can be typed into the address bar of the browser, rather than trusting any hyperlinks in the suspected phishing message.

Nearly all legitimate e-mail messages from companies to their customers contain an item of information that is not readily available to phishers. Some companies, for example PayPal, always address their customers by their username in emails, so if an email addresses the recipient in a generic fashion ("*Dear PayPal customer*") it is likely to be an attempt at phishing. Furthermore, PayPal offers various methods to determine spoof emails and advises users to forward suspicious emails to their spoof@paypal.com domain to investigate and warn other customers. Emails from banks and credit card companies often include partial account numbers. However, recent research has shown that the public do not typically distinguish between the first few digits and the last few digits of an account number—a significant problem since the first few digits are often the same for all clients of a financial institution. People can be trained to have their suspicion aroused if the message does not contain any specific personal information. Phishing attempts in early 2006, however, used personalized information, which makes it unsafe to assume that the presence of personal information alone guarantees that a message is legitimate. Furthermore, another recent study concluded in part that the presence of personal information does not significantly affect the success rate of phishing attacks, which suggests that most people do not pay attention to such details.

The Anti-Phishing Working Group, an industry and law enforcement association, has suggested that conventional phishing techniques could become obsolete in the future as people are increasingly aware of the social engineering techniques used by phishers. They predict that pharming and other uses of malware will become more common tools for stealing information.

Everyone can help educate the public by encouraging safe practices, and by avoiding dangerous ones. Unfortunately, even well-known players are known to incite users to hazardous behavior, e.g. by requesting their users to reveal their passwords for third party services, such as email.

Browsers Alerting Users to Fraudulent Websites

Another popular approach to fighting phishing is to maintain a list of known phishing sites and to check websites against the list. Microsoft's IE7 browser, Mozilla Firefox 2.0, Safari 3.2, and Opera all contain this type of anti-phishing measure. Firefox 2 used Google anti-phishing software. Opera 9.1 uses live blacklists from Phishtank, cyscon and GeoTrust, as well as live whitelists from GeoTrust. Some implementations of this approach send the visited URLs to a central service to be checked, which has raised concerns about privacy. According to a report by Mozilla in late 2006, Firefox 2 was found to be more effective than Internet Explorer 7 at detecting fraudulent sites in a study by an independent software testing company.

Screenshot of Firefox 2.0.0.1 Phising suspicious site warning

An approach introduced in mid-2006 involves switching to a special DNS service that filters out known phishing domains: this will work with any browser, and is similar in principle to using a hosts file to block web adverts.

To mitigate the problem of phishing sites impersonating a victim site by embedding its images (such as logos), several site owners have altered the images to send a message to the visitor that a site may be fraudulent. The image may be moved to a new filename and the original permanently replaced, or a server can detect that the image was not requested as part of normal browsing, and instead send a warning image.

Augmenting Password Logins

The Bank of America's website is one of several that ask users to select a personal image (marketed as SiteKey), and display this user-selected image with any forms that request a password. Users of the bank's online services are instructed to enter a password only when they see the image they selected. However, several studies suggest that few users refrain from entering their passwords when images are absent. In addition, this feature (like other forms of two-factor authentication) is susceptible to other attacks, such as those suffered by Scandinavian bank Nordea in late 2005, and Citibank in 2006.

A similar system, in which an automatically generated "Identity Cue" consisting of a colored word within a colored box is displayed to each website user, is in use at other financial institutions.

Security skins are a related technique that involves overlaying a user-selected image onto the login form as a visual cue that the form is legitimate. Unlike the website-based image schemes, however, the image itself is shared only between the user and the browser, and not between the user and the website. The scheme also relies on a mutual authentication protocol, which makes it less vulnerable to attacks that affect user-only authentication schemes.

Still another technique relies on a dynamic grid of images that is different for each login attempt. The user must identify the pictures that fit their pre-chosen categories (such as dogs, cars and flowers). Only after they have correctly identified the pictures that fit their categories are they allowed to enter their alphanumeric password to complete the login. Unlike the static images used on the Bank of America website, a dynamic image-based authentication method creates a one-time passcode for the login, requires active participation from the user, and is very difficult for a phishing website to correctly replicate because it would need to display a different grid of randomly generated images that includes the user's secret categories.

Eliminating Phishing Mail

Specialized spam filters can reduce the number of phishing emails that reach their addressees' inboxes, or provide post-delivery remediation, analyzing and removing spear phishing attacks upon delivery through email provider-level integration. These approaches rely on machine learning and natural language processing approaches to classify phishing emails. Email address authentication is another new approach.

Monitoring and Takedown

Several companies offer banks and other organizations likely to suffer from phishing scams round-the-clock services to monitor, analyze and assist in shutting down phishing websites. Individuals can contribute by reporting phishing to both volunteer and industry groups, such as cyscon or PhishTank. Individuals can also contribute by reporting phone phishing attempts to Phone Phishing,Federal Trade Commission. Phishing web pages and emails can be reported to Google. The Internet Crime Complaint Center noticeboard carries phishing and ransomware alerts.

Transaction Verification and Signing

Solutions have also emerged using the mobile phone (smartphone) as a second channel for verification and authorization of banking transactions.

Limitations of Technical Responses

An article in Forbes in August 2014 argues that the reason phishing problems persist even after a decade of anti-phishing technologies being sold is that phishing is "a technological medium to exploit human weaknesses" and that technology cannot fully compensate for human weaknesses.

Legal Responses

On January 26, 2004, the U.S. Federal Trade Commission filed the first lawsuit against a suspected phisher. The defendant, a Californian teenager, allegedly created a webpage designed to look like the America Online website, and used it to steal credit card information. Other countries have followed this lead by tracing and arresting phishers. A phishing kingpin, Valdir Paulo de Almeida, was arrested in Brazil for leading one of the largest phishing crime rings, which in two years stole between US$18 million and US$37 million. UK authorities jailed two men in June 2005 for their role in a phishing scam, in a case connected to the U.S. Secret Service Operation Firewall, which targeted notorious "carder" websites. In 2006 eight people were arrested by Japanese police on suspicion of phishing fraud by creating bogus Yahoo Japan Web sites, netting themselves ¥100 million (US$870,000). The arrests continued in 2006 with the FBI Operation Cardkeeper detaining a gang of sixteen in the U.S. and Europe.

In the United States, Senator Patrick Leahy introduced the *Anti-Phishing Act of 2005* in Congress on March 1, 2005. This bill, if it had been enacted into law, would have subjected criminals who created fake web sites and sent bogus emails in order to defraud consumers to fines of up to US$250,000 and prison terms of up to five years. The UK strengthened its legal arsenal against phishing with the Fraud Act 2006, which introduces a general offence of fraud that can carry up to a ten-year prison sentence, and prohibits the development or possession of phishing kits with intent to commit fraud.

Companies have also joined the effort to crack down on phishing. On March 31, 2005, Microsoft filed 117 federal lawsuits in the U.S. District Court for the Western District of Washington. The lawsuits accuse "John Doe" defendants of obtaining passwords and confidential information. March 2005 also saw a partnership between Microsoft and the Australian government teaching law enforcement officials how to combat various cyber crimes, including phishing. Microsoft announced a planned further 100 lawsuits outside the U.S. in March 2006, followed by the commencement, as of November 2006, of 129 lawsuits mixing criminal and civil actions. AOL reinforced its efforts against phishing in early 2006 with three lawsuits seeking a total of US$18 million under the 2005 amendments to the Virginia Computer Crimes Act, and Earthlink has joined in by helping to identify six men subsequently charged with phishing fraud in Connecticut.

In January 2007, Jeffrey Brett Goodin of California became the first defendant convicted by a jury under the provisions of the CAN-SPAM Act of 2003. He was found guilty of sending thousands of emails to America Online users, while posing as AOL's billing department, which prompted customers to submit personal and credit card information. Facing a possible 101 years in prison for the CAN-SPAM violation and ten other counts including wire fraud, the unauthorized use of credit cards, and the misuse of AOL's trademark, he was sentenced to serve 70 months. Goodin had been in custody since failing to appear for an earlier court hearing and began serving his prison term immediately.

Social Engineering (Security)

PROTECT YOUR INFO!
OPSEC ALERT

What is social engineering?

Social engineering is the art of manipulating people into performing actions or divulging confidential information, rather than by breaking in or using technical cracking techniques. While similar to a confidence trick or simple fraud, the term typically applies to trickery or deception for the purpose of information gathering, fraud or computer system access; in most cases the attacker never comes face-to-face with the victim. Social engineering using impersonation (e.g. to gain information over the phone, or to gate-crash) is known informally as blagging. In addition to criminal purposes, social engineering has also been employed by debt collectors, skip tracers, private investigators, bounty hunters and tabloid journalists. A study by Google researchers found that up to 90 percent of all domains involved in distributing fake antivirus software used social engineering techniques.

| TROOPER TO TROOPER   THE WIRE | PAGE 3

OPSEC alert

Social engineering, in the context of information security, refers to psychological manipulation of people into performing actions or divulging confidential information. A type of confidence trick for the purpose of information gathering, fraud, or system access, it differs from a traditional "con" in that it is often one of many steps in a more complex fraud scheme.

The term "social engineering" as an act of psychological manipulation is also associated with the social sciences, but its usage has caught-on among computer and information security professionals.

Techniques and Terms

All social engineering techniques are based on specific attributes of human decision-making known as cognitive biases. These biases, sometimes called "bugs in the human hardware", are exploited in various combinations to create attack techniques, some of which are listed below. The attacks used in social engineering can be used to steal employees' confidential information. The most common type of social engineering happens over the phone. Other examples of social engineering attacks are criminals posing as exterminators, fire marshals and technicians to go unnoticed as they steal company secrets.

One example of social engineering is an individual who walks into a building and posts an official-looking announcement to the company bulletin that says the number for the help desk has changed. So, when employees call for help the individual asks them for their passwords and IDs thereby gaining the ability to access the company's private information. Another example of social engineering would be that the hacker contacts the target on a social networking site and starts a conversation with the target. Slowly and gradually, the hacker gains trust of the target and then uses it to get access to sensitive information like password or bank account details.

Pretexting

Pretexting (adj. pretextual), also known in the UK as *blagging* or *bohoing*, is the act of creating and using an invented scenario (the pretext) to engage a targeted victim in a manner that increases the chance the victim will divulge information or perform actions that would be unlikely in ordinary circumstances. An elaborate lie, it most often involves some prior research or setup and the use of this information for impersonation (*e.g.*, date of birth, Social Security number, last bill amount) to establish legitimacy in the mind of the target.

This technique can be used to fool a business into disclosing customer information as well as by private investigators to obtain telephone records, utility records, banking records and other information directly from company service representatives. The information can then be used to establish even greater legitimacy under tougher questioning with a manager, *e.g.*, to make account changes, get specific balances, etc.

Pretexting can also be used to impersonate co-workers, police, bank, tax authorities, clergy, insurance investigators—or any other individual who could have perceived authority or right-to-know in the mind of the targeted victim. The pretexter must simply prepare answers to questions that might be asked by the victim. In some cases, all that is needed is a voice that sounds authoritative, an earnest tone, and an ability to think on one's feet to create a pretextual scenario.

Diversion Theft

Diversion theft, also known as the "Corner Game" or "Round the Corner Game", originated in the East End of London.

Diversion theft is a "con" exercised by professional thieves, normally against a transport or courier company. The objective is to persuade the people responsible for a legitimate delivery that the consignment is requested elsewhere—hence, "round the corner".

Phishing

Phishing is a technique of fraudulently obtaining private information. Typically, the phisher sends an e-mail that appears to come from a legitimate business—a bank, or credit card company—requesting "verification" of information and warning of some dire consequence if it is not provided. The e-mail usually contains a link to a fraudulent web page that seems legitimate—with company logos and content—and has a form requesting everything from a home address to an ATM card's PIN or a credit card number. For example, in 2003, there was a phishing scam in which users received e-mails supposedly from eBay claiming that the user's account was about to be suspended unless a link provided was clicked to update a credit card (information that the genuine eBay already had). Because it is relatively simple to make a Web site resemble a legitimate organization's site by mimicking the HTML code and logos the scam counted on people being tricked into thinking they were being contacted by eBay and subsequently, were going to eBay's site to update their account information. By spamming large groups of people, the "phisher" counted on the e-mail being read by a percentage of people who already had listed credit card numbers with eBay legitimately, who might respond.

IVR or Phone Phishing

Phone phishing (or "vishing") uses a rogue interactive voice response (IVR) system to recreate a legitimate-sounding copy of a bank or other institution's IVR system. The victim is prompted (typically via a phishing e-mail) to call in to the "bank" via a (ideally toll free) number provided in order to "verify" information. A typical "vishing" system will reject log-ins continually, ensuring the victim enters PINs or passwords multiple times, often disclosing several different passwords. More advanced systems transfer the victim to the attacker/defrauder, who poses as a customer service agent or security expert for further questioning of the victim.

Spear Phishing

Although similar to "phishing", spear phishing is a technique that fraudulently obtains private information by sending highly customized emails to few end users. It is the main difference between phishing attacks because phishing campaigns focus on sending out high volumes of generalized emails with the expectation that only a few people will respond. On the other hand, spear phishing emails require the attacker to perform additional research on their targets in order to "trick" end users into performing requested activities. The success rate of spear-phishing attacks is considerable higher than phishing attacks with people opening roughly 3% of phishing emails when compared to roughly 70% of potential attempts. However, when users actually open the emails phishing emails have a relatively modest 5% success rate to have the link or attachment clicked when compared to a spear-phishing attack's 50% success rate.

Water Holing

Water holing is a targeted social engineering strategy that capitalizes on the trust users have in websites they regularly visit. The victim feels safe to do things they would not do in a different situation. A wary person might, for example, purposefully avoid clicking a link in an unsolicited email, but the same person would not hesitate to follow a link on a website he or she often visits. So, the attacker prepares a trap for the unwary prey at a favored watering hole. This strategy has been successfully used to gain access to some (supposedly) very secure systems.

The attacker may set out by identifying a group or individuals to target. The preparation involves gathering information about websites the targets often visit from the secure system. The information gathering confirms that the targets visit the websites and that the system allows such visits. The attacker then tests these websites for vulnerabilities to inject code that may infect a visitor's system with malware. The injected code trap and malware may be tailored to the specific target group and the specific systems they use. In time, one or more members of the target group will get infected and the attacker can gain access to the secure system.

Baiting

Baiting is like the real-world Trojan horse that uses physical media and relies on the curiosity or greed of the victim. In this attack, attackers leave malware-infected floppy disks, CD-ROMs, or USB flash drives in locations people will find them (bathrooms, elevators, sidewalks, parking lots, etc.), give them legitimate and curiosity-piquing labels, and waits for victims. For example, an attacker may create a disk featuring a corporate logo, available from the target's website, and label it "Executive Salary Summary Q2 2012". The attacker then leaves the disk on the floor of an elevator or somewhere in the lobby of the target company. An unknowing employee may find it and insert the disk into a computer to satisfy his or her curiosity, or a good Samaritan may find it and return it to the company. In any case, just inserting the disk into a computer installs malware, giving attackers access to the victim's PC and, perhaps, the target company's internal computer network.

Unless computer controls block infections, insertion compromises PCs "auto-running" media. Hostile devices can also be used. For instance, a "lucky winner" is sent a free digital audio player compromising any computer it is plugged to. A "road apple" (the colloquial term for horse manure, suggesting the device's undesirable nature) is any removable media with malicious software left in opportunistic or conspicuous places. It may be a CD, DVD, or USB flash drive, among other media. Curious people take it and plug it into a computer, infecting the host and any attached networks. Hackers may give them enticing labels, such as "Employee Salaries" or "Confidential".

Quid Pro Quo

Quid pro quo means *something for something*:

- An attacker calls random numbers at a company, claiming to be calling back from technical support. Eventually this person will hit someone with a legitimate problem, grateful that someone is calling back to help them. The attacker will "help" solve the problem and, in the process, have the user type commands that give the attacker access or launch malware.

- In a 2003 information security survey, 90% of office workers gave researchers what they claimed was their password in answer to a survey question in exchange for a cheap pen. Similar surveys in later years obtained similar results using chocolates and other cheap lures, although they made no attempt to validate the passwords.

Tailgating

An attacker, seeking entry to a restricted area secured by unattended, electronic access control, e.g. by RFID card, simply walks in behind a person who has legitimate access. Following common courtesy, the legitimate person will usually hold the door open for the attacker or the attackers themselves may ask the employee to hold it open for them. The legitimate person may fail to ask for identification for any of several reasons, or may accept an assertion that the attacker has forgotten or lost the appropriate identity token. The attacker may also fake the action of presenting an identity token.

Other Types

Common confidence tricksters or fraudsters also could be considered "social engineers" in the wider sense, in that they deliberately deceive and manipulate people, exploiting human weaknesses to obtain personal benefit. They may, for example, use social engineering techniques as part of an IT fraud.

A very recent type of social engineering technique includes spoofing or hacking IDs of people having popular e-mail IDs such as Yahoo!, Gmail, Hotmail, etc. Among the many motivations for deception are:

- Phishing credit-card account numbers and their passwords.

- Cracking private e-mails and chat histories, and manipulating them by using common editing techniques before using them to extort money and creating distrust among individuals.

- Cracking websites of companies or organizations and destroying their reputation.

- Computer virus hoaxes.

- Convincing users to run malicious code within the web browser via self-XSS attack to allow access to their web account.

Countermeasures

Organizations reduce their security risks by:

Standard Framework Establishing frameworks of trust on an employee/personnel level (i.e., specify and train personnel when/where/why/how sensitive information should be handled)

Scrutinizing Information Identifying which information is sensitive and evaluating its exposure to social engineering and breakdowns in security systems (building, computer system, etc.).

Security Protocols Establishing security protocols, policies, and procedures for handling sensitive information.

Training to Employees Training employees in security protocols relevant to their position. (e.g., in situations such as tailgating, if a person's identity cannot be verified, then employees must be trained to politely refuse.)

Event Test Performing unannounced, periodic tests of the security framework.

Review Reviewing the above steps regularly: no solutions to information integrity are perfect.

Waste Management Using a waste management service that has dumpsters with locks on them, with keys to them limited only to the waste management company and the cleaning staff. Locating the dumpster either in view of employees so that trying to access it carries a risk of being seen or caught, or behind a locked gate or fence where the person must trespass before they can attempt to access the dumpster.

Notable Social Engineers

Kevin Mitnick

Reformed computer criminal and later security consultant Kevin Mitnick points out that it is much easier to trick someone into giving a password for a system than to spend the effort to crack into the system.

Christopher Hadnagy

Christopher Hadnagy is the security professional who wrote the first framework defining the physical and psychological principles of social engineering. He is most widely known for his books, podcast and the being the creator of the DEF CON Social Engineer Capture the Flag and the Social Engineer CTF for Kids.

Mike Ridpath

Mike Ridpath Security consultant, published author, and speaker. Emphasizes techniques and tactics for social engineering cold calling. Became notable after his talks where he would play recorded calls and explain his thought process on what he was doing to get passwords through the phone and his live demonstrations. As a child Ridpath was connected with Badir Brothers and was widely known within the phreaking and hacking community for his articles with popular underground ezines, such as, Phrack, B4B0 and 9x on modifying Oki 900s, blueboxing, satellite hacking and RCMAC.

Badir Brothers

Brothers Ramy, Muzher, and Shadde Badir—all of whom were blind from birth—managed to set up an extensive phone and computer fraud scheme in Israel in the 1990s using social engineering, voice impersonation, and Braille-display computers.

Law

In common law, pretexting is an invasion of privacy tort of appropriation.

Pretexting of Telephone Records

In December 2006, United States Congress approved a Senate sponsored bill making the pretexting of telephone records a federal felony with fines of up to $250,000 and ten years in prison for individuals (or fines of up to $500,000 for companies). It was signed by President George W. Bush on 12 January 2007.

Federal Legislation

The 1999 "GLBA" is a U.S. Federal law that specifically addresses pretexting of banking records as an illegal act punishable under federal statutes. When a business entity such as a private investigator, SIU insurance investigator, or an adjuster conducts any type of deception, it falls under the authority of the Federal Trade Commission (FTC). This federal agency has the obligation and authority to ensure that consumers are not subjected to any unfair or deceptive business practices. US Federal Trade Commission Act, Section 5 of the FTCA states, in part: "Whenever the Commission shall have reason to believe that any such person, partnership, or corporation has been or is using any unfair method of competition or unfair or deceptive act or practice in or affecting commerce, and if it shall appear to the Commission that a proceeding by it in respect thereof would be to the interest of the public, it shall issue and serve upon such person, partnership, or corporation a complaint stating its charges in that respect."

The statute states that when someone obtains any personal, non-public information from a financial institution or the consumer, their action is subject to the statute. It relates to the consumer's relationship with the financial institution. For example, a pretexter using false pretenses either to get a consumer's address from the consumer's bank, or to get a consumer to disclose the name of his or her bank, would be covered. The determining principle is that pretexting only occurs when information is obtained through false pretenses.

While the sale of cell telephone records has gained significant media attention, and telecommunications records are the focus of the two bills currently before the United States Senate, many other types of private records are being bought and sold in the public market. Alongside many advertisements for cell phone records, wireline records and the records associated with calling cards are advertised. As individuals shift to VoIP telephones, it is safe to assume that those records will be offered for sale as well. Currently, it is legal to sell telephone records, but illegal to obtain them.

1st Source Information Specialists

U.S. Rep. Fred Upton (R-Kalamazoo, Michigan), chairman of the Energy and Commerce Subcommittee on Telecommunications and the Internet, expressed concern over the easy access to personal mobile phone records on the Internet during a House Energy & Commerce Committee hearing on "Phone Records For Sale: *Why Aren't Phone Records Safe From Pretexting?*" Illinois became the first state to sue an online records broker when Attorney General Lisa Madigan sued 1st Source Information Specialists, Inc. A spokeswoman for Madigan's office said. The Florida-based company operates several Web sites that sell mobile telephone records, according to a copy of the suit. The attorneys general of Florida and Missouri quickly followed Madigan's lead, filing suits respectively, against 1st Source Information Specialists and, in Missouri's case, one other records broker – First Data Solutions, Inc.

Several wireless providers, including T-Mobile, Verizon, and Cingular filed earlier lawsuits against records brokers, with Cingular winning an injunction against First Data Solutions and 1st Source Information Specialists. U.S. Senator Charles Schumer (D-New York) introduced legislation in February 2006 aimed at curbing the practice. The Consumer Telephone Records Protection Act of 2006 would create felony criminal penalties for stealing and selling the records of mobile phone, landline, and Voice over Internet Protocol (VoIP) subscribers.

HP

Patricia Dunn, former chairwoman of Hewlett Packard, reported that the HP board hired a private investigation company to delve into who was responsible for leaks within the board. Dunn acknowledged that the company used the practice of pretexting to solicit the telephone records of board members and journalists. Chairman Dunn later apologized for this act and offered to step down from the board if it was desired by board members. Unlike Federal law, California law specifically forbids such pretexting. The four felony charges brought on Dunn were dismissed.

In Popular Culture

- In the TV show *White Collar*, Matt Bomer played a highly intelligent and multitalented con artist working as an FBI criminal informant.

- In the movie *Identity Thief*, Melissa McCarthy played a fraudster who used pretexting to get the name, credit card number and Social Security number of an executive (Jason Bateman) enabling her to steal his identity and commit credit card fraud.

- In the film *Hackers*, the protagonist used pretexting when he asked a security guard for the telephone number to a TV station's modem while posing as an important company executive.

- In Jeffrey Deaver's book *The Blue Nowhere*, social engineering to obtain confidential information is one of the methods used by the killer, Phate, to get close to his victims.

- In the movie *Live Free or Die Hard*, Justin Long is seen pretexting that his father is dying from a heart attack to have an On-Star Assist representative start what will become a stolen car.

- In the movie *Sneakers*, one of the characters poses as a low level security guard's superior in order to convince him that a security breach is just a false alarm.

- In the movie *The Thomas Crown Affair*, one of the characters poses over the telephone as a museum guard's superior in order to move the guard away from his post.

- In the James Bond movie *Diamonds Are Forever*, Bond is seen gaining entry to the Whyte laboratory with a then-state-of-the-art card-access lock system by "tailgating". He merely waits for an employee to come to open the door, then posing himself as a rookie at the lab, fakes inserting a non-existent card while the door is unlocked for him by the employee.

- In the television show *Rockford Files*, The character Jim Rockford used pretexting often in his private investigation work.

- In the TV show *The Mentalist*, protagonist Patrick Jane often uses pretexting to trick criminals into confessing to the crimes they committed.

- In the TV show *Burn Notice*, many characters are seen using social engineering; in Michael Westen's psych profile it is stated that he is very skilled in social engineering.

- In the TV show *Psych*, protagonist Shawn Spencer often uses pretexting to gain access to locations he would otherwise not be allowed into without police credentials.

- In the videogame *Watch Dogs*, protagonist Aiden Pearce states that he studied social engineering when growing up into a life of crime and uses social engineering tactics to manipulate other characters throughout the game to get the information he wants.

- In the TV show *Mr. Robot*, Darlene scatters USB flash drives (containing malware) outside a prison entrance, baiting a curious guard into compromising the prison's internal network when he plugs one of the drives into his computer workstation.

- In the movie *Who Am I*, the main characters are seen using various social engineering techniques.

- In French novels from Maxime Frantini [Journal d'un hacker, L'ombre et la lumière, la Cavale, La détermination du fennec], hacker hero Ylian Estevez mainly uses social engineering for its attacks.

- In the movie *Mars Needs Women* The entire film is one elaborate example after another of social engineering carried out by the aliens who are shown engaging in and utilizing these techniques to attain their thule ultima: The capture of 5 Earth women for reproductive purposes to re-infuse their planet's female to male ratio, in a cold and calculating manner until their scheme is thwarted by their own leader, "Dop" (Tommy Kirk) after he develops romantic feelings towards one of their intended abductees; female Earth scientist Dr. Marjorie Bolen portrayed by Yvonne Craig.

Cyberterrorism

Cyberterrorism is the use of the Internet to conduct violent acts that result in or threaten the loss of life or significant bodily harm in order to achieve political gains through intimidation. It is also sometimes considered the act of Internet terrorism in terrorist activities, including acts of deliberate, large-scale disruption of computer networks, especially of personal computers attached to the Internet, by the means of tools such as computer viruses.

Cyberterrorism is a controversial term. Some authors choose a very narrow definition, relating to deployments, by known terrorist organizations, of disruption attacks against information systems for the primary purpose of creating alarm and panic. Some other authors choose a much too broad definition which tends to falsely include cybercrime when in reality, cyberterrorism and cybercrime are two very different issues and must be defined separately. Terrorism online should be considered cyberterrorism when there has been fear inflicted on a group of people, whereas cybercrime is the act of committing a felony or crime online typically without the use of fear. By these narrow and broad definitions, it is difficult to identify which instances of online terrorism are cyberterrorism or cybercrime.

Cyberterrorism can be also defined as the intentional use of computer, networks, and public internet to cause destruction and harm for personal objectives. Experienced cyberterrorists who are very skilled in terms of hacking can deal massive damage to government systems, hospital records, and national security programs, often which leaves a country in turmoil and in fear of further attacks. The objectives of such terrorists may be political or ideological since this can be seen as a form of terrorism.

There is much concern from government and media sources about potential damages that could be caused by cyberterrorism, and this has prompted efforts by government agencies such as the Federal Bureau of Investigations (FBI) and the Central Intelligence Agency (CIA) to put an end to cyber attacks and cyberterrorism.

There have been several major and minor instances of cyberterrorism. Al-Qaeda utilized the internet to communicate with supporters and even to recruit new members. Estonia, a Baltic country which is constantly evolving in terms of technology, became a battleground for cyberterror in April, 2007 after disputes regarding the removal of a WWII soviet statue located Estonia's capital Tallinn.

Overview

There is debate over the basic definition of the scope of cyberterrorism. There is variation in qualification by motivation, targets, methods, and centrality of computer use in the act. Depending on context, cyberterrorism may overlap considerably with cybercrime, cyberwar or ordinary terrorism. Eugene Kaspersky, founder of Kaspersky Lab, now feels that "cyberterrorism" is a more accurate term than "cyberwar". He states that "with today's attacks, you are clueless about who did it or when they will strike again. It's not cyber-war, but cyberterrorism." He also equates large-scale cyber weapons, such as the Flame Virus and NetTraveler Virus which his company discovered, to biological weapons, claiming that in an interconnected world, they have the potential to be equally destructive.

If cyberterrorism is treated similarly to traditional terrorism, then it only includes attacks that threaten property or lives, and can be defined as the leveraging of a target's computers and information, particularly via the Internet, to cause physical, real-world harm or severe disruption of infrastructure.

There are some who say that cyberterrorism does not exist and is really a matter of hacking or information warfare. They disagree with labelling it terrorism because of the unlikelihood of the creation of fear, significant physical harm, or death in a population using electronic means, considering current attack and protective technologies.

If a strict definition is assumed, then there have been no or almost no identifiable incidents of cyberterrorism, although there has been much public concern.

However, there is an old saying that death or loss of property are the side products of terrorism, the main purpose of such incidents is to *create terror* in peoples mind. If any incident in the cyber world can *create terror*, it may be called cyberterrorism.

Defining Cyberterrorism

Assigning a concrete definition to cyberterrorism can be hard, due to the difficulty of defining the term terrorism itself. Multiple organizations have created their own definitions, most of which are overly broad. There is also controversy concerning overuse of the term, hyperbole in the media, and by security vendors trying to sell "solutions".

The term can also be used in a variety of different ways, but is also limited on when it can be used. An attack on an Internet business can be labeled cyberterrorism, however when it is done for economic motivations rather than ideological it is typically regarded as cybercrime. Cyberterrorism is also limited to actions by individuals, independent groups, or organizations. Any form of cyber warfare conducted by governments and states would be regulated and punishable under international law.

Cyberterrorism is defined by the Technolytics Institute as "The premeditated use of disruptive activities, or the threat thereof, against computers and/or networks, with the intention to cause harm or further social, ideological, religious, political or similar objectives. Or to intimidate any person in furtherance of such objectives." The term appears first in defense literature, surfacing in reports by the U.S. Army War College as early as 1998.

The National Conference of State Legislatures, an organization of legislators created to help policymakers with issues such as economy and homeland security defines cyberterrorism as:

> [T]he use of information technology by terrorist groups and individuals to further their agenda. This can include use of information technology to organize and execute attacks against networks, computer systems and telecommunications infrastructures, or for exchanging information or making threats electronically. Examples are hacking into computer systems, introducing viruses to vulnerable networks, web site defacing, Denial-of-service attacks, or terroristic threats made via electronic communication.

NATO defines cyberterrorism as, "a cyberattack using or exploiting computer or communication networks to cause sufficient destruction or disruption to generate fear or to intimidate a society into an ideological goal"

The National Infrastructure Protection Center defines it as, "A criminal act perpetrated by the use of computers and telecommunications capabilities resulting in violence, destruction, and/or disruption of services to create fear by causing confusion and certainty within a given population conform to a political, social, or ideological agent."

Lastly, the FBI defines it as, "premeditated, politically motivated attack against information, computer systems, computer programs, and data which results in violence against non-combatant targets by subnational groups or clandestine agents".

Across these definitions, they all share the view that cyberterrorism is politically and/or ideologically inclined. One area of debate is the difference between cyberterrorism and hacktivism. Hacktivism is," the marriage of hacking with political activism". Both items are politically driven, and involve using computers, however cyberterrorism is primarily used to cause harm. It becomes an issue because acts of violence on the computer can be labeled either cyberterrorism or hacktivism.

Types of Cyberterror Capability

The following three levels of cyberterror capability is defined by Monterey group

- Simple-Unstructured: The capability to conduct basic hacks against individual systems using tools created by someone else. The organization possesses little target analysis, command and control, or learning capability.

- Advanced-Structured: The capability to conduct more sophisticated attacks against multiple systems or networks and possibly, to modify or create basic hacking tools. The organization possesses an elementary target analysis, command and control, and learning capability.

- Complex-Coordinated: The capability for a coordinated attack capable of causing mass-disruption against integrated, heterogeneous defenses (including cryptography). Ability to create sophisticated hacking tools. Highly capable target analysis, command and control, and organization learning capability.

Concerns

As the Internet becomes more pervasive in all areas of human endeavor, individuals or groups can use the anonymity afforded by cyberspace to threaten citizens, specific groups (i.e. with membership based on ethnicity or belief), communities and entire countries, without the inherent threat of capture, injury, or death to the attacker that being physically present would bring. Many groups such as Anonymous, use tools such as denial-of-service attack to attack and censor groups who oppose them, creating many concerns for freedom and respect for differences of thought.

Many believe that cyberterrorism is an extreme threat to countries' economies, and fear an attack could potentially lead to another Great Depression. Several leaders agree that cyberterrorism has the highest percentage of threat over other possible attacks on U.S. territory. Although natural disasters are considered a top threat and have proven to be devastating to people and land, there is ultimately little that can be done to prevent such events from happening. Thus, the expectation is to focus more on preventative measures that will make Internet attacks impossible for execution.

As the Internet continues to expand, and computer systems continue to be assigned increased responsibility while becoming more complex and interdependent, sabotage or terrorism via the Internet may become a more serious threat and is possibly one of the top 10 events to "end the human race." The Internet of Things promises to further merge the virtual and physical worlds, which some experts see as a powerful incentive for states to use terrorist proxies in furtherance of objectives.

Dependence on the internet is rapidly increasing on a worldwide scale, creating a platform for international cyber terror plots to be formulated and executed as a direct threat to national security. For terrorists, cyber-based attacks have distinct advantages over physical attacks. They can be conducted remotely, anonymously, and relatively cheaply, and they do not require significant investment in weapons, explosive and personnel. The effects can be widespread and profound. Incidents of cyberterrorism are likely to increase. They will be conducted through denial of service attacks, malware, and other methods that are difficult to envision today.

In an article about cyber attacks by Iran and North Korea, the *New York Times* observes, "The appeal of digital weapons is similar to that of nuclear capability: it is a way for an outgunned, outfinanced nation to even the playing field. 'These countries are pursuing cyberweapons the same way they are pursuing nuclear weapons,' said James A. Lewis, a computer security expert at the Center for Strategic and International Studies in Washington. 'It's primitive; it's not top of the line, but it's good enough and they are committed to getting it.'"

History

Public interest in cyberterrorism began in the late 1980s, when the term was coined by Barry C. Collin. As 2000 approached, the fear and uncertainty about the millennium bug heightened, as did the potential for attacks by cyber terrorists. Although the millennium bug was by no means a terrorist attack or plot against the world or the United States, it did act as a catalyst in sparking the fears of a possibly large-scale devastating cyber-attack. Commentators noted that many of the facts of such incidents seemed to change, often with exaggerated media reports.

The high-profile terrorist attacks in the United States on September 11, 2001 and the ensuing War on Terror by the US led to further media coverage of the potential threats of cyberterrorism in the years following. Mainstream media coverage often discusses the possibility of a large attack making use of computer networks to sabotage critical infrastructures with the aim of putting human lives in jeopardy or causing disruption on a national scale either directly or by disruption of the national economy.

Authors such as Winn Schwartau and John Arquilla are reported to have had considerable financial success selling books which described what were purported to be plausible scenarios of mayhem caused by cyberterrorism. Many critics claim that these books were unrealistic in their assessments of whether the attacks described (such as nuclear meltdowns and chemical plant explosions) were possible. A common thread throughout what critics perceive as cyberterror-hype is that of non-falsifiability; that is, when the predicted disasters fail to occur, it only goes to show how lucky we've been so far, rather than impugning the theory.

In 2016, for the first time ever, the Department of Justice charged Ardit Ferizi with cyberterrorisim. He is accused of allegedly hacking into a military website and stealing the names, addresses, and other personal information of government and military personnel and selling it to ISIS

International Response

Conventions

As of 2016 there have been seventeen conventions and major legal instruments that specifically deal with terrorist activities and can also be applied to terrorism.

- 1963: Convention on Offences and Certain Other Acts Committed on Board Aircraft

- 1970: Convention for the Suppression of Unlawful Seizure of Aircraft

- 1971: Convention for the Suppression of Unlawful Acts Against the Safety of Civil Aviation

- 1973: Convention on the Prevention and Punishment of Crimes against Internationally Protected Persons

- 1979: International Convention against the Taking of Hostages

- 1980: Convention on the Physical Protection of Nuclear Material

- 1988: Protocol for the Suppression of Unlawful Acts of Violence at Airports Serving International Civil Aviation

- 1988: Protocol for the Suppression of Unlawful Acts against the Safety of Fixed Platforms Located on the Continental Shelf

- 1988: Convention for the Suppression of Unlawful Acts against the Safety of Maritime Navigation

- 1989: Supplementary to the Convention for the Suppression of Unlawful Acts against the Safety of Civil Aviation

- 1991: Convention on the Marking of Plastic Explosives for the Purpose of Detection

- 1997: International Convention for the Suppression of Terrorist Bombings

- 1999: International Convention for the Suppression of the Financing of Terrorism

- 2005: Protocol to the Convention for the Suppression of Unlawful Acts against the Safety of Maritime Navigation

- 2005: International Convention for the Suppression of Acts of Nuclear Terrorism

- 2010: Protocol Supplementary to the Convention for the Suppression of Unlawful Seizure of Aircraft

- 2010: Convention on the Suppression of Unlawful Acts Relating to International Civil Aviation

International Institutions

As of 2016 the United Nations only has one agency that specializes in cyberterrorism, the International Telecommunications Union.

U.S. Military/Protections against Cyberterrorism

The US Department of Defense (DoD) charged the United States Strategic Command with the duty of combating cyberterrorism. This is accomplished through the Joint Task Force-Global Network Operations, which is the operational component supporting USSTRATCOM in defense of the DoD's Global Information Grid. This is done by integrating GNO capabilities into the operations of all DoD computers, networks, and systems used by DoD combatant commands, services and agencies.

On November 2, 2006, the Secretary of the Air Force announced the creation of the Air Force's newest MAJCOM, the Air Force Cyber Command, which would be tasked to monitor and defend American interest in cyberspace. The plan was however replaced by the creation of Twenty-Fourth Air Force which became active in August 2009 and would be a component of the planned United States Cyber Command.

On December 22, 2009, the White House named its head of Computer security as Howard Schmidt to coordinate U.S Government, military and intelligence efforts to repel hackers. He left the position in May, 2012. Michael Daniel was appointed to the position of White House Coordinator of Cyber Security the same week and continues in the position during the second term of the Obama administration.

More recently, Obama signed an executive order to enable the US to impose sanctions on either individuals or entities that are suspected to be participating in cyber related acts. These acts can be threats to our national security, financial issues or foreign policy issues.

Estonia and NATO

The Baltic state of Estonia was target to a massive denial-of-service attack that ultimately rendered the country offline and shut out from services dependent on Internet connectivity in April 2007. The infrastructure of Estonia including everything from online banking and mobile phone networks to government services and access to health care information was disabled for a time. The tech-dependent state experienced severe turmoil and there was a great deal of concern over the nature and intent of the attack.

The cyber attack was a result of an Estonian-Russian dispute over the removal of a bronze statue depicting a World War II-era Soviet soldier from the center of the capital, Tallinn. In the midst of the armed conflict with Russia, Georgia likewise was subject to sustanined and coordinated attacks on its electronic infrastructure in August 2008. In both of these cases, circumstantial evidence point to coordinated Russian attacks, but attribution of the attacks is difficult; though both the countries blame Moscow for contributing to the cyber attacks, proof establishing legal culpability is lacking.

Estonia joined NATO in 2004, which prompted NATO to carefully monitor its member state's response to the attack. NATO also feared escalation and the possibility of cascading effects beyond Estonia's border to other NATO members. In 2008, directly as a result of the attacks, NATO opened a new center of excellence on cyberdefense to conduct research and training on cyber warfare in Tallinn.

The chaos resulting from the attacks in Estonia illustrated to the world the dependence countries had on information technology. This dependence then makes countries vulnerable to future cyber attacks and terrorism.

China

The Chinese Defense Ministry confirmed the existence of an online defense unit in May 2011. Composed of about thirty elite internet specialists, the so-called "Cyber Blue Team," or "Blue Army," is officially claimed to be engaged in cyber-defense operations, though there are fears the unit has been used to penetrate secure online systems of foreign governments.

Pakistan

Pakistan Government has also taken steps to curb the menace of cyber terrorism and extremist propaganda. National Counter Terrorism Authority (Nacta) is working on joint programs with different NGOs and other cyber security organizations in Pakistan to combat this problem. Surf Safe Pakistan is one such example. Now people in Pakistan can report extremist and terrorist related content online on Surf Safe Pakistan portal. Tier3 Cyber Security services Pakistan led the development of the Surf Safe Portal. The National Counter Terrorism Authority (NACTA) provides the Federal Government's leadership for the Surf Safe Campaign.

Examples

An operation can be done by anyone anywhere in the world, for it can be performed thousands of miles away from a target. An attack can cause serious damage to a critical infrastructure which may result in casualties. Attacking an infrastructure can be power grids, monetary systems, dams, media, and personal information.

Some attacks are conducted in furtherance of political and social objectives, as the following examples illustrate:

- In 1996, a computer hacker allegedly associated with the White Supremacist movement temporarily disabled a Massachusetts ISP and damaged part of the ISP's record keeping system. The ISP had attempted to stop the hacker from sending out worldwide racist messages under the ISP's name. The hacker signed off with the threat, "you have yet to see true electronic terrorism. This is a promise."

- In 1998, Spanish protesters bombarded the Institute for Global Communications (IGC) with thousands of bogus e-mail messages. E-mail was tied up and undeliverable to the ISP's users, and support lines were tied up with people who couldn't get their mail. The protestors also spammed IGC staff and member accounts, clogged their Web page with bogus credit card orders, and threatened to employ the same tactics against organizations using IGC services. They demanded that IGC stop hosting the Web site for the Euskal Herria Journal, a New York-based publication supporting Basque independence. Protestors said IGC supported terrorism because a section on the Web pages contained materials on the terrorist group ETA, which claimed responsibility for assassinations of Spanish political and security officials, and attacks on military installations. IGC finally relented and pulled the site because of the "mail bombings."

- In 1998, ethnic Tamil guerrillas attempted to disrupt Sri Lankan embassies by sending large volumes of e-mail. The embassies received 800 e-mails a day over a two-week period. The messages read "We are the Internet Black Tigers and we're doing this to disrupt your communications." Intelligence authorities characterized it as the first known attack by terrorists against a country's computer systems.

- During the Kosovo conflict in 1999, NATO computers were blasted with e-mail bombs and hit with denial-of-service attacks by hacktivists protesting the NATO bombings. In addition, businesses, public organizations, and academic institutes received highly politicized virus-laden e-mails from a range of Eastern European countries, according to reports. Web defacements were also common. After the Chinese Embassy was accidentally bombed in Belgrade, Chinese hacktivists posted messages such as "We won't stop attacking until the war stops!" on U.S. government Web sites.

- Since December 1997, the Electronic Disturbance Theater (EDT) has been conducting Web sit-ins against various sites in support of the Mexican Zapatistas. At a designated time, thousands of protestors point their browsers to a target site using software that floods the target with rapid and repeated download requests. EDT's software has also been used by animal rights groups against organizations said to abuse animals. Electrohippies, another group of hacktivists, conducted Web sit-ins against the WTO when they met in Seattle in late 1999. These sit-ins all require mass participation to have much effect, and thus are more suited to use by activists than by terrorists.

- In 2000, a Japanese Investigation revealed that the government was using software developed by computer companies affiliated with Aum Shinrikyo, the doomsday sect responsible for the sarin gas attack on the Tokyo subway system in 1995. "The government found 100 types of software programs used by at least 10 Japanese government agencies, including the Defense Ministry, and more than 80 major Japanese companies, including Nippon Telegraph and Telephone." Following the discovery, the Japanese government suspended use of Aum-developed programs out of concern that Aum-related companies may have compromised security by breaching firewalls. gaining access to sensitive systems or information, allowing invasion by outsiders, planting viruses that could be set off later, or planting malicious code that could cripple computer systems and key data system.

- In March 2013, the New York Times reported on a pattern of cyber attacks against U.S. financial institutions believed to be instigated by Iran as well as incidents affecting South Korean financial institutions that originate with the North Korean government.

- In August 2013, media companies including the New York Times, Twitter and the Huffington Post lost control of some of their websites Tuesday after hackers supporting the Syrian government breached the Australian Internet company that manages many major site addresses. The Syrian Electronic Army, a hacker group that has previously attacked media organisations that it considers hostile to the regime of Syrian president Bashar al-Assad, claimed credit for the Twitter and Huffington Post hacks in a series of Twitter messages. Electronic records showed that NYTimes.com, the only site with an hours-long outage, redirected visitors to a server controlled by the Syrian group before it went dark.

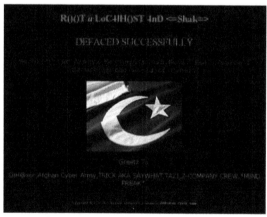

The website of Air Botswana, defaced by a group calling themselves the "Pakistan Cyber Army"

- Pakistani Cyber Army is the name taken by a group of hackers who are known for their defacement of websites, particularly Indian, Chinese, and Israeli companies and governmental organizations, claiming to represent Pakistani nationalist and Islamic interests. The group is thought to have been active since at least 2008, and maintains an active presence on social media, especially Facebook. Its members have claimed responsibility for the hijacking of websites belonging to Acer, BSNL, India's CBI, Central Bank, and the State Government of Kerala.

Sabotage

Non-political acts of sabotage have caused financial and other damage. In 2000, disgruntled employee Vitek Boden caused the release of 800,000 litres of untreated sewage into waterways in Maroochy Shire, Australia.

More recently, in May 2007 Estonia was subjected to a mass cyber-attack in the wake of the removal of a Russian World War II war memorial from downtown Tallinn. The attack was a distributed denial-of-service attack in which selected sites were bombarded with traffic to force them offline; nearly all Estonian government ministry networks as well as two major Estonian bank networks were knocked offline; in addition, the political party website of Estonia's current Prime Minister Andrus Ansip featured a counterfeit letter of apology from Ansip for removing the memorial statue. Despite speculation that the attack had been coordinated by the Russian government, Estonia's defense minister admitted he had no conclusive evidence linking cyber attacks to Russian authorities. Russia called accusations of its involvement "unfounded," and neither NATO nor European Commission experts were able to find any conclusive proof of official Russian government participation. In January 2008 a man from Estonia was convicted for launching the attacks against the Estonian Reform Party website and fined.

During the Russia-Georgia War, on 5 August 2008, three days before Georgia launched its invasion of South Ossetia, the websites for OSInform News Agency and OSRadio were hacked. The OSinform website at osinform.ru kept its header and logo, but its content was replaced by a feed to the Alania TV website content. Alania TV, a Georgian government supported television station aimed at audiences in South Ossetia, denied any involvement in the hacking of the websites. Dmitry Medoyev, at the time the South Ossetian envoy to Moscow, claimed that Georgia was attempting to cover up information on events which occurred in the lead up to the war. One such cyber attack caused the Parliament of Georgia and Georgian Ministry of Foreign Affairs websites to be replaced by images comparing Georgian president Mikheil Saakashvili to Adolf Hitler. Other attacks involved denials of service to numerous Georgian and Azerbaijani websites, such as when Russian hackers allegedly disabled the servers of the Azerbaijani Day.Az news agency.

Website Defacement and Denial of Service

Even more recently, in October 2007, the website of Ukrainian president Viktor Yushchenko was attacked by hackers. A radical Russian nationalist youth group, the Eurasian Youth Movement, claimed responsibility.

In 1999 hackers attacked NATO computers. The computers flooded them with email and hit them with a denial of service (DoS). The hackers were protesting against the NATO bombings of the Chinese embassy in Belgrade. Businesses, public organizations and academic institutions were bombarded with highly politicized emails containing viruses from other European countries.

In Fiction

- The Japanese cyberpunk manga, *Ghost in the Shell* (as well as its popular movie and TV adaptations) centers around an anti-cyberterrorism and cybercrime unit. In its mid-21st century Japan setting such attacks are made all the more threatening by an even more widespread use of technology including cybernetic enhancements to the human body allowing people themselves to be direct targets of cyberterrorist attacks.

- Dan Brown's *Digital Fortress*.

- Amy Eastlake's *Private Lies*.

- In the movie *Live Free or Die Hard*, John McClane (Bruce Willis) takes on a group of cyberterrorists intent on shutting down the entire computer network of the United States.

- The movie *Eagle Eye* involves a super computer controlling everything electrical and networked to accomplish the goal.

- The plots of *24* Day 4 and Day 7 include plans to breach the nation's nuclear plant grid and then to seize control of the entire critical infrastructure protocol.

- The Tom Clancy created series Netforce was about a FBI/Military team dedicated to combating cyberterrorists.

- Much of the plot of *Mega Man Battle Network* is centered around cyberterrorism.

- In the 2009 Japanese animated film *Summer Wars*, an artificial intelligence cyber-terrorist attempts to take control over the world's missiles in order to "win" against the main characters that attempted to keep it from manipulating the world's electronic devices.

- In the 2012 film Skyfall, part of the James Bond franchise, main villain Raoul Silva (Javier Bardem) is an expert cyberterrorist who is responsible for various cyberterrorist incidents in the past.

- Cyberterrorism plays a role in the 2012 video game *Call of Duty: Black Ops II*, first when main antagonist Raul Menendez cripples the Chinese economy with a cyberattack and frames the United States for it, starting a new Cold War between the two powers. Later, another cyberattack with a computer worm leads to Menendez seizing control of the entire U.S drone fleet. Finally, one of the game's endings leads to another attack similar to the latter, this time crippling the U.S' electrical and water distribution grids. An alternate ending depicts the cyberattack failing after it is stopped by one of the game's characters pivotal to the storyline.

- The plot of the 2013 video game *Watch Dogs* is heavily influenced by cyber-terrorism. In which players take control of the game's protagonist, Aiden Pierce, an accused murder suspect, who hacks into a ctOS (Central Operating System), giving him complete control of Chicago's mainframe in order to hunt down his accusers.

- The video game *Metal Slug 4* focuses on Marco and Fio, joined by newcomers Nadia and Trevor, to battle a terrorist organization known as Amadeus that is threatening the world with a computer virus.

- The visual novel *Baldr Force* has the main character Tooru Souma joining a military organization to fight cyberterrorism to avenge the death of his friend.

- The Japanese manga and live action *Bloody Monday* is highly influenced by hacking and cracking. The main character Takagi Fujimaru is a Super Elite hacker which use his hacking knowledge to fight against his enemies.

- In the 2016 movie Death Note: Light Up the New World society is afflicted with cyber-terrorism.

Extortion

Loot and Extortion. Statues at Trago Mills, poking fun at the Inland Revenue.

Extortion (also called shakedown, outwrestling and exaction) is a criminal offense of obtaining money, property, or services from an individual or institution, through coercion. It is sometimes euphemistically referred to as a "protection racket" since the racketeers often phrase their demands as payment for "protection" from (real or hypothetical) threats from unspecified other parties. Extortion is commonly practiced by organized crime groups. The actual obtainment of money or property is not required to commit the offense. Making a threat of violence which refers to a requirement of a payment of money or property to halt future violence is sufficient to commit the offense. Exaction refers not only to extortion or the demanding and obtaining of something through force, but additionally, in its formal definition, means the infliction of something such as pain and suffering or making somebody endure something unpleasant.

Extortion is distinguished from robbery. In robbery, whether armed or not, the offender takes property from the victim by the immediate use of force or fear that force will be immediately used (as in the classic line, "Your money or your life.") Extortion, which is not limited to the taking of property, involves the verbal or written *instillation* of fear that something will happen to the victim if they do not comply with the extortionist's will. Another key distinction is that extortion always involves a verbal or written threat, whereas robbery does not. In United States federal law, extortion can be committed with or without the use of force and with or without the use of a weapon.

In blackmail, which always involves extortion, the extortionist threatens to reveal information about a victim or their family members that is potentially embarrassing, socially damaging, or incriminating unless a demand for money, property, or services is met.

The term *extortion* is often used metaphorically to refer to usury or to price-gouging, though neither is legally considered extortion. It is also often used loosely to refer to everyday situations where one person feels indebted against their will, to another, in order to receive an essential service or avoid legal consequences.

Neither extortion nor blackmail requires a threat of a criminal act, such as violence, merely a threat used to elicit actions, money, or property from the object of the extortion. Such threats include the filing of reports (true or not) of criminal behavior to the police, revelation of damaging facts (such as pictures of the object of the extortion in a compromising position), etc.

United States

In the United States, extortion may also be committed as a federal crime across a computer system, phone, by mail or in using any instrument of interstate commerce. Extortion requires that the individual sent the message willingly and knowingly as elements of the crime. The message only has to be sent (but does not have to reach the intended recipient) to commit the crime of extortion.

United Kingdom

England and Wales

In England and Wales extorting property and money by coercion may be the felony of Blackmail which covers any "unwarranted demand with menaces" including physical threats. See section 21 of the Theft Act 1968 plus sections 29 and 30 of the Larceny Act 1916. A group of people may also be committing conspiracy.

Cyberextortion

Cyberextortion is when an individual or group uses the internet as an offensive force. The group or individual usually sends a company a threatening email stating that they have received confidential information about their company and will exploit a security leak or launch an attack that will harm the company's network. The message sent through the email usually demands money in exchange for the prevention of the attack.

Cases

In March 2008, Anthony Digati was arrested on federal charges of extortion through interstate communication. Digati put $50,000 into a variable life insurance policy by New York Life Insurance Company and wanted a return of $198,303.88. When the firm didn't comply, he threatened to send out 6 million spam emails. He registered a domain in February 2008 that contained New York Life's name in the URL to display false public statements about the company and increased his demand to $3 million. According to prosecutors, Digati's intent was not to inform or educate but he wanted to "damage the reputation of New York Life and cost the company millions of dollars in revenue,". New York Life contacted the Federal Bureau of Investigation and Digati was apprehended.

On February 15, 2011, Spanish police apprehended a man who attempted to blackmail Nintendo over customer information he had stolen. The man stole personal information about 4,000 users and emailed Nintendo Ibérica, Nintendo's Spanish division, and accused the company of data negligence. He threatened the company that he would make the information public and complain to the Spanish Data Agency if his demands were not met. After Nintendo ignored his demands, he published some of the information on an Internet forum. Nintendo notified authorities and the man was arrested in Málaga. No information has been revealed as to what the man demanded from Nintendo.

Similar Crimes

- Badger game: The victim or "mark"—for example, such as a married person—is tricked into a compromising position to make them vulnerable to blackmail.

- Clip joint: A clip joint or fleshpot is an establishment, usually a strip club or entertainment bar, typically one claiming to offer adult entertainment or bottle service, in which customers are tricked into paying money and receive poor goods or services, or none, in return.

- Coercion: the practice of compelling a person or manipulating them to behave in an involuntary way (whether through action or inaction) by use of threats, intimidation, trickery, or some other form of pressure or force. These are used as leverage, to force the victim to act in the desired way.

- Confidence trick (also known as a bunko, con, flim flam, gaffle, grift, hustle, scam, scheme, swindle, bamboozle or finnese): an attempt to defraud a person or group by gaining their confidence.

- Cryptovirology: a software scam in which a public key cryptography system crafts fake keys which encrypt the user's data, but cannot decrypt them unless the user pays for the real key.

- Dognapping: The crime of taking a dog from its owner, which usually occurs in purebred dogs, the profit from which can run up to thousands of dollars.

- Loan sharking: A loan shark is a person or body that offers unsecured loans at high interest rates to individuals, often backed by blackmail or threats of violence.

- Price gouging: a pejorative term for a seller pricing much higher than is considered reasonable or fair. In precise, legal usage, it is the name of a felony that applies in some of the United States only during civil emergencies.

- Racket: A service that is fraudulently offered to solve a problem, such as for a problem that does not actually exist, will not be affected, or would not otherwise exist.

- Sextortion: Forcing individuals to send sexual images or perform sexual services.

- Taxation: the taking of money and/or property from private citizens by the state. Taxation occurs under the pretence that it is in service of the common good of society for the provision of services including public infrastructure and protection from potential harm. It is a monetary equivalent of expropriation, eminent domain and other involuntary forms of wealth redistribution. Though still widespread, taxation is not universally regarded as non-criminal in nature insofar as it is involuntary and implicitly backed by a threat of violence from agents of the state.

- Terrorism: most simply, policy intended to intimidate or cause terror. It is more commonly understood as an act which is intended to create fear (terror), is perpetrated for an ideological goal (as opposed to a materialistic goal or a lone attack), and deliberately target or disregard the safety of non-combatants. Some definitions also include acts of unlawful violence or unconventional warfare, but at present, the international community has been unable to formulate a universally agreed, legally binding, criminal law definition of terrorism.

- Tiger kidnapping: the taking of an innocent hostage to make a loved one or associate of the victim do something, e.g. a child is taken hostage to force the shopkeeper to open the safe; the term originates from the prior observation of the victim, like a tiger does with its prey. Ransoms are often used alongside these.

Cyberwarfare

Cyberwarfare involves the use and targeting of computers and networks in warfare. It involves both offensive and defensive operations pertaining to the threat of cyberattacks, espionage and sabotage. There has been controversy over whether such operations can duly be called "war". Nevertheless, nations have been developing their capabilities and engaged in cyberwarfare either as an aggressor, defendant, or both.

Definition

Cyberwarfare has been defined as "actions by a nation-state to penetrate another nation's computers or networks for the purposes of causing damage or disruption", but other definitions also include non-state actors, such as terrorist groups, companies, political or ideological extremist groups, hacktivists, and transnational criminal organizations.

Some governments have made it an integral part of their overall military strategy, with some having invested heavily in cyberwarfare capability. Cyberwarfare is essentially a formalized version of penetration testing in which a government entity has established it as a warfighting capability.

This capability uses the same set of penetration testing methodologies but applies them, in the case of United States doctrine, in a strategical way to

- Prevent cyber attacks against critical infrastructure

- Reduce national vulnerability to cyber attacks

- Minimize damage and recovery time from cyber attacks

Offensive operations are also part of these national level strategies for officially declared wars as well as undeclared secretive operations.

Types of Threat

- Cyberattacks, where immediate damage or disruption is caused are the main concern.

- Cyber espionage, which can provide the information needed to make a successful cyberattack or scandal to launch an information warfare.

Espionage

Traditional espionage is not an act of war, nor is cyber-espionage, and both are generally assumed to be ongoing between major powers.

Despite this assumption, some incidents can cause serious tensions between nations, and are often described as "attacks". For example:

- Massive spying by the US on many countries, revealed by Edward Snowden.

- After the NSA's spying on Germany's Chancellor Angela Merkel was revealed, the Chancellor compared the NSA with the Stasi.

- The NSA recording nearly every cell phone conversation in the Bahamas, without the Bahamian government's permission, and similar programmes in Kenya, the Philippines, Mexico and Afghanistan.

- The "Titan Rain" probes of American defence contractors computer systems since 2003.

- The Office of Personnel Management data breach, in the US, widely attributed to China.

Sabotage

Computers and satellites that coordinate other activities are vulnerable components of a system and could lead to the disruption of equipment. Compromise of military systems, such as C4ISTAR components that are responsible for orders and communications could lead to their interception or malicious replacement. Power, water, fuel, communications, and transportation infrastructure all may be vulnerable to disruption. According to Clarke, the civilian realm is also at risk, noting that the security breaches have already gone beyond stolen credit card numbers, and that potential targets can also include the electric power grid, trains, or the stock market.

In mid July 2010, security experts discovered a malicious software program called Stuxnet that had infiltrated factory computers and had spread to plants around the world. It is considered "the first attack on critical industrial infrastructure that sits at the foundation of modern economies," notes *The New York Times*.

Stuxnet, while extremely effective in delaying Iran's nuclear program for the development of nuclear weaponry, came at a high cost. For the first time, it became clear that not only could cyber weapons be defensive but they could be offensive. The large decentralization and scale of cyberspace makes it extremely difficult to direct from a policy perspective. Non-state actors can play as large a part in the cyberwar space as state actors, which leads to dangerous, sometimes disastrous, consequences. Small groups of highly skilled malware developers are able to as effectively impact global politics and cyber warfare as large governmental agencies. A major aspect of this ability lies in the willingness of these groups to share their exploits and developments on the web as a form of arms proliferation. This allows lesser hackers to become more proficient in creating the large scale attacks that once only a small handful were skillful enough to manage. In addition, thriving black markets for these kinds of cyber weapons are buying and selling these cyber capabilities to the highest bidder without regard for consequences.

Denial-of-service Attack

In computing, a denial-of-service attack (DoS attack) or distributed denial-of-service attack (DDoS attack) is an attempt to make a machine or network resource unavailable to its intended users. Perpetrators of DoS attacks typically target sites or services hosted on high-profile web servers such as banks, credit card payment gateways, and even root nameservers. DoS attacks may not be limited to computer-based methods, as strategic physical attacks against infrastructure can be just as devastating. For example, cutting undersea communication cables may severely cripple some regions and countries with regards to their information warfare ability.

Electrical Power Grid

The federal government of the United States admits that the electric power grid is susceptible to cyberwarfare. The United States Department of Homeland Security works with industries to identify vulnerabilities and to help industries enhance the security of control system networks, the federal government is also working to ensure that security is built in as the next generation of "smart grid" networks are developed. In April 2009, reports surfaced that China and Russia had infiltrated the U.S. electrical grid and left behind software programs that could be used to disrupt the system, according to current and former national security officials. The North American Electric Reliability Corporation (NERC) has issued a public notice that warns that the electrical grid is not adequately protected from cyber attack. China denies intruding into the U.S. electrical grid. One countermeasure would be to disconnect the power grid from the Internet and run the net with droop speed control only. Massive power outages caused by a cyber attack could disrupt the economy, distract from a simultaneous military attack, or create a national trauma.

Howard Schmidt, former Cyber-Security Coordinator of the US, commented on those possibilities:

It's possible that hackers have gotten into administrative computer systems of utility companies, but says those aren't linked to the equipment controlling the grid, at least not in developed countries. [Schmidt] has never heard that the grid itself has been hacked.

On 23 December 2015, what is believed to be a first known successful cyber attack on a power grid took place in Ukraine leading to temporary blackouts. The cyber attack is attributed to the Russian advanced persistent threat group called "Sandworm" and it was performed during an ongoing military confrontation.

Motivations

Military

In the U.S., General Keith B. Alexander, first head of the recently formed USCYBERCOM, told the Senate Armed Services Committee that computer network warfare is evolving so rapidly that there is a "mismatch between our technical capabilities to conduct operations and the governing laws and policies. Cyber Command is the newest global combatant and its sole mission is cyberspace, outside the traditional battlefields of land, sea, air and space." It will attempt to find and, when necessary, neutralize cyberattacks and to defend military computer networks.

Alexander sketched out the broad battlefield envisioned for the computer warfare command, listing the kind of targets that his new headquarters could be ordered to attack, including "traditional battlefield prizes – command-and-control systems at military headquarters, air defense networks and weapons systems that require computers to operate."

One cyber warfare scenario, Cyber ShockWave, which was wargamed on the cabinet level by former administration officials, raised issues ranging from the National Guard to the power grid to the limits of statutory authority.

The distributed nature of internet based attacks means that it is difficult to determine motivation and attacking party, meaning that it is unclear when a specific act should be considered an act of war.

Examples of cyberwarfare driven by political motivations can be found worldwide. In 2008, Russia began a cyber attack on the Georgian government website, which was carried out along with Georgian military operations in South Ossetia. In 2008, Chinese 'nationalist hackers' attacked CNN as it reported on Chinese repression on Tibet.

Jobs in cyberwarfare have become increasingly popular in the military. The United States Navy actively recruits for cyber warfare engineers. The US Army has their Cyber Command where they actively recruit for cryptologic network warfare specialists.

Civil

Potential targets in internet sabotage include all aspects of the Internet from the backbones of the web, to the internet service providers, to the varying types of data communication mediums and network equipment. This would include: web servers, enterprise information systems, client server systems, communication links, network equipment, and the desktops and laptops in businesses and homes. Electrical grids and telecommunication systems are also deemed vulnerable, especially due to current trends in automation.

Hacktivism

Politically motivated hacktivism, involves the subversive use of computers and computer networks to promote an agenda, and can potentially extend to attacks, theft and virtual sabotage that could be seen as cyberwarfare – or mistaken for it.

Private sector

Computer hacking represents a modern threat in ongoing global conflicts and industrial espionage and as such is presumed to widely occur. It is typical that this type of crime is underreported to the extent they are known. According to McAfee's George Kurtz, corporations around the world face millions of cyberattacks a day. "Most of these attacks don't gain any media attention or lead to strong political statements by victims." This type of crime is usually financially motivated.

Non-profit Research

But not all examinations with the issue of cyberwarfare are achieving profit or personal gain. There are still institutes and companies like the University of Cincinnati or the Kaspersky Security Lab which are trying to increase the sensibility of this topic by researching and publishing of new security threats.

By Region

The Internet security company McAfee stated in their 2007 annual report that approximately 120 countries have been developing ways to use the Internet as a weapon and target financial markets, government computer systems and utilities.

Asia

China

Foreign Policy magazine puts the size of China's "hacker army" at anywhere from 50,000 to 100,000 individuals.

Diplomatic cables highlight US concerns that China is using access to Microsoft source code and 'harvesting the talents of its private sector' to boost its offensive and defensive capabilities.

A 2008 article in the *Culture Mandala: The Bulletin of the Centre for East-West Cultural and Economic Studies* by Jason Fritz alleges that the Chinese government from 1995 to 2008 was involved in a number of high-profile cases of espionage, primarily through the use of a "decentralized network of students, business people, scientists, diplomats, and engineers from within the Chinese Diaspora". A defector in Belgium, purportedly an agent, claimed that there were hundreds of spies in industries throughout Europe, and on his defection to Australia Chinese diplomat Chen Yonglin said there were over 1,000 such in that country. In 2007, a Russian executive was sentenced to 11 years for passing information about the rocket and space technology organization to China. Targets in the United States have included 'aerospace engineering programs, space shuttle design, C4ISR data, high-performance computers, Nuclear weapon design, cruise missile data, semiconductors, integrated circuit design, and details of US arms sales to Taiwan'.

While China continues to be held responsible for a string of cyber-attacks on a number of public and private institutions in the United States, India, Russia, Canada, and France, the Chinese government denies any involvement in cyber-spying campaigns. The administration maintains the position that China is not the threat but rather the victim of an increasing number of cyber-attacks. Most reports about China's cyber warfare capabilities have yet to be confirmed by the Chinese government.

According to Fritz, China has expanded its cyber capabilities and military technology by acquiring foreign military technology. Fritz states that the Chinese government uses "new space-based surveillance and intelligence gathering systems, Anti-satellite weapon, anti-radar, infrared decoys, and false target generators" to assist in this quest, and that they support their "informationization" of their military through "increased education of soldiers in cyber warfare; improving the information network for military training, and has built more virtual laboratories, digital libraries and digital campuses." Through this informationization, they hope to prepare their forces to engage in a different kind of warfare, against technically capable adversaries. Many recent news reports link China's technological capabilities to the beginning of a new 'cyber cold war.'

In response to reports of cyberattacks by China against the United States, Amitai Etzioni of the Institute for Communitarian Policy Studies has suggested that China and the United States agree to a policy of mutually assured restraint with respect to cyberspace. This would involve allowing both states to take the measures they deem necessary for their self-defense while simultaneously agreeing to refrain from taking offensive steps; it would also entail vetting these commitments.

Operation Shady RAT is an ongoing series of cyber attacks starting mid-2006, reported by Internet security company McAfee in August 2011. China is widely believed to be the state actor behind these attacks which hit at least 72 organizations including governments and defense contractors.

India

The Department of Information Technology created the Indian Computer Emergency Response Team (CERT-In) in 2004 to thwart cyber attacks in India. That year, there were 23 reported cyber security breaches. In 2011, there were 13,301. That year, the government created a new subdivision, the National Critical Information Infrastructure Protection Centre (NCIIPC) to thwart attacks against energy, transport, banking, telecom, defence, space and other sensitive areas.

The Executive Director of the Nuclear Power Corporation of India (NPCIL) stated in February 2013 that his company alone was forced to block up to ten targeted attacks a day. CERT-In was left to protect less critical sectors.

A high-profile cyber attack on 12 July 2012 breached the email accounts of about 12,000 people, including those of officials from the Ministry of External Affairs, Ministry of Home Affairs, Defence Research and Development Organisation (DRDO), and the Indo-Tibetan Border Police (ITBP). A government-private sector plan being overseen by National Security Advisor (NSA) Shivshankar Menon began in October 2012, and intends to beef up India's cyber security capabilities in the light of a group of experts findings that India faces a 470,000 shortfall of such experts despite the country's reputation of being an IT and software powerhouse.

In February 2013, Information Technology Secretary J. Satyanarayana stated that the NCIIPC was finalizing policies related to national cyber security that would focus on domestic security solutions, reducing exposure through foreign technology. Other steps include the isolation of various security agencies to ensure that a synchronised attack could not succeed on all fronts and the planned appointment of a National Cyber Security Coordinator. As of that month, there had been no significant economic or physical damage to India related to cyber attacks.

On 26 November 2010, a group calling itself the Indian Cyber Army hacked the websites belonging to the Pakistan Army and the others belong to different ministries, including the Ministry of Foreign Affairs, Ministry of Education, Ministry of Finance, Pakistan Computer Bureau, Council of Islamic Ideology, etc. The attack was done as a revenge for the Mumbai terrorist attacks.

On 4 December 2010, a group calling itself the Pakistan Cyber Army hacked the website of India's top investigating agency, the Central Bureau of Investigation (CBI). The National Informatics Center (NIC) has begun an inquiry.

In July 2016, Cymmetria researchers discovered and revealed the cyber attack dubbed 'Patchwork', which compromised an estimated 2500 corporate and government agencies using code stolen from GitHub and the dark web. Examples of weapons used are an exploit for the Sandworm vulnerability (CVE-2014-4114), a compiled AutoIt script, and UAC bypass code dubbed UACME. Targets are believed to be mainly military and political assignments around Southeast Asia and the South China Sea and the attackers are believed to be of Indian origin and gathering intelligence from influential parties.

Kyrgyzstan

In 2007 the website of the Central Electoral Commission of Kyrgyzstan was defaced during its election. The message left on the website read "This site has been hacked by Dream of Estonian organization". During the election campaigns and riots preceding the election, there were cases of Denial-of-service attacks against the Kyrgyz ISPs.

Philippines

The Chinese are being blamed after a cybersecurity company F-Secure Labs found a malware Nan-HaiShu which targeted the Philippines Department of Justice that which sent information in an infected machine to a server with a Chinese IP address. The malware which is considered particularly sophisticated in nature was introduced by phishing emails that were designed to look like they were coming from an authentic sources. The information sent is believed to be relating to the South China Sea legal case.

Russia

When Russia was still the Soviet Union in 1982, a portion of its Trans-Siberia pipeline within its territory exploded, allegedly due to computer malware implanted in the pirated Canadian software by the Central Intelligence Agency. The malware caused the SCADA system running the pipeline to malfunction. The "Farewell Dossier" provided information on this attack, and wrote that compromised computer chips would become a part of Soviet military equipment, flawed turines would be placed in the gas pipeline, and defective plans would disrupt the output of chemical plants and a tractor factor. This caused the "most monumental nonnuclear explosion and fire ever seen from space." However, the Soviet Union did not blame the United States of the Attack.

Russian, South Ossetian, Georgian and Azerbaijani sites were attacked by hackers during the 2008 South Ossetia War.

Russian-led Cyberattacks

It has been claimed that Russian security services organized a number of denial of service attacks as a part of their cyber-warfare against other countries, most notably the 2007 cyberattacks on Estonia and the 2008 cyberattacks on Russia, South Ossetia, Georgia, and Azerbaijan. One identified young Russian hacker said that he was paid by Russian state security services to lead hacking attacks on NATO computers. He was studying computer sciences at the *Department of the Defense of Information*. His tuition was paid for by the FSB.

South Korea

In July 2009, there were a series of coordinated denial of service attacks against major government, news media, and financial websites in South Korea and the United States. While many thought the attack was directed by North Korea, one researcher traced the attacks to the United Kingdom.

In July 2011, the South Korean company SK Communications was hacked, resulting in the theft of the personal details (including names, phone numbers, home and email addresses and resident registration numbers) of up to 35 million people. A trojaned software update was used to gain access to the SK Communications network. Links exist between this hack and other malicious activity and it is believed to be part of a broader, concerted hacking effort.

With ongoing tensions on the Korean Peninsula, South Korea's defense ministry stated that South Korea was going to improve cyber-defense strategies in hopes of preparing itself from possible cyber attacks. In March 2013, South Korea's major banks – Shinhan Bank, Woori Bank and NongHyup Bank – as well as many broadcasting stations – KBS, YTN and MBC – were hacked and more than 30,000 computers were affected; it is one of the biggest attacks South Korea has faced in years. Although it remains uncertain as to who was involved in this incident, there has been immediate assertions that North Korea is connected, as it threatened to attack South Korea's government institutions, major national banks and traditional newspapers numerous times – in reaction to the sanctions it received from nuclear testing and to the continuation of Foal Eagle, South Korea's annual joint military exercise with the United States. North Korea's cyber warfare capabilities raise the alarm for South Korea, as North Korea is increasing its manpower through military academies specializing in hacking. Current figures state that South Korea only has 400 units of specialized personnel, while North Korea has more than 3,000 highly trained hackers; this portrays a huge gap in cyber warfare capabilities and sends a message to South Korea that it has to step up and strengthen its Cyber Warfare Command forces. Therefore, in order to be prepared from future attacks, South Korea and the United States will discuss further about deterrence plans at the Security Consultative Meeting (SCM). At SCM, they plan on developing strategies that focuses on accelerating the deployment of ballistic missiles as well as fostering its defense shield program, known as the Korean Air and Missile Defense.

Europe

Estonia

In April 2007, Estonia came under cyber attack in the wake of relocation of the Bronze Soldier of Tallinn. The largest part of the attacks were coming from Russia and from official servers of the authorities of Russia. In the attack, ministries, banks, and media were targeted. This attack on Estonia, a seemingly small Baltic nation, was so effective because of how most of the nation is run online. Estonia has implemented an e-government, where bank services, political elections and taxes are all done online.This attack really hurt Estonia's economy and the people of Estonia. At least 150 people were injured on the first day due to riots in the streets.

Germany

In 2013, Germany revealed the existence of their 60-person Computer Network Operation unit. The German intelligence agency, BND, announced it was seeking to hire 130 "hackers" for a new "cyber defence station" unit. In March 2013, BND president Gerhard Schindler announced that his agency had observed up to five attacks a day on government authorities, thought mainly to originate in China. He confirmed the attackers had so far only accessed data and expressed concern that the stolen information could be used as the basis of future sabotage attacks against arms manufacturers, telecommunications companies and government and military agencies. Shortly after Edward Snowden leaked details of the U.S. National Security Agency's cyber surveillance system, German Interior Minister Hans-Peter Friedrich announced that the BND would be given an additional budget of 100 million Euros to increase their cyber surveillance capability from 5% of total internet traffic in Germany to 20% of total traffic, the maximum amount allowed by German law.

Netherlands

In the Netherlands, Cyber Defense is nationally coordinated by the National Cyber Security Centrum (nl) (NCSC). The Dutch Ministry of Defense laid out a cyber strategy in 2011. The first focus is to improve the cyber defense handled by the Joint IT branch (JIVC). To improve intel operations the intel community in the Netherlands (including the military intel organization MIVD) has set up the Joint Sigint Cyber Unit (JSCU). The ministry of Defense is furthermore setting up an offensive cyber force, called Defensie Cyber Command (DCC), which will be operational in the end of 2014.

Sweden

In January 2017, Sweden's armed forces were subjected to a cyber-attack that caused them to shutdown a so-called Caxcis IT system used in military exercises.

Ukraine

According to CrowdStrike from 2014 to 2016, the Russian APT Fancy Bear used Android malware to target the Ukrainian Army's Rocket Forces and Artillery. They distributed an infected version of an Android app whose original purpose was to control targeting data for the D-30 Howitzer artillery. The app, used by Ukrainian officers, was loaded with the X-Agent spyware and posted online on military forums. The attack was claimed by CrowdStrike to be successful, with more than 80% of Ukrainian D-30 Howitzers destroyed, the highest percentage loss of any artillery pieces in the army (a percentage that had never been previously reported and would mean the loss of nearly the entire arsenal of the biggest artillery piece of the Ukrainian Armed Forces). According to the Ukrainian army this number is incorrect and that losses in artillery weapons "were way below those reported" and that that these losses "have nothing to do with the stated cause".

In 2014, the Russians were suspected to use a cyber weapon called "Snake", or "Ouroboros," to conduct a cyber attack on Ukraine during a period of political turmoil. The Snake tool kit began spreading into Ukrainian computer systems in 2010. It performed Computer Network Exploitation (CNE), as well as highly sophisticated Computer Network Attacks (CNA).

On December 23, 2015 the BlackEnergy malware was used in a cyberattack on Ukraine's powergrid that left more than 200,000 people temporarily without power. A mining company and a large railway operator were also victims of the attack.

United Kingdom

MI6 reportedly infiltrated an Al Qaeda website and replaced the instructions for making a pipe bomb with the recipe for making cupcakes.

In October 2010, Iain Lobban, the director of the Government Communications Headquarters (GCHQ), said the UK faces a "real and credible" threat from cyber attacks by hostile states and criminals and government systems are targeted 1,000 times each month, such attacks threatened the UK's economic future, and some countries were already using cyber assaults to put pressure on other nations.

On 12 November 2013, financial organisations in London conducted cyber war games dubbed 'Waking Shark 2' to simulate massive internet-based attacks against bank and other financial organisations. The Waking Shark 2 cyber war games followed a similar exercise in Wall Street.

Middle East

Iran

Iran has been both victim and predator of several cyberwarfare operations. Iran is considered an emerging military power in the field.

In September 2010, Iran was attacked by the Stuxnet worm, thought to specifically target its Natanz nuclear enrichment facility. The worm is said to be the most advanced piece of malware ever discovered and significantly increases the profile of cyberwarfare.

Israel

In the 2006 war against Hezbollah, Israel alleges that cyber-warfare was part of the conflict, where the Israel Defense Forces (IDF) intelligence estimates several countries in the Middle East used Russian hackers and scientists to operate on their behalf. As a result, Israel attached growing importance to cyber-tactics, and became, along with the U.S., France and a couple of other nations, involved in cyber-war planning. Many international high-tech companies are now locating research and development operations in Israel, where local hires are often veterans of the IDF's elite computer units. Richard A. Clarke adds that "our Israeli friends have learned a thing or two from the programs we have been working on for more than two decades."

In September 2007, Israel carried out an airstrike on Syria dubbed Operation Orchard. U.S. industry and military sources speculated that the Israelis may have used cyberwarfare to allow their planes to pass undetected by radar into Syria.

North America

United States

Cyberwarfare in the United States is a part of the American military strategy of proactive cyber defence and the use of cyberwarfare as a platform for attack. The new United States military strategy makes explicit that a cyberattack is *casus belli* just as a traditional act of war.

In 2013 Cyberwarfare was, for the first time, considered a larger threat than Al Qaeda or terrorism, by many U.S. intelligence officials. Representative Mike Rogers, chairman of the U.S. House Permanent Select Committee on Intelligence, for instance, said in late July 2013, that "most Americans" do not realize that the United States is currently in the middle of a "cyber war."

U.S. government security expert Richard A. Clarke, in his book *Cyber War* (May 2010), defines "cyberwarfare" as "actions by a nation-state to penetrate another nation's computers or networks for the purposes of causing damage or disruption." *The Economist* describes cyberspace as "the fifth domain of warfare," and William J. Lynn, U.S. Deputy Secretary of Defense, states that "as a doctrinal matter, the Pentagon has formally recognized cyberspace as a new domain in warfare . . . [which] has become just as critical to military operations as land, sea, air, and space."

In 2009, president Barack Obama declared America's digital infrastructure to be a "strategic national asset," and in May 2010 the Pentagon set up its new U.S. Cyber Command (USCYBER-COM), headed by General Keith B. Alexander, director of the National Security Agency (NSA), to defend American military networks and attack other countries' systems. The EU has set up ENISA (European Union Agency for Network and Information Security) which is headed by Prof. Udo Helmbrecht and there are now further plans to significantly expand ENISA's capabilities. The United Kingdom has also set up a cyber-security and "operations centre" based in Government Communications Headquarters (GCHQ), the British equivalent of the NSA. In the U.S. however, Cyber Command is only set up to protect the military, whereas the government and corporate infrastructures are primarily the responsibility respectively of the Department of Homeland Security and private companies.

In February 2010, top American lawmakers warned that the "threat of a crippling attack on telecommunications and computer networks was sharply on the rise." According to The Lipman Report, numerous key sectors of the U.S. economy along with that of other nations, are currently at risk, including cyber threats to public and private facilities, banking and finance, transportation, manufacturing, medical, education and government, all of which are now dependent on computers for daily operations. In 2009, president Obama stated that "cyber intruders have probed our electrical grids."

The Economist writes that China has plans of "winning informationised wars by the mid-21st century". They note that other countries are likewise organizing for cyberwar, among them Russia, Israel and North Korea. Iran boasts of having the world's second-largest cyber-army. James Gosler, a government cybersecurity specialist, worries that the U.S. has a severe shortage of computer security specialists, estimating that there are only about 1,000 qualified people in the country today, but needs a force of 20,000 to 30,000 skilled experts. At the July 2010 Black Hat computer security conference, Michael Hayden, former deputy director of national intelligence, challenged thousands of attendees to help devise ways to "reshape the Internet's security architecture", explaining, "You guys made the cyberworld look like the north German plain."

In January 2012, Mike McConnell, the former director of national intelligence at the National Security Agency under president George W. Bush told the Reuters news agency that the U.S. has already launched attacks on computer networks in other countries. McConnell did not name the country that the U.S. attacked but according to other sources it may have been Iran. In June 2012 *the New York Times* reported that president Obama had ordered the cyber attack on Iranian nuclear enrichment facilities.

In August 2010, the U.S. for the first time warned publicly about the Chinese military's use of civilian computer experts in clandestine cyber attacks aimed at American companies and government agencies. The Pentagon also pointed to an alleged China-based computer spying network dubbed

GhostNet that was revealed in a research report last year. The Pentagon stated:

> "The People's Liberation Army is using "information warfare units" to develop viruses to attack enemy computer systems and networks, and those units include civilian computer professionals. Commander Bob Mehal, will monitor the PLA's buildup of its cyberwarfare capabilities and will continue to develop capabilities to counter any potential threat."

The United States Department of Defense sees the use of computers and the Internet to conduct warfare in cyberspace as a threat to national security. The United States Joint Forces Command describes some of its attributes:

> Cyberspace technology is emerging as an "instrument of power" in societies, and is becoming more available to a country's opponents, who may use it to attack, degrade, and disrupt communications and the flow of information. With low barriers to entry, coupled with the anonymous nature of activities in cyberspace, the list of potential adversaries is broad. Furthermore, the globe-spanning range of cyberspace and its disregard for national borders will challenge legal systems and complicate a nation's ability to deter threats and respond to contingencies.

In February 2010, the United States Joint Forces Command released a study which included a summary of the threats posed by the internet:

> With very little investment, and cloaked in a veil of anonymity, our adversaries will inevitably attempt to harm our national interests. Cyberspace will become a main front in both irregular and traditional conflicts. Enemies in cyberspace will include both states and non-states and will range from the unsophisticated amateur to highly trained professional hackers. Through cyberspace, enemies will target industry, academia, government, as well as the military in the air, land, maritime, and space domains. In much the same way that airpower transformed the battlefield of World War II, cyberspace has fractured the physical barriers that shield a nation from attacks on its commerce and communication. Indeed, adversaries have already taken advantage of computer networks and the power of information technology not only to plan and execute savage acts of terrorism, but also to influence directly the perceptions and will of the U.S. Government and the American population.

On 6 October 2011, it was announced that Creech AFB's drone and Predator fleet's command and control data stream had been keylogged, resisting all attempts to reverse the exploit, for the past two weeks. The Air Force issued a statement that the virus had "posed no threat to our operational mission".

On 21 November 2011, it was widely reported in the U.S. media that a hacker had destroyed a water pump at the Curran-Gardner Township Public Water District in Illinois. However, it later turned out that this information was not only false, but had been inappropriately leaked from the Illinois Statewide Terrorism and Intelligence Center.

According to the *Foreign Policy* magazine, NSA's Tailored Access Operations (TAO) unit "has successfully penetrated Chinese computer and telecommunications systems for almost 15 years, generating some of the best and most reliable intelligence information about what is going on inside the People's Republic of China."

On 24 November 2014. The Sony Pictures Entertainment hack was a release of confidential data belonging to Sony Pictures Entertainment (SPE).

In June 2015, the United States Office of Personnel Management (OPM) announced that it had been the target of a data breach targeting the records of as many as four million people. Later, FBI Director James Comey put the number at 18 million. The *Washington Post* has reported that the attack originated in China, citing unnamed government officials.

In 2016, Jeh Johnson the United States Secretary of Homeland Security and James Clapper the U.S. Director of National Intelligence issued a joint statement accusing Russia of interfering with the 2016 United States presidential election. The New York Times reported the Obama administration has formally accused Russia of stealing and disclosing Democratic National Committee emails. Under U.S. law (50 U.S.C.Title 50 – War and National Defense, Chapter 15 – National Security, Subchapter III Accountability for Intelligence Activities) there must be a formal *Presidential finding* prior to authorizing a covert attack. U.S. vice president Joe Biden said on the American news interview program *Meet The Press* that the United States will respond. The New York Times noted that Biden's comment "seems to suggest that Mr. Obama is prepared to order — or has already ordered — some kind of covert action". On December 29 the United States imposed the most extensive sanctions against Russia since the Cold War, expelling 35 Russian diplomats from the United States.

The United States has used cyberattacks for tactical advantage in Afghanistan.

In 2014 Barack Obama ordered an intensification of cyberwarfare against North Korea's missile program for sabotaging test launches in their opening seconds.

In March 2017, WikiLeaks has published more than 8,000 documents on the CIA. The confidential documents, codenamed Vault 7 and dated from 2013–2016, include details on CIA's software capabilities, such as the ability to compromise cars, smart TVs, web browsers (including Google Chrome, Microsoft Edge, Mozilla Firefox, and Opera Software ASA), and the operating systems of most smartphones (including Apple's iOS and Google's Android), as well as other operating systems such as Microsoft Windows, macOS, and Linux.

American *"Kill Switch Bill"*

On 19 June 2010, United States Senator Joe Lieberman (I-CT) introduced a bill called "Protecting Cyberspace as a National Asset Act of 2010", which he co-wrote with Senator Susan Collins (R-ME) and Senator Thomas Carper (D-DE). If signed into law, this controversial bill, which the American media dubbed the *"Kill switch bill"*, would grant the president emergency powers over parts of the Internet. However, all three co-authors of the bill issued a statement that instead, the bill "[narrowed] existing broad presidential authority to take over telecommunications networks".

Cyberpeace

The German civil rights panel "FIfF" runs a campaign for cyberpeace – for the control of cyberweapons and surveillance technology and against the militarization of cyberspace and the development and stockpiling of offensive exploits and malware. Measures for cyberpeace include policymakers developing new rules and norms for warfare, individuals and organizations building new tools and secure infrastructures, promoting open source, the establishment of cyber security centers, auditing of critical infrastructure cybersecurity, obligations to disclose vulnerabilities, disarmament, defensive security strategies, decentralization, education and widely applying relevant tools and infrastructures, encryption and other cyberdefenses.

Cyberpeacemaking may also refer to new ways of using cyberspace to strengthen or bring about general peace.

Cyber Counterintelligence

Cyber counter-intelligence are measures to identify, penetrate, or neutralize foreign operations that use cyber means as the primary tradecraft methodology, as well as foreign intelligence service collection efforts that use traditional methods to gauge cyber capabilities and intentions.

- On 7 April 2009, The Pentagon announced they spent more than $100 million in the last six months responding to and repairing damage from cyber attacks and other computer network problems.

- On 1 April 2009, U.S. lawmakers pushed for the appointment of a White House cyber security "czar" to dramatically escalate U.S. defenses against cyber attacks, crafting proposals that would empower the government to set and enforce security standards for private industry for the first time.

- On 9 February 2009, the White House announced that it will conduct a review of the nation's cyber security to ensure that the Federal government of the United States cyber security initiatives are appropriately integrated, resourced and coordinated with the United States Congress and the private sector.

- In the wake of the 2007 cyberwar waged against Estonia, NATO established the Cooperative Cyber Defence Centre of Excellence (CCD CoE) in Tallinn, Estonia, in order to enhance the organization's cyber defence capability. The center was formally established on 14 May 2008, and it received full accreditation by NATO and attained the status of International Military Organization on 28 October 2008. Since Estonia has led international efforts to fight cybercrime, the United States Federal Bureau of Investigation says it will permanently base a computer crime expert in Estonia in 2009 to help fight international threats against computer systems.

- In 2015, the Department of Defense released an updated cyber strategy memorandum detailing the present and future tactics deployed in the service of defense against cyberwarfare. In this memorandum, three cybermissions are laid out. The first cybermission seeks to arm and maintain existing capabilities in the area of cyberspace, the second cybermission focuses on prevention of cyberwarfare, and the third cybermission includes strategies for retaliation and preemption (as distinguished from prevention).

One of the hardest issues in cyber counterintelligence is the problem of "Attribution". Unlike conventional warfare, figuring out who is behind an attack can be very difficult. However Defense Secretary Leon Panetta has claimed that the United States has the capability to trace attacks back to their sources and hold the attackers "accountable".

Controversy Over Terms

There is debate on whether the term "cyberwarfare" is accurate.

Eugene Kaspersky, founder of Kaspersky Lab, concludes that "cyberterrorism" is a more accurate term than "cyberwar". He states that "with today's attacks, you are clueless about who did it or when they will strike again. It's not cyber-war, but cyberterrorism." He also equates large-scale cyber weapons, such as Flame and NetTraveler which his company discovered, to biological weapons, claiming that in an interconnected world, they have the potential to be equally destructive.

In October 2011 the *Journal of Strategic Studies*, a leading journal in that field, published an article by Thomas Rid, "Cyber War Will Not Take Place" which argued that all politically motivated cyber attacks are merely sophisticated versions of sabotage, espionage, or subversion – and that it is unlikely that cyber war will occur in the future.

Howard Schmidt, an American cybersecurity expert, argued in March 2010 that "there is no cyber-war... I think that is a terrible metaphor and I think that is a terrible concept. There are no winners in that environment."

Other experts, however, believe that this type of activity already constitutes a war. The warfare analogy is often seen intended to motivate a militaristic response when that is not necessarily appropriate. Ron Deibert, of Canada's Citizen Lab, has warned of a "militarization of cyberspace".

The European cybersecurity expert Sandro Gaycken argued for a middle position. He considers cyberwar from a legal perspective an unlikely scenario, due to the reasons lined out by Rid (and, before him, Sommer), but the situation looks different from a strategic point of view. States have to consider military-led cyber operations an attractive activity, within and without war, as they offer a large variety of cheap and risk-free options to weaken other countries and strengthen their own positions. Considered from a long-term, geostrategic perspective, cyber offensive operations can cripple whole economies, change political views, agitate conflicts within or among states, reduce their military efficiency and equalize the capacities of high-tech nations to that of low-tech nations, and use access to their critical infrastructures to blackmail them.

Legality, Rules

Various parties have attempted to come up with international legal frameworks to clarify what is and is not acceptable, but none have yet to be widely accepted.

The Tallinn Manual, published in 2013, is an academic, non-binding study on how international law, in particular the jus ad bellum and international humanitarian law, apply to cyber conflicts and cyber warfare. It was written at the invitation of the Tallinn-based NATO Cooperative Cyber Defence Centre of Excellence by an international group of approximately twenty experts between 2009 and 2012.

The Shanghai Cooperation Organisation (members of which include China and Russia) defines cyberwar to include dissemination of information "harmful to the spiritual, moral and cultural spheres of other states". In September 2011, these countries proposed to the UN Secretary General a document called "International code of conduct for information security".

In contrast, the United States' approach focuses on physical and economic damage and injury, putting political concerns under freedom of speech. This difference of opinion has led to reluctance in the West to pursue global cyber arms control agreements. However, American General Keith B. Alexander did endorse talks with Russia over a proposal to limit military attacks in cyberspace. In June 2013, Barack Obama and Vladimir Putin agreed to install a secure *Cyberwar-Hotline* providing "a direct secure voice communications line between the US cybersecurity coordinator and the Russian deputy secretary of the security council, should there be a need to directly manage a crisis situation arising from an ICT security incident" (White House quote).

A Ukrainian professor of International Law, Alexander Merezhko, has developed a project called the International Convention on Prohibition of Cyberwar in Internet. According to this project, cyberwar is defined as the use of Internet and related technological means by one state against the political, economic, technological and information sovereignty and independence of another state. Professor Merezhko's project suggests that the Internet ought to remain free from warfare tactics and be treated as an international landmark. He states that the Internet (cyberspace) is a "common heritage of mankind".

On the February 2017 RSA Conference Microsoft president Brad Smith suggested global rules – a "Digital Geneva Convention" – for cyber attacks that "ban the nation-state hacking of all the civilian aspects of our economic and political infrastructures". He also stated that an independent organization could investigate and publicly disclose evidence that attributes nation-state attacks to specific countries. Furthermore, he said that the technology sector should collectively and neutrally work together to protect Internet users and pledge to remain neutral in conflict and not aid governments in offensive activity and to adopt a coordinated disclosure process for software and hardware vulnerabilities.

In Films

Documentaries

- *Cyber War Threat* (2015)
- *Darknet, Hacker, Cyberwar* (2017)
- *Zero Days* (2016)

Malware

Malware, short for malicious software, is an umbrella term used to refer to a variety of forms of hostile or intrusive software, including computer viruses, worms, trojan horses, ransomware, spyware, adware, scareware, and other malicious programs. It can take the form of executable code, scripts, active content, and other software. Malware is defined by its malicious intent, acting against the requirements of the computer user - and so does not include software that causes unintentional harm due to some deficiency.

Programs supplied officially by companies, can be considered malware if they secretly act against the interests of the computer user. An example is the Sony rootkit, a Trojan embedded into CDs sold by Sony, which silently installed and concealed itself on purchasers' computers with the intention of preventing illicit copying; it also reported on users' listening habits, and unintentionally created vulnerabilities that were exploited by unrelated malware.

Software such as anti-virus and firewalls are used to protect against activity identified as malicious, and to recover from attacks.

Purposes

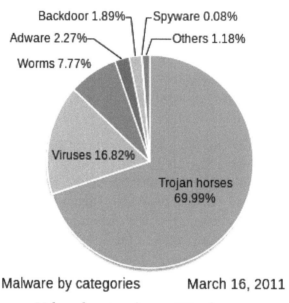

Malware by categories on 16 March 2011.

Many early infectious programs, including the first Internet Worm, were written as experiments or pranks. Today, malware is used by both black hat hackers and governments, to steal personal, financial, or business information.

Malware is sometimes used broadly against government or corporate websites to gather guarded information, or to disrupt their operation in general. However, malware is often used against individuals to gain information such as personal identification numbers or details, bank or credit card numbers, and passwords.

Since the rise of widespread broadband Internet access, malicious software has more frequently been designed for profit. Since 2003, the majority of widespread viruses and worms have been designed to take control of users' computers for illicit purposes. Infected "zombie computers" are used to send email spam, to host contraband data such as child pornography, or to engage in distributed denial-of-service attacks as a form of extortion.

Programs designed to monitor users' web browsing, display unsolicited advertisements, or redirect affiliate marketing revenues are called spyware. Spyware programs do not spread like viruses; instead they are generally installed by exploiting security holes. They can also be hidden and packaged together with unrelated user-installed software.

Ransomware affects an infected computer in some way, and demands payment to reverse the damage. For example, programs such as CryptoLocker encrypt files securely, and only decrypt them on payment of a substantial sum of money.

Some malware is used to generate money by click fraud, making it appear that the computer user has clicked an advertising link on a site, generating a payment from the advertiser. It was estimated in 2012 that about 60 to 70% of all active malware used some kind of click fraud, and 22% of all ad-clicks were fraudulent.

In addition to criminal money-making, malware can be used for sabotage, often for political motives. Stuxnet, for example, was designed to disrupt very specific industrial equipment. There have been politically motivated attacks that have spread over and shut down large computer networks, including massive deletion of files and corruption of master boot records, described as "computer killing". Such attacks were made on Sony Pictures Entertainment (25 November 2014, using malware known as Shamoon or W32.Disttrack) and Saudi Aramco (August 2012).

Infectious Malware

The best-known types of malware, viruses and worms, are known for the manner in which they spread, rather than any specific types of behavior. The term *computer virus* is used for a program that embeds itself in some other executable software (including the operating system itself) on the target system without the user's consent and when that is run causes the virus to spread to other executables. On the other hand, a *worm* is a stand-alone malware program that *actively* transmits itself over a network to infect other computers. These definitions lead to the observation that a virus requires the user to run an infected program or operating system for the virus to spread, whereas a worm spreads itself.

Concealment

These categories are not mutually exclusive, so malware may use multiple techniques. This section only applies to malware designed to operate undetected, not sabotage and ransomware.

Viruses

A computer program usually hidden within another seemingly innocuous program that produces copies of itself and inserts them into other programs or files, and that usually performs a malicious action (such as destroying data).

Trojan Horses

A *trojan*, is a malicious computer program which misrepresents itself to appear useful, routine, or interesting in order to persuade a victim to install it. The term is derived from the Ancient Greek story of the Trojan Horse used to invade the city of Troy by stealth.

Trojans are generally spread by some form of social engineering, for example where a user is duped into executing an e-mail attachment disguised to be unsuspicious, (e.g., a routine form to be filled in), or by drive-by download. Although their payload can be anything, many modern forms act as a backdoor, contacting a controller which can then have unauthorized access to the affected computer. While Trojans and backdoors are not easily detectable by themselves, computers may appear to run slower due to heavy processor or network usage.

Unlike computer viruses and worms, Trojans generally do not attempt to inject themselves into other files or otherwise propagate themselves.

Rootkits

Once a malicious program is installed on a system, it is essential that it stays concealed, to avoid detection. Software packages known as *rootkits* allow this concealment, by modifying the host's operating system so that the malware is hidden from the user. Rootkits can prevent a malicious process from being visible in the system's list of processes, or keep its files from being read.

Some malicious programs contain routines to defend against removal, not merely to hide themselves. An early example of this behavior is recorded in the Jargon File tale of a pair of programs infesting a Xerox CP-V time sharing system:

> Each ghost-job would detect the fact that the other had been killed, and would start a new copy of the recently stopped program within a few milliseconds. The only way to kill both ghosts was to kill them simultaneously (very difficult) or to deliberately crash the system.

Backdoors

A backdoor is a method of bypassing normal authentication procedures, usually over a connection to a network such as the Internet. Once a system has been compromised, one or more backdoors may be installed in order to allow access in the future, invisibly to the user.

The idea has often been suggested that computer manufacturers preinstall backdoors on their systems to provide technical support for customers, but this has never been reliably verified. It was reported in 2014 that US government agencies had been diverting computers purchased by those considered "targets" to secret workshops where software or hardware permitting remote access by the agency was installed, considered to be among the most productive operations to obtain access to networks around the world. Backdoors may be installed by Trojan horses, worms, implants, or other methods.

Evasion

Since the beginning of 2015, a sizable portion of malware utilizes a combination of many techniques designed to avoid detection and analysis.

- The most common evasion technique is when the malware evades analysis and detection by fingerprinting the environment when executed.

- The second most common evasion technique is confusing automated tools' detection methods. This allows malware to avoid detection by technologies such as signature-based anti-virus software by changing the server used by the malware.

- The third most common evasion technique is timing-based evasion. This is when malware runs at certain times or following certain actions taken by the user, so it executes during certain vulnerable periods, such as during the boot process, while remaining dormant the rest of the time.

- The fourth most common evasion technique is done by obfuscating internal data so that automated tools do not detect the malware.

- An increasingly common technique is adware that uses stolen certificates to disable anti-malware and virus protection; technical remedies are available to deal with the adware.

Nowadays, one of the most sophisticated and stealthy ways of evasion is to use information hiding techniques, namely stegomalware.

Vulnerability

- In this context, and throughout, what is called the "system" under attack may be anything from a single application, through a complete computer and operating system, to a large network.

- Various factors make a system more vulnerable to malware.

Security Defects in Software

Malware exploits security defects (security bugs or vulnerabilities) in the design of the operating system, in applications (such as browsers, e.g. older versions of Microsoft Internet Explorer supported by Windows XP), or in vulnerable versions of browser plugins such as Adobe Flash Player, Adobe Acrobat or Reader, or Java SE. Sometimes even installing new versions of such plugins does not automatically uninstall old versions. Security advisories from plug-in providers announce security-related updates. Common vulnerabilities are assigned CVE IDs and listed in the US National Vulnerability Database. Secunia PSI is an example of software, free for personal use, that will check a PC for vulnerable out-of-date software, and attempt to update it.

Malware authors target bugs, or loopholes, to exploit. A common method is exploitation of a buffer overrun vulnerability, where software designed to store data in a specified region of memory does not prevent more data than the buffer can accommodate being supplied. Malware may provide data that overflows the buffer, with malicious executable code or data after the end; when this payload is accessed it does what the attacker, not the legitimate software, determines.

Insecure Design or User Error

Early PCs had to be booted from floppy disks. When built-in hard drives became common, the operating system was normally started from them, but it was possible to boot from another boot device if available, such as a floppy disk, CD-ROM, DVD-ROM, USB flash drive or network. It was common to configure the computer to boot from one of these devices when available. Normally none would be available; the user would intentionally insert, say, a CD into the optical drive to boot the computer in some special way, for example, to install an operating system. Even without booting, computers can be configured to execute software on some media as soon as they become available, e.g. to autorun a CD or USB device when inserted.

Malicious software distributors would trick the user into booting or running from an infected device or medium. For example, a virus could make an infected computer add autorunnable code to any USB stick plugged into it. Anyone who then attached the stick to another computer set to autorun from USB would in turn become infected, and also pass on the infection in the same way. More generally, any device that plugs into a USB port - even lights, fans, speakers, toys, or peripherals such as a digital microscope - can be used to spread malware. Devices can be infected during manufacturing or supply if quality control is inadequate.

This form of infection can largely be avoided by setting up computers by default to boot from the internal hard drive, if available, and not to autorun from devices. Intentional booting from another device is always possible by pressing certain keys during boot.

Older email software would automatically open HTML email containing potentially malicious JavaScript code. Users may also execute disguised malicious email attachments and infected executable files supplied in other ways.

Over-privileged Users and Over-privileged Code

In computing, privilege refers to how much a user or program is allowed to modify a system. In poorly designed computer systems, both users and programs can be assigned more privileges than they should be, and malware can take advantage of this. The two ways that malware does this is through overprivileged users and overprivileged code.

Some systems allow all users to modify their internal structures, and such users today would be considered over-privileged users. This was the standard operating procedure for early microcomputer and home computer systems, where there was no distinction between an *administrator* or *root*, and a regular user of the system. In some systems, non-administrator users are over-privileged by design, in the sense that they are allowed to modify internal structures of the system. In some environments, users are over-privileged because they have been inappropriately granted administrator or equivalent status.

Some systems allow code executed by a user to access all rights of that user, which is known as over-privileged code. This was also standard operating procedure for early microcomputer and home computer systems. Malware, running as over-privileged code, can use this privilege to subvert the system. Almost all currently popular operating systems, and also many scripting applications allow code too many privileges, usually in the sense that when a user executes code, the system allows that code all rights of that user. This makes users vulnerable to malware in the form of e-mail attachments, which may or may not be disguised.

Use of the Same Operating System

- Homogeneity can be a vulnerability. For example, when all computers in a network run the same operating system, upon exploiting one, one worm can exploit them all: In particular, Microsoft Windows or Mac OS X have such a large share of the market that an exploited vulnerability concentrating on either operating system could subvert a large number of systems. Introducing diversity purely for the sake of robustness, such as adding Linux computers, could increase short-term costs for training and maintenance. However, as long as all the nodes are not part of the same directory service for authentication, having a few diverse nodes could deter total shutdown of the network and allow those nodes to help with recovery of the infected nodes. Such separate, functional redundancy could avoid the cost of a total shutdown, at the cost of increased complexity and reduced usability in terms of single sign-on authentication.

Anti-malware Strategies

As malware attacks become more frequent, attention has begun to shift from viruses and spyware protection, to malware protection, and programs that have been specifically developed to combat malware.

Anti-virus and Anti-malware Software

A specific component of anti-virus and anti-malware software, commonly referred to as an on-access or real-time scanner, hooks deep into the operating system's core or kernel and functions in a manner similar to how certain malware itself would attempt to operate, though with the user's informed permission for protecting the system. Any time the operating system accesses a file, the on-access scanner checks if the file is a 'legitimate' file or not. If the file is identified as malware by the scanner, the access operation will be stopped, the file will be dealt with by the scanner in a pre-defined way (how the anti-virus program was configured during/ post installation), and the user will be notified. This may have a considerable performance impact on the operating system, though the degree of impact is dependent on how well the scanner was programmed. The goal is to stop any operations the malware may attempt on the system before they occur, including activities which might exploit bugs or trigger unexpected operating system behavior.

Anti-malware programs can combat malware in two ways:

1. They can provide real time protection against the installation of malware software on a computer. This type of malware protection works the same way as that of antivirus protection in that the anti-malware software scans all incoming network data for malware and blocks any threats it comes across.

2. Anti-malware software programs can be used solely for detection and removal of malware software that has already been installed onto a computer. This type of anti-malware software scans the contents of the Windows registry, operating system files, and installed programs on a computer and will provide a list of any threats found, allowing the user to choose which files to delete or keep, or to compare this list to a list of known malware components, removing files that match.

Real-time protection from malware works identically to real-time antivirus protection: the software scans disk files at download time, and blocks the activity of components known to represent malware. In some cases, it may also intercept attempts to install start-up items or to modify browser settings. Because many malware components are installed as a result of browser exploits or user error, using security software (some of which are anti-malware, though many are not) to "sandbox" browsers (essentially isolate the browser from the computer and hence any malware induced change) can also be effective in helping to restrict any damage done.

Examples of Microsoft Windows antivirus and anti-malware software include the optional Microsoft Security Essentials (for Windows XP, Vista, and Windows 7) for real-time protection, the Windows Malicious Software Removal Tool (now included with Windows (Security) Updates on "Patch Tuesday", the second Tuesday of each month), and Windows Defender (an optional download in the case of Windows XP, incorporating MSE functionality in the case of Windows 8 and later). Additionally, several capable antivirus software programs are available for free download from the Internet (usually restricted to non-commercial use). Tests found some free programs to be competitive with commercial ones. Microsoft's System File Checker can be used to check for and repair corrupted system files.

Some viruses disable System Restore and other important Windows tools such as Task Manager and Command Prompt. Many such viruses can be removed by rebooting the computer, entering Windows safe mode with networking, and then using system tools or Microsoft Safety Scanner.

Hardware implants can be of any type, so there can be no general way to detect them.

Website Security Scans

As malware also harms the compromised websites (by breaking reputation, blacklisting in search engines, etc.), some websites offer vulnerability scanning. Such scans check the website, detect malware, may note outdated software, and may report known security issues.

"Air Gap" Isolation or "Parallel Network"

As a last resort, computers can be protected from malware, and infected computers can be prevented from disseminating trusted information, by imposing an "air gap" (i.e. completely disconnecting them from all other networks). However, malware can still cross the air gap in some situations. For example, removable media can carry malware across the gap. In December 2013 researchers in Germany showed one way that an apparent air gap can be defeated.

"AirHopper", "BitWhisper", "GSMem" and "Fansmitter" are four techniques introduced by researchers that can leak data from air-gapped computers using electromagnetic, thermal and acoustic emissions.

Grayware

Grayware is a term applied to unwanted applications or files that are not classified as malware, but can worsen the performance of computers and may cause security risks.

It describes applications that behave in an annoying or undesirable manner, and yet are less serious or troublesome than malware. Grayware encompasses spyware, adware, fraudulent dialers, joke programs, remote access tools and other unwanted programs that harm the performance of computers or cause inconvenience. The term came into use around 2004.

Another term, potentially unwanted program (PUP) or potentially unwanted application (PUA), refers to applications that would be considered unwanted despite often having been downloaded by the user, possibly after failing to read a download agreement. PUPs include spyware, adware, and fraudulent dialers. Many security products classify unauthorised key generators as grayware, although they frequently carry true malware in addition to their ostensible purpose.

Software maker Malwarebytes lists several criteria for classifying a program as a PUP. Some adware (using stolen certificates) disables anti-malware and virus protection; technical remedies are available.

History of Viruses and Worms

Before Internet access became widespread, viruses spread on personal computers by infecting the executable boot sectors of floppy disks. By inserting a copy of itself into the machine code instructions in these executables, a virus causes itself to be run whenever a program is run or the disk is booted. Early computer viruses were written for the Apple II and Macintosh, but they became more widespread with the dominance of the IBM PC and MS-DOS system. Executable-infecting viruses are dependent on users exchanging software or boot-able floppies and thumb drives so they spread rapidly in computer hobbyist circles.

The first worms, network-borne infectious programs, originated not on personal computers, but on multitasking Unix systems. The first well-known worm was the Internet Worm of 1988, which infected SunOS and VAX BSD systems. Unlike a virus, this worm did not insert itself into other programs. Instead, it exploited security holes (vulnerabilities) in network server programs and started itself running as a separate process. This same behavior is used by today's worms as well.

With the rise of the Microsoft Windows platform in the 1990s, and the flexible macros of its applications, it became possible to write infectious code in the macro language of Microsoft Word and similar programs. These *macro viruses* infect documents and templates rather than applications (executables), but rely on the fact that macros in a Word document are a form of executable code.

Academic Research

The notion of a self-reproducing computer program can be traced back to initial theories about the operation of complex automata. John von Neumann showed that in theory a program could reproduce itself. This constituted a plausibility result in computability theory. Fred Cohen experimented with computer viruses and confirmed Neumann's postulate and investigated other properties of malware such as detectability and self-obfuscation using rudimentary encryption. His doctoral dissertation was on the subject of computer viruses. The combination of cryptographic technology as part of the payload of the virus, exploiting it for attack purposes was initialized and investigated from the mid 1990s, and includes initial ransomware and evasion ideas.

International Cybercrime

There is no commonly agreed single definition of "cybercrime". It refers to illegal internet-mediated activities that often take place in global electronic networks. Cybercrime is "international" or "transnational" – there are 'no cyber-borders between countries'. International cybercrimes often challenge the effectiveness of domestic and international law and law enforcement. Because existing laws in many countries are not tailored to deal with cybercrime, criminals increasingly conduct crimes on the Internet in order to take advantages of the less severe punishments or difficulties of being traced. No matter in developing or developed countries, governments and industries have gradually realized the colossal threats of cybercrime on economic and political security and public interests. However, complexity in types and forms of cybercrime increases the difficulty to fight back. In this sense, fighting cybercrime calls for international cooperation. Various organizations and governments have already made joint efforts in establishing global standards of legislation and law enforcement both on a regional and on an international scale. U.S.-China's cooperation is one of the most striking progress recently because they are the top two source countries of cybercrime.

Information and communication technology (ICT) plays an important role in helping ensure interoperability and security based on global standards. General countermeasures have been adopted in cracking down cybercrime, such as legal measures in perfecting legislation and technical measures in tracking down crimes over the network, Internet content control, using public or private proxy and computer forensics, encryption and plausible deniability, etc. Due to the heterogeneity of law enforcement and technical countermeasures of different countries, this article will mainly focus on legislative and regulatory initiatives of international cooperation.

Typology

In terms of cybercrime, we may often associate it with various forms of Internet attacks, such as hacking, Trojans, malware (keyloggers), botnet, Denial-of-Service (DoS), spoofing, phishing, and vishing. Though cybercrime encompasses a broad range of illegal activities, it can be generally divided into five categories:

Intrusive Offences

Illegal Access: "Hacking" is one of the major forms of offences that refers to unlawful access to a computer system.

Data Espionage: Offenders can intercept communications between users (such as e-mails) by targeting communication infrastructure such as fixed lines or wireless, and any Internet service (e.g., e-mail servers, chat or VoIP communications).

Data Interference: Offenders can violate the integrity of data and interfere with them by deleting, suppressing, or altering data and restricting access to them.

Content-related Offences

Pornographic Material (Child-Pornography): Sexually related content was among the first content to be commercially distributed over the Internet.

Racism, Hate Speech, Glorification of Violence: Radical groups use mass communication systems such as the Internet to spread propaganda.

Religious Offences: A growing number of websites present material that is in some countries covered by provisions related to religious offences, e.g., anti-religious written statements.

Spam: Offenders send out bulk mails by unidentified source and the mail server often contains useless advertisements and pictures.

Copyright and Trademark-related Offences

Common copyright offences: cyber copyright infringement of software, music or films.

Trademark violations: A well-known aspect of global trade. The most serious offences include phishing and domain or name-related offences, such as cybersquatting.

Computer-related Offences

Fraud: online auction fraud, advance fee fraud, credit card fraud, Internet banking

Forgery: manipulation of digital documents.

Identity theft: It refers to stealing private information including Social Security Numbers (SSN), passport numbers, Date of birth, addresses, phone numbers, and passwords for non-financial and financial accounts.

Combination Offences

Cyberterrorism: The main purposes of it are propaganda, information gathering, preparation of real-world attacks, publication of training material, communication, terrorist financing and attacks against critical infrastructure.

Cyberwarfare: It describes the use of ICTs in conducting warfare using the Internet.

Cyberlaundering: Conducting crime through the use of virtual currencies, online casinos etc.

Threats

Similar to conventional crime, economic benefits, power, revenge, adventure, ideology and lust are the core driving forces of cybercrime. Major threats caused by those motivations can be categorized as following:

Economic security, reputation and social trust are severely challenged by cyber fraud, counterfeiting, impersonation and concealment of identity, extortion, electronic money laundering, copyright infringement and tax evasion.

Public interest and national security/integrity can be threatened by dissemination of offensive material —e.g., pornographic, defamatory or inflammatory/intrusive communication— cyber stalking/harassment, Child pornography and paedophilia, electronic vandalism/terrorism.

Privacy, domestic and even diplomatic information security are harmed by unauthorized access and misuse of ICT, denial of services, and illegal interception of communication.

Domestic, as well as international security are threatened by cybercrime due to its transnational characteristic. No single country can really handle this big issue on their own. It is imperative for us to collaborate and defend cybercrime on a global scale.

International Trends

As more and more criminals are aware of potentially large economic gains that can be achieved with cybercrime, they tend to switch from simple adventure and vandalism to more targeted attacks, especially platforms where valuable information highly concentrates, such as computer, mobile devices and the Cloud. There are several emerging international trends of cybercrime.

- Platform switch: Cybercrime is switching its battle ground from Windows-system PCs to other platforms, including mobile phones, tablet computers, and VoIP. Because a significant threshold in vulnerabilities has been reached. PC vendors are building better security into their products by providing faster updates, patches and user alert to potential flaws. Besides, global mobile devices' penetration—from smart phones to tablet PCs—accessing the Internet by 2013 will surpass 1 billion, creating more opportunities for cybercrime. The massively successful banking Trojan, Zeus is already being adapted for the mobile platform. Smishing, or SMS phishing, is another method cyber criminals are using to exploit mobile devices, which users download after falling prey to a social engineering ploy, is designed to defeat the SMS-based two-factor authentication most banks use to confirm online funds transfers by customers. VoIP systems are being used to support vishing (telephone-based phishing) schemes, which are now growing in popularity.

- Social engineering scams: It refers to a non-technical kind of intrusion, in the form of e-mails or social networking chats, that relies heavily on human interaction and often involves fooling potential victims into downloading malware or leaking personal data. Social engineering is nevertheless highly effective for attacking well-protected computer systems with the exploitation of trust. Social networking becomes an increasingly important tool for cyber criminals to recruit money mules to assist their money laundering operations around the globe. Spammers are not only spoofing social networking messages to persuade targets to click on links in emails — they are taking advantage of users' trust of their social networking connections to attract new victims.

- Highly targeted: The newest twist in "hypertargeting" is malware that is meant to disrupt industrial systems — such as the Stuxnet network worm, which exploits zero-day vulnerabilities in Microsoft. The first known copy of the worm was discovered in a plant in Germany. A subsequent variant led to a widespread global outbreak.

- Dissemination and use of malware: malware generally takes the form of a virus, a worm, a Trojan horse, or spyware. In 2009, the majority of malware connects to host Web sites registered in the U.S.A. (51.4%), with China second (17.2%), and Spain third (15.7%). A primary means of malware dissemination is email. It is truly international in scope.

- Intellectual property theft (IP theft): It is estimated that 90% of the software, DVDs, and CDs sold in some countries are counterfeit, and that the total global trade in counterfeit goods is more than $600 billion a year. In the USA alone, IP theft costs businesses an estimated $250 billion annually, and 750,000 jobs.

International Legislative Responses and Cooperation

G8

Group of Eight (G8) is made up of the heads of eight industrialized countries: the U.S., the United Kingdom, Russia, France, Italy, Japan, Germany, and Canada.

In 1997, G8 released a Ministers' Communiqué that includes an action plan and principles to combat cybercrime and protect data and systems from unauthorized impairment. G8 also mandates that all law enforcement personnel must be trained and equipped to address cybercrime, and designates all member countries to have a point of contact on a 24 hours a day/7 days a week basis.

United Nations

In 1990 the UN General Assembly adopted a resolution dealing with computer crime legislation. In 2000 the UN GA adopted a resolution on combating the criminal misuse of information technology. In 2002 the UN GA adopted a second resolution on the criminal misuse of information technology.

ITU

The International Telecommunication Union (ITU), as a specialized agency within the United Nations, plays a leading role in the standardization and development of telecommunications and cybersecurity issues. The ITU was the lead agency of the World Summit on the Information Society (WSIS).

In 2003, Geneva Declaration of Principles and the Geneva Plan of Action were released, which highlights the importance of measures in the fight against cybercrime.

In 2005, the Tunis Commitment and the Tunis Agenda were adopted for the Information Society.

Council of Europe

Council of Europe is an international organisation focusing on the development of human rights and democracy in its 47 European member states.

In 2001, the Convention on Cybercrime, the first international convention aimed at Internet criminal behaviors, was co-drafted by the Council of Europe with the addition of USA, Canada, and Japan and signed by its 46 member states. But only 25 countries ratified later. It aims at providing the basis of an effective legal framework for fighting cybercrime, through harmonization of cybercriminal offences qualification, provision for laws empowering law enforcement and enabling international cooperation.

Regional Responses

APEC

Asia-Pacific Economic Cooperation (APEC) is an international forum that seeks to promote promoting open trade and practical economic cooperation in the Asia-Pacific Region. In 2002, APEC issued Cybersecurity Strategy which is included in the Shanghai Declaration. The strategy outlined six areas for co-operation among member economies including legal developments, information sharing and co-operation, security and technical guidelines, public awareness, and training and education.

OECD

The Organisation for Economic Co-operation and Development (OECD) is an international economic organisation of 34 countries founded in 1961 to stimulate economic progress and world trade.

In 1990, the Information, Computer and Communications Policy (ICCP) Committee created an Expert Group to develop a set of guidelines for information security that was drafted until 1992 and then adopted by the OECD Council. In 2002, OECD announced the completion of "Guidelines for the Security of Information Systems and Networks: Towards a Culture of Security".

European Union

The coat of arms of the European Cybercrime Centre

In 2001, the European Commission published a communication titled "Creating a Safer Information Society by Improving the Security of Information Infrastructures and Combating Computer-related Crime".

In 2002, EU presented a proposal for a "Framework Decision on Attacks against Information Systems". The Framework Decision takes note of Convention on Cybercrime, but concentrates on the harmonisation of substantive criminal law provisions that are designed to protect infrastructure elements.

Commonwealth

In 2002, the Commonwealth of Nations presented a model law on cybercrime that provides a legal framework to harmonise legislation within the Commonwealth and enable international cooperation. The model law was intentionally drafted in accordance with the Convention on Cybercrime.

ECOWAS

The Economic Community of West African States (ECOWAS) is a regional group of west African Countries founded in 1975 it has fifteen member states. In 2009, ECOWAS adopted the Directive on Fighting Cybercrime in ECOWAS that provides a legal framework for the member states, which includes substantive criminal law as well as procedural law.

GCC

In 2007, the Arab League and Gulf Cooperation Council (GCC) recommended at a conference seeking a joint approach that takes into consideration international standards.

Voluntary Industry Response

During the past few years, public-private partnerships have emerged as a promising approach for tackling cybersecurity issues around the globe. Executive branch agencies (e.g., the Federal Trade Commission in US), regulatory agencies (e.g., Australian Communications and Media Authority), separate agencies (e.g., ENISA in the EU) and industry (e.g., MAAWG, ...) are all involved in partnership.

In 2004, the London Action Plan was founded, which aims at promoting international spam enforcement cooperation and address spam related problems, such as online fraud and deception, phishing, and dissemination of viruses.

Case Analysis

U.S.

According to Sophos, the U.S. remains the top-spamming country and the source of about one-fifth of the world's spam. Since fighting cybercrime involves great amount of sophisticated legal and other measures, only milestones rather than full texts are provideds here.

Legal and Regulatory Measures

The first federal computer crime statute was the Computer Fraud and Abuse Act of 1984 (CFAA).

In 1986, Electronic Communications Privacy Act (ECPA) was an amendment to the federal wiretap law.

"National Infrastructure Protection Act of 1996".

"Cyberspace Electronic Security Act of 1999".

"Patriot Act of 2001".

Digital Millennium Copyright Act (DMCA) was enacted in 1998.

Cyber Security Enhancement Act (CSEA) was passed in 2002.

Can-spam law issued in 2003 and subsequent implementation measures were made by FCC and FTC.

In 2005 the USA passed the Anti-Phishing Act which added two new crimes to the US Code.

In 2009, the Obama Administration released Cybersecurity Report and policy. Cybersecurity Act of 2010, a bill seeking to increase collaboration between the public and the private sector on cybersecurity issues.

A number of agencies have been set up in the U.S. to fight against cybercrime, including the FBI, National Infrastructure Protection Center, National White Collar Crime Center, Internet Fraud Complaint Center, Computer Crime and Intellectual Property Section of the Department of Justice (DoJ), Computer Hacking and Intellectual Property Unit of the DoJ, and Computer Emergency Readiness Team/Coordination Center (CERT/CC) at Carnegie-Mellon, and so on.

CyberSafe is a public service project designed to educate end users of the Internet about the critical need for personal computer security.

Technical Measures

Cloud computing: It can make infrastructures more resilient to attacks and functions as data back-up as well. However, as the Cloud concentrates more and more sensitive data, it becomes increasingly attractive to cybercriminals.

Better encryption methods are developed to deal with phishing, smishing and other illegal data interception activities.

The Federal Bureau of Investigation has set up special technical units and developed Carnivore, a computer surveillance system which can intercept all packets that are sent to and from the ISP where it is installed, to assist in the investigation of cybercrime.

Industry Collaboration

Public-private partnership: in 2006, the Internet Corporation for Assigned Names and Numbers (ICANN) signed an agreement with the United States Department of Commerce (United States Department of Commerce) that they partnered through the Multistakeholder Model of consultation.

In 2008, the second annual Cyber Storm conference was exercised, involving nine states, four foreign governments, 18 federal agencies and 40 private companies.

In 2010, National Cyber Security Alliance's public awareness campaign was launched in partnership with the U.S. Department of Homeland Security, the Federal Trade Commission, and others.

Incentives for ISP: Though the cost of security measures increases, Internet Service Providers (ISP) are encouraged to fight against cybercrime to win consumer support, good reputation and brand image among consumer and peer ISP as well.

International Cooperation

USA has signed and also ratified Convention on Cybercrime.

United States has actively participated in G8/OECD/APEC/OAS/U.S.-China cooperation in cracking down international cyber crime.

Future Challenges

Privacy in tracking down cybercrime is being challenged and becomes a controversial issue.

Public-private partnership. As the U.S. government gets more involved in the development of IT products, many companies worry this may stifle their innovation, even undermining efforts to develop more secure technology products. New legislative proposals now being considered by the U.S. Congress could be potentially intrusive on private industry, which may prevent enterprises from responding effectively to emerging and changing threats. Cyber attacks and security breaches are increasing in frequency and sophistication, they are targeting organizations and individuals with malware and anonymization techniques that can evade current security controls. Current perimeter-intrusion detection, signature-based malware, and anti-virus solutions are providing little defense. Relatively few organizations have recognized organized cyber criminal networks, rather than hackers, as their greatest potential cyber security threat; even fewer are prepared to address this threat.

China

In January 2009, China was ranked No.3 spam-producing country in the world, according to data compiled by security vendor Sophos. Sophos now ranks China as spam producer No.20, right behind Spain.

China's underground economy is booming with estimated 10 billion RMB in 2009. Hacking, malware and spam are immensely popular. With patriotic hacktivism, people hack to defend the country.

Legal and Regulatory Measures

Criminal Law – the basic law identifies the law enforcement concerning cybercrime.

In 2000, the Decision on Internet Security of the Standing Committee of the NPC was passed.

In 2000, China issued a series of Internet rules that prohibit anyone to propagate pornography, virus and scams.

In 2003, China signed UN General Assembly Resolution 57/239 on "Creation of a global culture of cybersecurity".

In 2003, China signed Geneva Declaration of Principles of the World Summit on the Information Society.

In 2006, an anti-spam initiative was launched.

In July 2006, the ASEAN Regional Forum (ARF), which included China, issued a statement that its members should implement cybercrime and cybersecurity laws "in accordance with their national conditions and by referring to relevant international instruments".

In 2009, ASEAN-China framework agreement on network and information security emergency response were adopted.

In 2009, agreement within the Shanghai Cooperation Organization on information security was made.

Technical Measures

Internet censorship: China has made it tougher to register new Internet domains and has put on stricter content control to help reduce spam.

"Golden Shield Project" or "The Great Firewall of China": a national Internet control and censorship project. In 2009, Green Dam software: It restricts access to a secret list of sites, and monitors users'activity.

Operating system change: China is trying to get around this by using Linux, though with a lot of technical impediments to solve.

Industry Collaboration

Internet Society of China — the group behind China's anti-spam effort — is working on standards and better ways of cooperating to fight cybercrime.

ISPs have become better at working with customers to cut down on the spam problem.

International Cooperation

In 2005, China signed up for the London Action Plan on spam, an international effort to curb the problem.

Anti-Spam "Beijing Declaration"2006 International Anti-Spam Summit was held.

The APEC Working Group on Telecommunications agreed an action plan for 2010-2015 that included "fostering a safe and trusted ICT environment".

In January 2011, the United States and China committed for the first time at head of state level to work together on a bilateral basis on issues of cybersecurity. "Fighting Spam to Build Trust" will be the first effort to help overcome the trust deficit between China and the United States on cybersecurity. Cyber Security China Summit 2011 will be held in Shanghai.

Achievement and Future Challenges

Successfully cracking down spam volume in 2009. However, insufficient criminal laws and regulations are great impediments in fighting cybercrime. A lack of electronic evidence laws or regulations, low rank of existing internet control regulations and technological impediments altogether limit the efficiency of Chinese governments' law enforcement.

References

- Hoofnagle, Chris Jay, Identity Theft: Making the Known Unknowns Known. Harvard Journal of Law and Technology, Vol. 21, Fall 2007

- Gantz, John; Rochester, Jack B. (2005). Pirates of the Digital Millennium. Upper Saddle River, NJ 07458: Prentice Hall. ISBN 0-13-146315-2

- Ghosh, Ayush (2013). "Seclayer: A plugin to prevent phishing attacks". IUP Journal of Information Technology, 9(4), 52–64

- Hoffman, Sandra K (2009). Identity Theft : A Reference Handbook. Santa Barbara, US: ABC-CLIO. pp. 42–44. ISBN 9781598841442 – via Contemporary World Issues

- Gable, Kelly A. "Cyber-Apocalypse Now: Securing the Internet against Cyberterrorism and Using Universal Jurisdiction as a Deterrent" Vanderbilt Journal of Transnational Law, Vol. 43, No. 1

- Arata, Michael J. (2010). For Dummies : Identity Theft For Dummies (1). Hoboken, US: For Dummies. pp. 43–45. ISBN 9780470622735 – via ProQuest ebrary

- Collins, Sean (April 2012). "Stuxnet: the emergence of a new cyber weapon and its implications". Journal of Policing, Intelligence and Counter Terrorism. 7 (1). Retrieved 6 June 2015

- Anderson, Ross J. (2008). Security engineering: a guide to building dependable distributed systems (2nd ed.). Indianapolis, IN: Wiley. p. 1040. ISBN 978-0-470-06852-6. Chapter 2, page 17

- Gorman, Siobhan. (8 April 2009) Electricity Grid in U.S. Penetrated By Spies. The Wall Street Journal. Retrieved 8 November 2011

- Mitnick, K (2002): "The Art of Deception", p. 103 Wiley Publishing Ltd: Indianapolis, Indiana; United States of America. ISBN 0-471-23712-4

- Barrett, Devlin (5 June 2015). "U.S. Suspects Hackers in China Breached About four (4) Million People's Records, Officials Say". Wall Street Journal. Retrieved 5 June 2015

- Bodmer, Kilger, Carpenter, & Jones (2012). Reverse Deception: Organized Cyber Threat Counter-Exploitation. New York: McGraw-Hill Osborne Media. ISBN 0071772499, ISBN 978-0071772495

- Lee, Carol E.; Sonne, Paul (December 30, 2016). "U.S. Sanctions Russia Over Election Hacking; Moscow Threatens to Retaliate" – via Wall Street Journal

- Singer, P.W.; Friedman, Allan (2014). Cybersecurity and Cyberwar: What Everyone Needs to Know. Oxford: Oxford University Press. p. 156. ISBN 978-0-19-991809-6

- Rid, Thomas (October 2011). "Cyber War Will Not Take Place". Journal of Strategic Studies. 35: 5–32. doi:10.1080/01402390.2011.608939. Retrieved 21 October 2011

- Mazanec, Brain M. (2015). The Evolution of Cyber War. USA: University of Nebraska Press. pp. 235–236. ISBN 9781612347639

- Gorman, Siobhan. (4 June 2010) WSJ: U.S. Backs Talks on Cyber Warfare. The Wall Street Journal. Retrieved 8 November 2011

- Mazanec, Brain M. (2015). The Evolution of Cyber War. USA: University of Nebraska Press. pp. 221–222. ISBN 9781612347639

- Hanspach, Michael; Goetz, Michael (November 2013). "On Covert Acoustical Mesh Networks in Air". Journal of Communications. doi:10.12720/jcm.8.11.758-767

- Hofkirchner, Wolfgang; Burgin, Mark. The Future Information Society: Social and Technological Problems. World Scientific. ISBN 9789813108981. Retrieved 22 May 2017

3

Psychological Warfare in Cybercrime

One of the common forms of bullying is cyberbullying. It includes spreading rumors, abusing, making sexual remarks, hateful comments and disclosing an individual's personal information. Bullying can harm a person to an extent where they can develop suicidal tendencies. Cybercrime is best understood in confluence with the major topics listed in the following chapter.

Cyberbullying

Cyberbullying or cyberharassment is a form of bullying or harassment using electronic forms of contact. Cyberbullying has become increasingly common, especially among teenagers. Harmful bullying behavior can include posting rumors about a person, threats, sexual remarks, disclose victims' personal information, or pejorative labels (i.e., hate speech). Bullying or harassment can be identified by repeated behavior and an intent to harm. Victims may have lower self-esteem, increased suicidal ideation, and a variety of emotional responses, retaliating, being scared, frustrated, angry, and depressed. Individuals have reported that cyberbullying can be more harmful than traditional bullying.

Awareness in the United States has risen in the 2010s, due in part to high-profile cases. Several states in the US and in other countries have laws specific to regulating cyberbullying. These laws can be designed to specifically target teen cyberbullying, while others use laws extending from the scope of physical harassment. In cases of adult cyberharassment, these reports are usually filed beginning with local police. Research has demonstrated a number of serious consequences of cyberbullying victimization.

Internet trolling is a common form of bullying over the Internet in an online community (such as in online gaming or social media) in order to elicit a reaction, disruption, or for their own personal amusement. Cyberstalking is another form of bullying or harassment that uses electronic communications to stalk a victim may pose a credible threat to the safety of the victim.

Definitions

A frequently used definition of cyberbullying is "an aggressive, intentional act or behavior that is carried out by a group or an individual, using electronic forms of contact, repeatedly and over time against a victim who cannot easily defend him or herself." There are many variations of the definition, such as the National Crime Prevention Council's more specific definition: "the process of using the Internet, cell phones or other devices to send or post text or images intended to hurt or embarrass another person."

Cyberbullying is often similar to traditional bullying, with some notable distinctions. Victims of cyberbullying may not know the identity of their bully, or why the bully is targeting them. The harassment can have wide-reaching effects on the victim, as the content used to harass the victim can be spread and shared easily among many people and often remains accessible for a long time after the initial incident.

The terms *cyberharassment* and *cyberbullying* are sometimes used synonymously, though some people use cyberbullying specifically to refer to harassment among minors or in a school setting.

Cyberstalking

Cyberstalking is a form of online harassment in which the perpetrator uses electronic communications to stalk a victim. Cyberstalking is considered more dangerous than other forms of cyberbullying because it generally involves a credible threat to the safety of the victim. Cyberstalkers may send repeated messages intended to threaten or harass their victim. They may encourage others to do the same, either explicitly or by impersonating their victim and asking others to contact them.

Trolling

Internet trolls intentionally try to provoke or offend others in order to elicit a reaction. Trolls and cyberbullies do not always have the same goals: while some trolls engage in cyberbullying, others may be engaged in comparatively harmless mischief. A troll may be disrupt either for their own amusement or because they are genuinely a combative person.

Methods Used

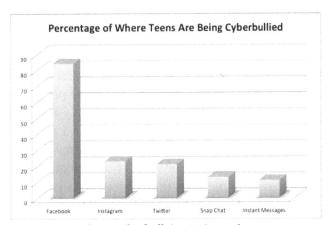

Where Cyberbullying Is Occurring.

Manuals to educate the public, teachers and parents summarize, "Cyberbullying is being cruel to others by sending or posting harmful material using a cell phone or the internet." Research, legislation and education in the field are ongoing. Research has identified basic definitions and guidelines to help recognize and cope with what is regarded as abuse of electronic communications.

- Cyberbullying involves repeated behavior with intent to harm.

- Cyberbullying is perpetrated through harassment, cyberstalking, denigration (sending or posting cruel rumors and falsehoods to damage reputation and friendships), impersonation, and exclusion (intentionally and cruelly excluding someone from an online group)

Cyberbullying can be as simple as continuing to send emails or text messages harassing someone who has said they want no further contact with the sender. It may also include public actions such as repeated threats, sexual remarks, pejorative labels (i.e., hate speech) or defamatory false accusations, ganging up on a victim by making the person the subject of ridicule in online forums, hacking into or vandalizing sites about a person, and posting false statements as fact aimed a discrediting or humiliating a targeted person. Cyberbullying could be limited to posting rumors about a person on the internet with the intention of bringing about hatred in others' minds or convincing others to dislike or participate in online denigration of a target. It may go to the extent of personally identifying victims of crime and publishing materials severely defaming or humiliating them.

Cyberbullies may disclose victims' personal data (e.g. real name, home address, or workplace/ schools) at websites or forums or may use impersonation, creating fake accounts, comments or sites posing as their target for the purpose of publishing material in their name that defames, discredits or ridicules them. This can leave the cyberbully anonymous which can make it difficult for the offender to be caught or punished for their behavior, although not all cyberbullies maintain their anonymity. Text or instant messages and emails between friends can also constitute cyberbullying if what is said or displayed is hurtful to the participants.

Cyberbullying by email from a fictional friend@hotmail.com

The recent use of mobile applications and rise of smartphones have yielded to a more accessible form of cyberbullying. It is expected that cyberbullying via these platforms will be associated with bullying via mobile phones to a greater extent than exclusively through other more stationary internet platforms. In addition, the combination of cameras and Internet access and the instant availability of these modern smartphone technologies yield themselves to specific types of cyberbullying not found in other platforms. It is likely that those cyberbullied via mobile devices will experience a wider range of cyberbullying types than those exclusively bullied elsewhere.

While most cases are considered to be cyberbullying, some teens argue that most events are simply drama. For example, Danah Boyd writes, "teens regularly used that word [drama] to describe various forms of interpersonal conflict that ranged from insignificant joking around to serious jealousy-driven relational aggression. Whereas adults might have labeled many of these practices as bullying, teens saw them as drama."

In Social Media

Cyberbullying can take place on social media sites such as Facebook, Myspace, and Twitter. "By 2008, 93% of young people between the ages of 12 and 17 were online. In fact, youth spend more time with media than any single other activity besides sleeping." The last decade has witnessed a surge of cyberbullying, bullying that occurs through the use of electronic communication technologies, such as e-mail, instant messaging, social media, online gaming, or through digital messages or images sent to a cellular phone.

There are many risks attached to social media sites, and cyberbullying is one of the larger risks. One million children were harassed, threatened or subjected to other forms of cyberbullying on Facebook during the past year, while 90 percent of social-media-using teens who have witnessed online cruelty say they have ignored mean behavior on social media, and 35 percent have done this frequently. 95 percent of social-media-using teens who have witnessed cruel behavior on social networking sites say they have seen others ignoring the mean behavior, and 55 percent witness this frequently.

According to a 2013 Pew Research study, eight out of 10 teens who use social media share more information about themselves than they have in the past. This includes location, images, and contact information. "The most recent case of cyber-bullying and illegal activity on Facebook involved a memorial page for the young boys who lost their lives to suicide due to anti-gay bullying. The page quickly turned into a virtual grave desecration and platform condoning gay teen suicide and the murdering of homosexuals. Photos were posted of executed homosexuals, desecrated photos of the boys who died and supposed snuff photos of gays who have been murdered. Along with this were thousands of comments encouraging murder sprees against gays, encouragement of gay teen suicide, death threats etc. In addition, the page continually exhibited pornography to minors." In order to protect children, it's important that personal information such as age, birthday, school/church, phone number, etc. be kept confidential.

Cyberbullying can also take place through the use of websites belonging to certain groups to effectively request the targeting of another individual or group. An example of this is the bullying of climate scientists and activists.

In Gaming

Online harassment in gaming culture can occur in online gaming

Of those who reported having experienced online harassment in a Pew Research poll, 16% said the most recent incident occurred in an online game. A study from National Sun Yat-sen University observed that children who enjoyed violent video games were significantly more likely to both experience and perpetrate cyberbullying.

Another study that discusses the direct correlation between exposure to violent video games and cyber bullying also took into account personal factors such as; "duration of playing online games, alcohol consumption in the last 3 months, parents drunk in the last 3 months, anger, hostility, ADHD, and a sense of belonging" as potential contributing factors of cyberbullying.

Gaming was a more common venue for men to experience harassment, whereas women's' harassment tended to occur via social media. Most respondents considered gaming culture to be equally welcoming to both genders, though 44% thought it favored men. Keza MacDonald writes in The Guardian that sexism exists in gaming culture, but is not mainstream within it. Sexual harassment in gaming generally involves slurs directed towards women, sex role stereotyping, and overaggressive language. U.S. President Barack Obama made reference to harassment of women gamers during remarks in honor of Women's History Month.

Competitive gaming scenes have been less welcoming of women that has broader gaming culture. In an internet-streamed fighting game competition, one female gamer forfeited a match after the coach of her team, Aris Bakhtanians, stated, "The sexual harassment is part of the culture. If you remove that from the fighting game community, it's not the fighting game community" The comments were widely condemned by gamers, with comments in support of sexual harassment "drowned out by a vocal majority of people expressing outrage, disappointment and sympathy." The incident built momentum for action to counter sexual harassment in gaming.

In a number of instances, game developers have been subjected to harassment and death threats by players upset by changes to a game or by a developer's online policies. Harassment also occurs in reaction to critics such as Jack Thompson or Anita Sarkeesian, whom some fans see as a threat to the medium. Various individuals have been harassed in connection with the Gamergate controversy. Harassment related to gaming is not of a notably different severity or tenor compared to online harassment motivated by other subcultures or advocacy issues.

Sabotage among rival crowdfunding campaigns is a recurring problem for projects related to gaming.

In Search Engines

Information cascades happen when users start passing on information they assume to be true, but cannot know to be true, based on information on what other users are doing. Information cascades can be accelerated by search engines' ranking technologies and their tendency to return results relevant to a user's previous interests. This type of information spreading is hard to stop. Information cascades over social media and the Internet may also be harmless, and may contain truthful information.

Bullies use Google bombs (a term applicable to any search engine) to increase the eminence of favored posts sorted by the most popular searches, done by linking to those posts from as many other web pages as possible. Examples include the campaign for the neologism "santorum" organized by the LGBT lobby. Google bombs can manipulate the Internet's search engines regardless of how authentic the pages are, but there is a way to counteract this type of manipulation as well.

Law Enforcement

A majority of states have laws that explicitly include electronic forms of communication within stalking or harassment laws. Most law enforcement agencies have cyber-crime units and often

Internet stalking is treated with more seriousness than reports of physical stalking. Help and resources can be searched by state or area.

Schools

The safety of schools is increasingly becoming a focus of state legislative action. There was an increase in cyber-bullying enacted legislation between 2006 and 2010. Initiatives and curriclulum requirements also exist in the UK (the Ofsted eSafety guidance) and Australia (Overarching Learning Outcome 13).

In 2012, a group of teenagers in New Haven, Connecticut developed an application to help fight bullying. Called "Back Off Bully" (BOB), the web app is an anonymous resource for computer, smart phone or iPad. When someone witnesses or is the victim of bullying, they can immediately report the incident. The app asks questions about time, location and how the bullying is happening, as well as providing positive action and empowerment over the incident, the reported information helps by going to a database where administrators study it. Common threads are spotted so others can intervene and break the bully's pattern. BOB, the brainchild of fourteen teens in a design class, is being considered as standard operating procedure at schools across the state. Recent studies carried out among 66 high school teachers have concluded that prevention programs proved ineffective to date.

Protection

There are laws that only address online harassment of children or focus on child predators as well as laws that protect adult cyberstalking victims, or victims of any age. Currently, there are 45 cyberstalking (and related) laws on the books. While some sites specialize in laws that protect victims age 18 and under, Working to Halt Online Abuse is a help resource containing a list of current and pending cyberstalking-related United States federal and state laws. It also lists those states that do not have laws yet and related laws from other countries. The Global Cyber Law Database (GCLD) aims to become the most comprehensive and authoritative source of cyber laws for all countries.

Age

Children report negative online behaviors occurring from the second grade. According to research, boys initiate negative online activity earlier than girls do. However, by middle school, girls are more likely to engage in cyberbullying than boys. Whether the bully is male or female, his or her purpose is to intentionally embarrass others, harass, intimidate, or make threats online to one another. This bullying occurs via email, text messaging, posts to blogs, and websites.

Studies in the psycho-social effects of cyberspace have begun to monitor the impacts cyber-bullying may have on the victims, and the consequences it may lead to. Consequences of cyber-bullying are multi-faceted, and affect online and offline behavior. Research on adolescents reported that changes in the victims' behavior as a result of cyber-bullying could be positive. Victims "created a cognitive pattern of bullies, which consequently helped them to recognize aggressive people."

However, the Journal of Psychosocial Research on Cyberspace abstract reports critical impacts in almost all of the respondents', taking the form of lower self-esteem, loneliness, disillusionment, and distrust of people. The more extreme impacts were self-harm. Children have killed each other and committed suicide after having been involved in a cyberbullying incident. Some cases of digital self-harm have been reported, where an individual engages in cyberbullying against themselves, or purposefully and knowingly exposes themselves to cyberbullying.

Adults

Stalking online has criminal consequences just as physical stalking. A target's understanding of why cyberstalking is happening is helpful to remedy and take protective action to restore remedy. Cyberstalking is an extension of physical stalking. Among factors that motivate stalkers are: envy, pathological obsession (professional or sexual), unemployment or failure with own job or life; intention to intimidate and cause others to feel inferior; the stalker is delusional and believes he/she "knows" the target; the stalker wants to instill fear in a person to justify his/her status; belief they can get away with it (anonymity).

The US federal cyberstalking law is designed to prosecute people for using electronic means to repeatedly harass or threaten someone online. There are resources dedicated to assisting adult victims deal with cyberbullies legally and effectively. One of the steps recommended is to record everything and contact police.

Research

Australia

The nationwide Australian Covert Bullying Prevalence Survey (Cross et al., 2009) assessed cyber-bullying experiences among 7,418 students. Rates of cyber-bullying increased with age, with 4.9% of students in Year 4 reporting cyberbullying compared to 7.9% in year nine. Cross et al., (2009) reported that rates of bullying and harassing others were lower, but also increased with age. Only 1.2% of Year 4 students reported cyber-bullying others compared to 5.6% of Year 9 students.

China

Over the mainland of China, cyberbullying seems has yet to receive adequate scholarly. A study investigated the risk factors of cyberbullying, illustrated a sample of 1438 high school students from central China. Data had shown 34.84% were participated bullied and 56.88% had been bullied by online. Students who spend more time on internet have themselves experienced traditional bullying as victims will be more likely to experience cyberbullying through different social media in instant-message.

A study investigated cyberbullying in Hong Kong chose 48 people out of 7654 students from elementary school to high school who were classify as potential aggressors that related to cyber-bullying. 31 out of 48 students declared they barely participate in cyber-attack. In is more general among high school students (28 out of 36 students) to participate in social media platform. These students took a survey about cyberbullying: 58% admitted they changed nickname for others, 56.3% for humiliation, 54.2% make fun of someone, 54.2% for spread out rumors. The Hong Kong Federation of Youth Groups had interviewed 1820 teenagers, 17.5% indicated the experience of cyberbully. For example: insult, coarse abuse, publishes personal private pictures with candid camera, and spread out in social media without permission.

European Union

In a study published in 2011, across 25 EU member states studied, the average 6% of the children (9–16 years old) have been bullied and only 3% of them confessed to be a bully. However, in an earlier publication of Hasenbrink et al. (2009), reporting on the results from a meta analysis from European Union countries, the authors estimated (via median results) that approximately 18% of European young people had been "bullied/harassed/stalked" via the internet and mobile phones. Cyber-harassment rates for young people across the EU member states ranged from 10% to 52%. The decreasing numbers can caused by developing increasingly specific methods, dividing the tasks into different variables.

Finland

In addition to the current research, Sourander et al. (2010) conducted a population-based cross-sectional study that took place in Finland. The authors of this study took the self-reports of 2215 Finish adolescents between the ages of 13 to 16 years old about cyberbullying and cyber-victimization during the past 6 months. It was found that, amongst the total sample, 4.8% were cybervictims only, 7.4% were cyberbullies only, and 5.4% were cyberbully-victims.

The authors of this study were able to conclude that cyberbullying as well as cybervictimization is associated not only with psychiatric issues, but psychosomatic issues. Many adolescents in the study reported headaches or difficulty sleeping. The authors believe that their results indicate a greater need for new ideas on how to prevent cyberbullying and what to do when it occurs. It is clearly a worldwide problem that needs to be taken seriously.

Ireland

The journal article titled "Exploring traditional and cyberbullying among Irish adolescent" studies the Health Behaviour in School-aged Children (HBSC) pilot survey was carried out by 8 post-primary schools across Ireland in which 318 students aged 15–18 years old completed. 59% of these students were boys and 41% were girls. The participation in this survey was completely voluntary for the student and content had to be obtained from the parents as well as students and also the school itself. This survey was also anonymous and confidential. It took one class or 40 minutes to complete by the students. This survey asked questions on traditional forms of bullying as well as cyber bullying, risk behaviours and self-reported health and life satisfaction.

66% of these students said that they have never been bullied. 14% reported that they were victims of the traditional forms of bullying. 10% reported that they were victims of cyber bullying and the remaining 10% said that they were victims of both traditional forms of bullying as well as cyber bullying. It was mostly boys that said they were victims of just traditional forms of bullying, but it was reported that it was mostly girls that were victims of both traditional forms of bullying and cyber bullying. 20% of the students in this survey said that they have been cyber bullied showing that cyber bullying is on the rise. Arrow D.I.T claims that twenty-three percent of 9–16 year olds in Ireland have been bullied on-line or of-line, compared to nineteen percent in Europe. Although, on-line bullying in Ireland at 4% according to Arrow D.I.T is lower than the European average which stands at 6%, and half that of the UK where 8% reported being cyberbullied. As a result, traditional forms of bullying in Ireland is higher than their European counterparts, but lower when it comes to cyberbullying.

Japan

According to recent research, in Japan, 17 percent (compared with a 25-country average of 37 percent) of youth between the ages of 8 and 17 have been victim to online bullying activities. The number shows that online bullying is a serious concern in Japan. Teenagers who spend more than 10 hours a week on Internet are more likely to become the target of online bullying. Only 28 percent of the survey participants understood what cyberbullying is. However, they do notice the severity of the issue since 63 percent of the surveyed worry about being targeted as victims of cyberbullying.

With the advance of Internet technology, everyone can access the internet. Since teenagers find themselves congregating socially on the internet via social media, they become easy targets for cyberbullying. Forms of social media where cyberbullying occurs include but are not limited to email, text, chat rooms, mobile phones, mobile phone cameras and social websites (Facebook, Twitter). Some cyberbullies have set up websites or blogs to post the target's images, publicize their personal information, gossip about the target, express why they hate the target, request people to agree with the bully's view, and sending links to the target to make sure they are watching the activity.

Much cyberbullying is an act of relational aggression, which involves alienating the victim from his or her peers through gossip or ostracism. This kind of attack can be easily launched via texting or other online activities. Here is an example of a 19-year-old teenager sharing his real experience of cyberbullying. When he was in high school, his classmates posted his photo online, insulted him constantly, and asked him to die. Because of the constant harassment, he did attempt suicide twice. Even when he quit school, the attacks did not stop.

Cyberbullying can cause serious psychological impact to the victims. They often feel anxious, nervous, tired, and depressed. Other examples of negative psychological trauma include losing confidence as a result being socially isolated from their schoolmates or friends. Mental psychological problems can also show up in the form of headaches, skin problems, abdominal pain, sleep problems, bed-wetting, and crying. It may also lead victims to commit suicide to end bullying.

United States

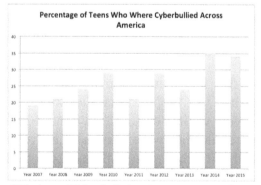

Percentage of Victims of Cyberbullying By Year Across the United States.

2000

A survey by the Crimes Against Children Research Center at the University of New Hampshire in 2000 found that 6% of the young people in the survey had experienced some form of harassment including threats and negative rumours and 2% had suffered distressing harassment.

2004

The 2004 I-Safe.org survey of 1,500 students between grades 4 and 8 found:

- 42% of children had been bullied while online. One in four have had it happen more than once.

- 35% had been threatened online. Nearly one in five had had it happen more than once.

- 21% had received mean or threatening e-mails or other messages.

- 58% admitted that someone had said mean or hurtful things to them online. More than four out of ten said it had happened more than once.

- 58% had not told their parents or an adult about something mean or hurtful that had happened to them online.

2005

The Youth Internet Safety Survey-2, conducted by the Crimes Against Children Research Center at the University of New Hampshire in 2005, found that 9% of the young people in the survey had experienced some form of harassment. The survey was a nationally representative telephone survey of 1,500 youth 10–17 years old. One third reported feeling distressed by the incident, with distress being more likely for younger respondents and those who were the victims of aggressive harassment (including being telephoned, sent gifts, or visited at home by the harasser). Compared to youth not harassed online, victims are more likely to have social problems. On the other hand, youth who harass others are more likely to have problems with rule breaking and aggression.

Hinduja and Patchin completed a study in the summer of 2005 of approximately 1,500 Internet-using adolescents and found that over one-third of youth reported being victimized online, and over 16% of respondents admitted to cyber-bullying others. While most of the instances of cyber-bullying involved relatively minor behavior (41% were disrespected, 19% were called names), over 12% were physically threatened and about 5% were scared for their safety. Notably, fewer than 15% of victims told an adult about the incident. Additional research by Hinduja and Patchin in 2007 found that youth who report being victims of cyber-bullying also experience stress or strain that is related to offline problem behaviors such as running away from home, cheating on a school test, skipping school, or using alcohol or marijuana. The authors acknowledge that both of these studies provide only preliminary information about the nature and consequences of online bullying, due to the methodological challenges associated with an online survey.

According to a 2005 survey by the National Children's Home charity and Tesco Mobile of 770 youth between the ages of 11 and 19, 20% of respondents revealed that they had been bullied via electronic means. Almost three-quarters (73%) stated that they knew the bully, while 26% stated that the offender was a stranger. 10% of responders indicated that another person has taken a picture and/or video of them via a cellular phone camera, consequently making them feel uncomfortable, embarrassed, or threatened. Many youths are not comfortable telling an authority figure about their cyber-bullying victimization for fear their access to technology will be taken from them; while 24% and 14% told a parent or teacher respectively, 28% did not tell anyone while 41% told a friend.

2006

According to the 2006 *Harris Interactive Cyberbullying Research Report*, commissioned by the National Crime Prevention Council, cyber-bullying is a problem that "affects almost half of all American teens".

2007

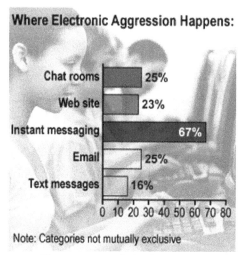

Distribution of cyberbullying venues used by young people in the US, according to the Centers for Disease Control

Studies published 2007 in the Journal of Adolescent Health indicated young people reporting being victims of electronic aggression in a range of 9% to 35%.

In 2007, Debbie Heimowitz, a Stanford University master's student, created Adina's Deck, a film based on Stanford accredited research. She worked in focus groups for ten weeks in three schools to learn about the problem of cyber-bullying in Northern California. The findings determined that over 60% of students had been cyber-bullied and were victims of cyber-bullying. The film is now being used in classrooms nationwide as it was designed around learning goals pertaining to problems that students had understanding the topic. The middle school of Megan Meier is reportedly using the film as a solution to the crisis in their town.

2008

In the summer of 2008, researchers Sameer Hinduja (Florida Atlantic University) and Justin Patchin (University of Wisconsin-Eau Claire) published a book on cyber-bullying that summarized the current state of cyber-bullying research. (*Bullying Beyond the Schoolyard: Preventing and Responding to Cyberbullying*). Their research documents that cyber-bullying instances have been increasing over the last several years. They also report findings from the most recent study of cyber-bullying among middle-school students. Using a random sample of approximately 2000 middle-school students from a large school district in the southern United States, about 10% of respondents had been cyber-bullied in the previous 30 days while over 17% reported being cyber-bullied at least once in their lifetime. While these rates are slightly lower than some of the findings from their previous research, Hinduja and Patchin point out that the earlier studies were predominantly conducted among older adolescents and Internet samples. That is, older youth use the Internet more frequently and are more likely to experience cyber-bullying than younger children.

2011

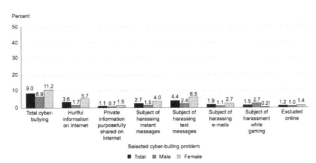

Students aged 12–18 who reported being cyber-bullied anywhere during the school year 2011

According to the 2011 National Crime Victimization Survey, conducted by the U.S. Department of Justice, Bureau of Justice Statistics, School Crime Supplement (SCS), 9% of students of ages 12–18 admittedly experienced cyberbullying during that school year (with a coefficient of variation between 30% and 50%).

2013

In the Youth Risk Behavior Survey 2013, the Center for Surveillance, Epidemiology, and Laboratory Services of the Centers for Disease Control and Prevention published results of its survey as part of the Youth Risk Behavior Surveillance System (YRBSS) in June 2014, indicating in table the percentage of school children being bullied through e-mail, chat rooms, instant messaging, Web sites, or texting ("electronically bullied") during the course of the year 2013.

2014

In 2014, Mehari, Farrell, and Le published a study that focused on the literature on cyberbullying among adolescents. They found that researchers have generally assumed that cyberbullying is distinct from aggression perpetrated in person. They suggest that the media through which aggression is perpetrated may be best conceptualized as a new dimension on which aggression can be classified, rather than cyberbullying as a distinct counterpart to existing forms of aggression and that future research on cyberbullying should be considered within the context of theoretical and empirical knowledge of aggression in adolescence. Mary Howlett-Brandon's doctoral dissertation analyzed the National Crime Victimization Survey: Student Crime Supplement, 2009, to focus on the cyberbullying victimization of Black students and White students in specific conditions.

2015

WalletHub's 2015's *Best & Worst States at Controlling Bullying* report measured the relative levels of bullying in 42 states. According to the report, North Dakota, Illinois, Louisiana, Rhode Island, and Washington D.C. have the highest attempted suicide by high school students. The top 5 states with highest percentage of students being bullied on campus is Missouri, Michigan, Idaho, North Dakota, and Montana.

Cyberbullying on social media has usually been student-to-student but recently, students have been cyberbullying their teachers. High School students in Colorado created a Twitter site that bullies many teachers. The bullying ranges from obscenities to false accusations of inappropriate actions with students.

Legislation

United States

Legislation geared at penalizing cyberbullying has been introduced in a number of U.S. states including New York, Missouri, Rhode Island and Maryland. At least forty five states passed laws against digital harassment. Dardenne Prairie of Springfield, Missouri, passed a city ordinance making online harassment a misdemeanor. The city of St. Charles, Missouri has passed a similar ordinance. Missouri is among other states where lawmakers are pursuing state legislation, with a task forces expected to have "cyberbullying" laws drafted and implemented. In June, 2008, Rep. Linda Sanchez (D-Calif.) and Rep. Kenny Hulshof (R-Mo.) proposed a federal law that would criminalize acts of cyberbullying.

Lawmakers are seeking to address cyberbullying with new legislation because there's currently no specific law on the books that deals with it. A fairly new federal cyberstalking law might address such acts, according to Parry Aftab, but no one has been prosecuted under it yet. The proposed federal law would make it illegal to use electronic means to "coerce, intimidate, harass or cause other substantial emotional distress."

In August 2008, the California state legislature passed one of the first laws in the country to deal directly with cyberbullying. The legislation, Assembly Bill 86 2008, gives school administrators the authority to discipline students for bullying others offline or online. This law took effect, January 1, 2009. A law in New York's Albany County that criminalized cyberbullying was recently struck down as unconstitutional by the New York Court of Appeals in People v. Marquan M.

A recent ruling first seen in the UK determined that it is possible for an Internet Service Provider (ISP) to be liable for the content of sites which it hosts, setting a precedent that any ISP should treat a notice of complaint seriously and investigate it immediately.

18 U.S.C.   875(c) criminalizes the making of threats via Internet.

European Union

Since the 1990s, the United Kingdom and other European countries have been working to solve workplace bullying since there is no legislation regulating cyberbullying. The pervasive nature of technology has made the act of bullying online much easier. A 24-hour internet connection gives bullies a never ending opportunity to find and bully victims. Employers in the European Union have more legal responsibility to their employees than other countries. Since employers do not the ability to fire or hire an employee at will like in the United States, employers in Europe are held to a high standard in how their employees are treated. The Framework Agreement on Harassment and Violence at Work is a law that prevents bullying occurring in the workplace and holds employers accountable for providing fair working conditionsr. Lawyers pursuing cyberbullying cases use The Ordinance on Victimization at Work law, since they are not any laws specifically condemning cyberbullying.

In 1993, Sweden was the first European Union country to have a law against cyberbullying. The Ordinance on Victimization at Work protected victims from "recurrent reprehensible or distinctly negative actions which are directed which are directed against individual employees in an offensive manner and can result in those employees being placed outside the workplace community".

In 2002, France passed the Social Modernization Law, which added consequences to the French Labor Code for cyberbullying such as holding employers accountable for their involvement in harassment. The legislation states, "the employer can be held accountable if it is deemed by court of law that the conduct defile the employee emotionally or physical health in any manner". The United Kingdom does not have anti-bullying legislation. However, it does have the Protection From Harassment Act, an anti-stalking law. The United Kingdom courts have used this legislation in bullying cases. In 2007, the European Union developed the Framework Agreement on Harassment and Violence at Work. The law defines the responsibilities of an employer such as protecting his or her employees from bullies in a work environment and the psychological pain a victim faces from bullies during business hours.

TAKE A

STAND

AGAINST

CYBERBULLING

*HELP OTHERS WHEN
THEY NEED IT

This image portrays the support and awareness that many anti-cyberbullying campaigns
have in some countries around the world.

The United States and other countries have more extensive legislation on cyberbullying than the European Union. The amount of cyberbullying incidents on social media are widespread and have increased drastically. However, the process of getting a claim against a bully is not an easy one because of the victim's need to provide sufficient evidence to prove the existence of bullying.

As of mid-2015, countries in the European Union like the United Kingdom are in the process of creating law specially related to cyberbullying. Since the process takes time, the government is supporting schools programs to promote internet safety with the help of teachers and parents. This will allow government to take the time it needs to create the cyberbullying laws while helping students safeguarding themselves from cyberbullying as much as they can.

Research on Preventative Legislation

Researchers suggest that programs be put in place for prevention of cyberbullying. These programs would be incorporated into school curricula and would include online safety and instruction on how to use the Internet properly. This could teach the victim proper methods of potentially avoiding the cyberbully, such as blocking messages or increasing the security on their computer.

Within this suggested school prevention model, even in a perfect world, not one crime can be stopped fully. That is why it is suggested that within this prevention method, effective coping strategies should be introduced and adopted. As with any crime, people learn to cope with what has happened, and the same goes for cyberbullying. People can adopt coping strategies to combat future cyberbullying events. An example of a coping strategy would be a social support group composed of various victims of cyberbullying. That could come together and share experiences, with a formal speaker leading the discussion. Something like a support group can allow students to share their stories, and allows that feeling of them being alone to be removed.

Teachers should be involved in all prevention educational models, as they are essentially the "police" of the classroom. Most cyberbullying often goes unreported as the victim feels nothing can be done to help in their current situation. However, if given the proper tools with preventative measures and more power in the classroom, teachers can be of assistance to the problem of cyber-bullying. If the parent, teacher, and victim can work together, a possible solution or remedy can be found.

There have been many legislative attempts to facilitate the control of bullying and cyberbullying. The problem is due to the fact that some existing legislation is incorrectly thought to be tied to bullying and cyberbullying (terms such as libel and slander). The problem is they do not directly apply to it nor define it as its own criminal behavior. Anti-cyberbullying advocates even expressed concern about the broad scope of applicability of some of the bills attempted to be passed.

In the United States, attempts were made to pass legislation against cyberbullying. Few states attempted to pass broad sanctions in an effort to prohibit cyberbullying. Problem include how to define cyberbullying and cyberstalking, and if charges are pressed, whether it violates the bully's freedom of speech. B. Walther has said that "Illinois is the only state to criminalize 'electronic communication(s) sent for the purpose of harassing another person' when the activity takes place outside a public school setting." Again this came under fire for infringement on freedom of speech.

Harmful Effects

Research had demonstrated a number of serious consequences of cyberbullying victimization. For example, victims have lower self-esteem, increased suicidal ideation, and a variety of emotional responses, retaliating, being scared, frustrated, angry, and depressed. People have reported that Cyberbullying can be more harmful than traditional bullying because there is no escaping it.

One of the most damaging effects is that a victim begins to avoid friends and activities, often the very intention of the cyberbully.

Cyberbullying campaigns are sometimes so damaging that victims have committed suicide. There are at least four examples in the United States where cyberbullying has been linked to the suicide of a teenager. The suicide of Megan Meier is a recent example that led to the conviction of the adult perpetrator of the attacks. Another example of harmful effects is the death of Holly Grogan who ended her life by jumping of a 30-foot bridge near Gloucester in the UK . It was reported that a number of her schoolmates has posted a number of hateful messages on her Facebook page.

According to Lucie Russell, director of campaigns, policy and participation at youth mental health charity Young Minds, young people who suffer from mental disorder are vulnerable to cyberbullying as they are sometimes unable to shrug it off:

When someone says nasty things healthy people can filter that out, they're able to put a block between that and their self-esteem. But mentally unwell people don't have the strength and the self-esteem to do that, to separate it, and so it gets compiled with everything else. To them, it becomes the absolute truth – there's no filter, there's no block. That person will take that on, take it as fact.

Social media has allowed bullies to disconnect from the impact they may be having on others.

Intimidation, Emotional Damage, Suicide

According to the Cyberbullying Research Center, "there have been several high-profile cases involving teenagers taking their own lives in part because of being harassed and mistreated over the Internet, a phenomenon we have termed cyberbullicide – suicide indirectly or directly influenced by experiences with online aggression."

Cyberbullying is an intense form of psychological abuse, whose victims are more than twice as likely to suffer from mental disorders compared to traditional bullying.

The reluctance youth have in telling an authority figure about instances of cyberbullying has led to fatal outcomes. At least three children between the ages of 12 and 13 have committed suicide due to depression brought on by cyberbullying, according to reports by USA Today and the Baltimore Examiner. These would include the suicide of Ryan Halligan and the suicide of Megan Meier, the latter of which resulted in United States v. Lori Drew.

More recently, teenage suicides tied to cyberbullying have become more prevalent. The latest victim of cyberbullying through the use of mobile applications was Rebecca Ann Sedwick, who committed suicide after being terrorized through mobile applications such as Ask.fm, Kik Messenger and Voxer.

On Youth and Teenagers

The effects of cyberbullying vary. But, research illustrates that cyber bullying adversely affects youth to a higher degree than adolescents and adults. Youth are more likely to suffer since they are still growing mentally and physically. Jennifer N. Caudle, a certified family physician, describes the effects as "Kids that are bullied are likely to experience anxiety, depression, loneliness, unhappiness and poor sleep".

This image shows different aspects of cyberbullying that can take place on the internet which puts more emotional strain on the younger children and teenage who experience cyberbullying.

Most of the time cyberbullying goes unnoticed; the younger generation hides their bullying from anyone that can help to prevent the bullying from occurring and from getting worse. Between 20% and 40% of adolescents are victims of cyberbullying worldwide. The youth slowly change their behaviors and actions so they become more withdrawn and quiet than they are used to, but no one notices since the change is subtle. Cyberbullying will "become a serious problem in the future with an increase in the Internet and mobile phone usage among young people".

If preventive actions are not taken against cyberbullying, younger children in addition to teenagers will feel more lonely and depressed along with having a significant change in their eating and sleeping patterns as well as loss of interest in their normal activities. These changes will affect their growth and development into adulthood. Younger children and teenagers are 76.2% less likely to display suicidal behaviors and thoughts, but are still at risk depending on other factors such as mental health status, home care, relationships with others. The risk of suicide increases 35% to 45% when victims do not have any support from anyone in their life and cyberbullying amplifies the situation more.

Awareness

Campaigns

The Cybersmile Foundation is a cyberbullying charity committed to tackling all forms of online bullying, abuse, and hate campaigns. The charity was founded in 2010 in response to the increasing number of cyberbullying related incidents of depression, eating disorders, social isolation, self-harm and suicides devastating lives around the world. Cybersmile provides support to victims and their friends and families through social media interaction, email and helpline support. They also run an annual event, Stop Cyberbullying Day, to draw attention to the issue.

Spain

There are multiple non-profit organizations that fight cyberbullying and cyberstalking. They advise victims, provide awareness campaigns, and report offenses to the police. These NGOs include the *Protégeles, PantallasAmigas, Foundation Alia2*, the non-profit initiative *Actúa Contra el Ciberacoso*, the National Communications Technology Institute (INTECO), the Agency of Internet quality, the *Agencia Española de Protección de Datos*, the *Oficina de Seguridad del Internauta*, the Spanish Internet users' Association, the Internauts' Association, and the Spanish Association of Mothers and Parents Internauts. The Government of Castile and León has also created a *Plan de Prevención del Ciberacoso y Promoción de la Navegación Segura en Centro Escolares*, and the Government of the Canary Islands has created a portal on the phenomenon called *Viveinternet*.

United States

In March 2007, the Advertising Council in the United States, in partnership with the National Crime Prevention Council, U.S. Department of Justice, and Crime Prevention Coalition of America, joined to announce the launch of a new public service advertising campaign designed to educate preteens and teens about how they can play a role in ending cyber-bullying.

January 20, 2008 – the Boy Scouts of America's 2008 edition of *The Boy Scout Handbook* addresses how to deal with online bullying. A new First Class rank requirements adds: "Describe the three things you should avoid doing related to use of the Internet. Describe a cyberbully and how you should respond to one."

January 31, 2008 – KTTV Fox 11 News based in Los Angeles put out a report about organized cyber-bullying on sites like Stickam by people who call themselves "/b/rothas". The site had put out report on July 26, 2007, about a subject that partly featured cyberbullying titled "hackers on steroids".

June 2, 2008 – Parents, teens, teachers, and Internet executives came together at Wired Safety's International Stop Cyberbullying Conference, a two-day gathering in White Plains, New York and New York City. Executives from Facebook, Verizon, MySpace, Microsoft, and many others talked with hundreds about how to better protect themselves, personal reputations, children and businesses online from harassment. Sponsors of the conference included McAfee, AOL, Disney, Procter & Gamble, Girl Scouts of the USA, WiredTrust, Children's Safety Research and Innovation Centre, KidZui.com and others. Cyberharassment vs. cyberbullying was a forefront topic, where age makes a difference and abusive internet behavior by adults with repeated clear intent to harm, ridicule or damage a person or business was classified as stalking harassment vs. bullying by teens and young adults.

August 2012 – A new organized movement to make revenge porn illegal began in August 2012. It is known as End Revenge Porn. Currently revenge porn is only illegal in two states, but the demand for its criminalization is on the rise as digital technology has increased in the past few generations. The organization seeks to provide support for victims, educate the public, and gain activist support to bring new legislation before the United States Government.

In 2006, PACER.org created a week long event that was held once a year in October. Today, the campaign is a monthlong event and is now known as the National Bullying Prevention Awareness Month.

Canada

Originated in Canada, Anti-Bullying day is a day of celebration for those who choose to participate wearing a symbol of colours (Pink, Blue or Purple) as a stance against bullying. A B.C. teacher founded the Stop A Bully movement, which uses pink wristbands to represent the wearer's stance to stop bullying.

Pink Shirt Day was inspired by David Shepherd and Travis Price. Their high school friends organized a protest in sympathy for a Grade 9 boy who was bullied for wearing a pink shirt. Their stance from wearing pink has been a huge inspiration in the Great Vancouver Mainland. "We know that victims of bullying, witnesses of bullying and bullies themselves all experience the very real and long term negative impacts of bullying regardless of its forms – physical, verbal, written, or on-line (cyberbullying)".

The ERASE (Expect Respect and A Safe Education) is an initiative started by the province of British Columbia to foster safe schools and prevent bullying. It builds on already-effective programs set up by the provincial government to ensure consistent policies and practices regarding the prevention of bullying.

Community Support

A number organizations are in coalition to provide awareness, protection and recourse for the escalating problem. Some aim to inform and provide measures to avoid as well as effectively terminate cyberbullying and cyberharassment. Anti-bullying charity Act Against Bullying launched the CyberKind campaign in August 2009 to promote positive internet usage.

In 2007, YouTube introduced the first Anti-Bullying Channel for youth, (BeatBullying) engaging the assistance of celebrities to tackle the problem.

In March 2010, a 17-year-old girl named Alexis Skye Pilkington was found dead in her room by her parents. Her parents claimed that after repeated cyberbullying, she was driven to suicide. Shortly after her death, attacks resumed. Members of eBaums World began to troll teens' memorial pages on Facebook, with the comments including expressions of pleasure over the death, with pictures of what seemed to be a banana as their profile pictures. Family and friends of the deceased teen responded by creating Facebook groups denouncing cyberbullying and trolling, with logos of bananas behind a red circle with a diagonal line through it.

In response and partnership to the 2011 film *Bully*, a grassroots effort to stop cyberbullying called The Bully Project was created. Their goal is "sparked a national movement to stop bullying that is transforming children's lives and changing a culture of bullying into one of empathy and action."

Notable Cases

Teens in the United States

13-year-old Zoe Johnson from Wyoming, Michigan committed suicide in July 2015. Johnson had been a victim of cyberbullying for years and suffered from mild depression. It is believed that a message posted on her Facebook the day before her suicide may have been the turning point that pushed her towards suicide. After her death, people continued to post messages on her Facebook with one person posting the message "good ur gone".

14-year-old Carla Jamerson from Las Vegas, Nevada committed suicide in 2015. She was a victim of cyberbullying for years. Jamerson went to both the city and school police, but did not receive any help. After not receiving any help, she hanged herself.

Bullying of climate scientists and activists

As of 2011 and 2012, climate scientists and climate activists were being confronted with abusive emails from all over the world. These emails were sometimes sent in response to public statements that merely reported findings related to the widely accepted anthropogenic climate change and its consequences. Such emails were sent in response to suggestions posted on climate denial websites, which are effectively requests to engage in cyberbullying. Climate scientists and climate activists were also confronted with libelous Internet reports that aimed to silence them or destroy their reputations.

Sweden

In 2013, two Swedish teenage girls were convicted by the Swedish court in Gothenburg for writing derogatory, explicit remarks next to the pictures of 38 youngsters, mostly girls, via an anonymous

Instagram account. They were found guilty and sentenced to youth care and youth service as well as rioting at two schools.

Ireland

In 2012, three teenage Irish girls committed suicide within a few weeks. Their families and friends called for the websites they were bullied on to be banned. Ask.fm, an online Q&A website has received a lot of criticism. However, Ask.fm's co-founder Mark Terebin argues that "it is necessary to go deeper and to find a root of a problem. It's not about the site, the problem is about education, about moral values that were devaluated lately".

Cyberstalking

Cyberstalking is the use of the Internet or other electronic means to stalk or harass an individual, group, or organization. It may include false accusations, defamation, slander and libel. It may also include monitoring, identity theft, threats, vandalism, solicitation for sex, or gathering information that may be used to threaten, embarrass or harass.

Cyberstalking is often accompanied by realtime or offline stalking. In many jurisdictions, such as California, both are criminal offenses. Both are motivated by a desire to control, intimidate or influence a victim. A stalker may be an online stranger or a person whom the target knows. He may be anonymous and solicit involvement of other people online who do not even know the target.

Cyberstalking is a criminal offense under various state anti-stalking, slander and harassment laws. A conviction can result in a restraining order, probation, or criminal penalties against the assailant, including jail.

Definitions and Description

There have been a number of attempts by experts and legislators to define cyberstalking. It is generally understood to be the use of the Internet or other electronic means to stalk or harass an individual, a group, or an organization. Cyberstalking is a form of cyberbullying, and the terms are often used interchangeably in the media. Both may include false accusations, defamation, slander and libel. Cyberstalking may also include monitoring, identity theft, threats, vandalism, solicitation for sex, or gathering information that may be used to threaten or harass. Cyberstalking is often accompanied by real-time or offline stalking. Both are criminal offenses.

Stalking is a continuous process, consisting of a series of actions, each of which may be entirely legal in itself. Technology ethics professor Lambèr Royakkers defines cyberstalking as perpetrated by someone without a current relationship with the victim. About the abusive effects of cyberstalking, he writes that:

[Stalking] is a form of mental assault, in which the perpetrator repeatedly, unwantedly, and disruptively breaks into the life-world of the victim, with whom he has no relationship (or no longer has), with motives that are directly or indirectly traceable to the affective sphere. Moreover, the separated acts that make up the intrusion cannot by themselves cause the mental abuse, but do taken together (cumulative effect).

Distinguishing Cyberstalking from Other Acts

It is important to draw a distinction between cyber-trolling and cyber-stalking. Research has shown that actions that can be perceived to be harmless as a one-off can be considered to be trolling, whereas if it is part of a persistent campaign then it can be considered stalking.

Cyberstalking author Alexis Moore separates cyberstalking from identity theft, which is financially motivated. Her definition, which was also used by the Republic of the Philippines in their legal description, is as follows:

Cyberstalking is a technologically-based "attack" on one person who has been targeted specifically for that attack for reasons of anger, revenge or control. Cyberstalking can take many forms, including:

1. harassment, embarrassment and humiliation of the victim

2. emptying bank accounts or other economic control such as ruining the victim's credit score

3. harassing family, friends and employers to isolate the victim

4. scare tactics to instill fear and more

Identification and Detection

CyberAngels has written about how to identify cyberstalking:

When identifying cyberstalking "in the field," and particularly when considering whether to report it to any kind of legal authority, the following features or combination of features can be considered to characterize a true stalking situation: malice, premeditation, repetition, distress, obsession, vendetta, no legitimate purpose, personally directed, disregarded warnings to stop, harassment and threats.

A number of key factors have been identified in cyberstalking:

- False accusations. Many cyberstalkers try to damage the reputation of their victim and turn other people against them. They post false information about them on websites. They may set up their own websites, blogs or user pages for this purpose. They post allegations about the victim to newsgroups, chat rooms, or other sites that allow public contributions such as Wikipedia or Amazon.com.

- Attempts to gather information about the victim. Cyberstalkers may approach their victim's friends, family and work colleagues to obtain personal information. They may advertise for information on the Internet, or hire a private detective.

- Monitoring their target's online activities and attempting to trace their IP address in an effort to gather more information about their victims.

- Encouraging others to harass the victim. Many cyberstalkers try to involve third parties in the harassment. They may claim the victim has harmed the stalker or his/her family in some way, or may post the victim's name and telephone number in order to encourage others to join the pursuit.

- False victimization. The cyberstalker will claim that the victim is harassing him or her. Bocij writes that this phenomenon has been noted in a number of well-known cases.

- Attacks on data and equipment. They may try to damage the victim's computer by sending viruses.

- Ordering goods and services. They order items or subscribe to magazines in the victim's name. These often involve subscriptions to pornography or ordering sex toys then having them delivered to the victim's workplace.

- Arranging to meet. Young people face a particularly high risk of having cyberstalkers try to set up meetings between them.

- The posting of defamatory or derogatory statements. Using web pages and message boards to incite some response or reaction from their victim.

Prevalence and Impact

According to *Law Enforcement Technology*, cyberstalking has increased exponentially with the growth of new technology and new ways to stalk victims. "Disgruntled employees pose as their bosses to post explicit messages on social network sites; spouses use GPS to track their mates' every move. Even police and prosecutors find themselves at risk, as gang members and other organized criminals find out where they live — often to intimidate them into dropping a case."

In January 2009, the Bureau of Justice Statistics in the United States released the study "Stalking Victimization in the United States," which was sponsored by the Office on Violence Against Women. The report, based on supplemental data from the National Crime Victimization Survey, showed that one in four stalking victims had been cyberstalked as well, with the perpetrators using internet-based services such as email, instant messaging, GPS, or spyware. The final report stated that approximately 1.2 million victims had stalkers who used technology to find them. The Rape, Abuse and Incest National Network (RAINN), in Washington D.C. has released statistics that there are 3.4 million stalking victims each year in the United States. Of those, one in four reported experiencing cyberstalking.

According to Robin M. Kowalski, a social psychologist at Clemson University, cyberbullying has been shown to cause higher levels of anxiety and depression for victims than normal bullying. Kowalksi states that much of this stems from the anonymity of the perpetrators, which is a common feature of cyberstalking as well. According to a study by Kowalksi, of 3,700 bullied middle-school students, a quarter had been subjected to a form of harassment online.

Types

Stalking by Strangers

According to Joey Rushing, a District Attorney of Franklin County, Alabama, there isn't a single definition of a cyberstalker, and they can be either strangers to the victim or have a former/present relationship. "[Cyberstalkers] come in all shapes, sizes, ages and backgrounds. They patrol Web sites looking for an opportunity to take advantage of people."

Gender-based Stalking

Harassment and stalking because of gender online is common, and can include rape threats and other threats of violence, as well as the posting of the victim's personal information. It is blamed for limiting victims' activities online or driving them offline entirely, thereby impeding their participation in online life and undermining their autonomy, dignity, identity, and opportunities.

Of Intimate Partners

Cyberstalking of intimate partners is the online harassment of a current or former romantic partner. It is a form of domestic violence, and experts say its purpose is to control the victim in order to encourage social isolation and create dependency. Harassers may send repeated insulting or threatening e-mails to their victims, monitor or disrupt their victims' e-mail use, and use the victim's account to send e-mails to others posing as the victim or to purchase goods or services the victim does not want. They may also use the Internet to research and compile personal information about the victim, to use in order to harass him or her.

Of Celebrities and Public Persons

Profiling of stalkers shows that almost always they stalk someone they know or, via delusion, think they know, as is the case with stalkers of celebrities or public persons in which the stalkers feel they know the celebrity even though the celebrity does not know them. As part of the risk they take for being in the public eye, celebrities and public figures are often targets of lies or made-up stories in tabloids as well as by stalkers, some even seeming to be fans.

In one noted case in 2011, actress Patricia Arquette quit Facebook after alleged cyberstalking. In her last post, Arquette explained that her security warned her Facebook friends to never accept friend requests from people they do not actually know. Arquette stressed that just because people seemed to be fans did not mean they were safe. The media issued a statement that Arquette planned to communicate with fans exclusively through her Twitter account in the future.

By Anonymous Online Mobs

Web 2.0 technologies have enabled online groups of anonymous people to self-organize to target individuals with online defamation, threats of violence and technology-based attacks. These include publishing lies and doctored photographs, threats of rape and other violence, posting sensitive personal information about victims, e-mailing damaging statements about victims to their employers, and manipulating search engines to make damaging material about the victim more prominent. Victims frequently respond by adopting pseudonyms or going offline entirely.

Experts attribute the destructive nature of anonymous online mobs to group dynamics, saying that groups with homogeneous views tend to become more extreme. As members reinforce each others' beliefs, they fail to see themselves as individuals and lose a sense of personal responsibility for their destructive acts. In doing so they dehumanize their victims, becoming more aggressive when they believe they are supported by authority figures. Internet service providers and website owners are sometimes blamed for not speaking out against this type of harassment.

A notable example of online mob harassment was the experience of American software developer and blogger Kathy Sierra. In 2007 a group of anonymous individuals attacked Sierra, threatening her with rape and strangulation, publishing her home address and Social Security number, and posting doctored photographs of her. Frightened, Sierra cancelled her speaking engagements and shut down her blog, writing "I will never feel the same. I will never be the same."

Corporate Cyberstalking

Corporate cyberstalking is when a company harasses an individual online, or an individual or group of individuals harasses an organization. Motives for corporate cyberstalking are ideological, or include a desire for financial gain or revenge.

Perpetrators

Motives and Profile

Mental profiling of digital criminals has identified psychological and social factors that motivate stalkers as: envy; pathological obsession (professional or sexual); unemployment or failure with own job or life; intention to intimidate and cause others to feel inferior; the stalker is delusional and believes he/she "knows" the target; the stalker wants to instill fear in a person to justify his/her status; belief they can get away with it (anonymity); intimidation for financial advantage or business competition; revenge over perceived or imagined rejection.

Four Types of Cyberstalkers

Preliminary work by Leroy McFarlane and Paul Bocij has identified four types of cyberstalkers: the vindictive cyberstalkers noted for the ferocity of their attacks; the composed cyberstalker whose motive is to annoy; the intimate cyberstalker who attempts to form a relationship with the victim but turns on them if rebuffed; and collective cyberstalkers, groups with a motive. According to Antonio Chacón Medina, author of *Una nueva cara de Internet, El acoso* ("A new face of the Internet: stalking"), the general profile of the harasser is cold, with little or no respect for others. The stalker is a predator who can wait patiently until vulnerable victims appear, such as women or children, or may enjoy pursuing a particular person, whether personally familiar to them or unknown. The harasser enjoys and demonstrates their power to pursue and psychologically damage the victim.

Behaviors

Cyberstalkers find their victims by using search engines, online forums, bulletin and discussion boards, chat rooms, and more recently, through social networking sites, such as MySpace, Facebook, Bebo, Friendster, Twitter, and Indymedia, a media outlet known for self-publishing. They may engage in live chat harassment or flaming or they may send electronic viruses and unsolicited e-mails. Cyberstalkers may research individuals to feed their obsessions and curiosity. Conversely, the acts of cyberstalkers may become more intense, such as repeatedly instant messaging their targets.

More commonly they will post defamatory or derogatory statements about their stalking target on web pages, message boards, and in guest books designed to get a reaction or response from their victim, thereby initiating contact. In some cases, they have been known to create fake blogs in the name of the victim containing defamatory or pornographic content.

When prosecuted, many stalkers have unsuccessfully attempted to justify their behavior based on their use of public forums, as opposed to direct contact. Once they get a reaction from the victim, they will typically attempt to track or follow the victim's internet activity. Classic cyberstalking behavior includes the tracing of the victim's IP address in an attempt to verify their home or place of employment.

Some cyberstalking situations do evolve into physical stalking, and a victim may experience abusive and excessive phone calls, vandalism, threatening or obscene mail, trespassing, and physical assault. Moreover, many physical stalkers will use cyberstalking as another method of harassing their victims.

A 2007 study led by Paige Padgett from the University of Texas Health Science Center found that there was a false degree of safety assumed by women looking for love online.

Cyberstalking Legislation

Legislation on cyberstalking varies from country to country. Cyberstalking and cyberbullying are relatively new phenomena, but that does not mean that crimes committed through the network are not punishable under legislation drafted for that purpose. Although there are often existing laws that prohibit stalking or harassment in a general sense, legislators sometimes believe that such laws are inadequate or do not go far enough, and thus bring forward new legislation to address this perceived shortcoming. In the United States, for example, nearly every state has laws that address cyberstalking, cyberbullying, or both.

In countries such as the US, in practice, there is little legislative difference between the concepts of "cyberbullying" and "cyberstalking." The primary distinction is one of age; if adults are involved, the act is usually termed *cyberstalking,* while among children it is usually referred to as *cyberbullying.* However, this distinction is one of semantics, and many laws treat *bullying* and *stalking* as much the same issue.

Australia

In Australia, the Stalking Amendment Act (1999) includes the use of any form of technology to harass a target as forms of "criminal stalking."

Canada

In 2012, there was a high-profile investigation into the death of Amanda Todd, a young Canadian student who'd been blackmailed and stalked online before committing suicide. The Royal Canadian Mounted Police were criticized in the media for not naming one of her alleged stalkers as a person of interest.

Philippines

In the Fifteenth Congress of the Republic of the Philippines, a cyberstalking bill was introduced by Senator Manny Villar. The result was to "urge the Senate Committees on Science and Technology, and Public Information and Mass Media to conduct an inquiry, in aid of legislation, on the increasing occurrence of cyber stalking cases and the modus operandi adopted in the internet to perpetuate crimes with the end in view of formulating legislation and policy measures geared towards curbing cyber stalking and other cyber crimes and protect online users in the country."

United States

History, Current Legislation

Cyberstalking is a criminal offense under American anti-stalking, slander, and harassment laws. A conviction can result in a restraining order, probation, or criminal penalties against the assailant, including jail. Cyberstalking specifically has been addressed in recent U.S. federal law. For example, the Violence Against Women Act, passed in 2000, made cyberstalking a part of the federal interstate stalking statute. The current US Federal Anti-Cyber-Stalking law is found at 47 U.S.C. 223.

Still, there remains a lack of federal legislation to specifically address cyberstalking, leaving the majority of legislative at the state level. A few states have both stalking and harassment statutes that criminalize threatening and unwanted electronic communications. The first anti-stalking law was enacted in California in 1990, and while all fifty states soon passed anti-stalking laws, by 2009 only 14 of them had laws specifically addressing "high-tech stalking." The first U.S. cyberstalking law went into effect in 1999 in California. Other states have laws other than harassment or anti-stalking statutes that prohibit misuse of computer communications and e-mail, while others have passed laws containing broad language that can be interpreted to include cyberstalking behaviors, such as in their harassment or stalking legislation.

Sentences can range from 18 months in prison and a $10,000 fine for a fourth-degree charge to ten years in prison and a $150,000 fine for a second-degree charge.

States with Cyberstalking Legislation

- Alabama, Arizona, Connecticut, Hawaii, Illinois, New Hampshire, and New York have included prohibitions against harassing electronic, computer or e-mail communications in their harassment legislation.

- Alaska, Florida, Oklahoma, Wyoming, and California, have incorporated electronically communicated statements as conduct constituting stalking in their anti-stalking laws.

- Texas enacted the *Stalking by Electronic Communications Act*, 2001.

- Missouri revised its state harassment statutes to include stalking and harassment by telephone and electronic communications (as well as cyber-bullying) after the Megan Meier suicide case of 2006. In one of the few cases where a cyberstalking conviction was obtained the cyberstalker was a woman, which is also much rarer that male cyberstalkers. The conviction was overturned in on appeal in 2009 however.

- In Florida, HB 479 was introduced in 2003 to ban cyberstalking. This was signed into law on October 2003.

Age, Legal Limitations

While some laws only address online harassment of children, there are laws that protect adult cyberstalking victims. While some sites specialize in laws that protect victims age 18 and under, current and pending cyberstalking-related United States federal and state laws offer help to victims of all ages.

Most stalking laws require that the perpetrator make a credible threat of violence against the victim; others include threats against the victim's immediate family; and still others require the alleged stalker's course of conduct constitute an implied threat. While some conduct involving annoying or menacing behavior might fall short of illegal stalking, such behavior may be a prelude to stalking and violence and should be treated seriously.

Online identity stealth blurs the line on infringement of the rights of would-be victims to identify their perpetrators. There is a debate on how internet use can be traced without infringing on protected civil liberties.

Specific Cases

There have been a number of high-profile legal cases in the United States related to cyberstalking, many of which have involved the suicides of young students. In thousands of other cases, charges either weren't brought for the cyber harassment or were unsuccessful in obtaining convictions. As in all legal instances, much depends on public sympathy towards the victim, the quality of legal representation and other factors that can greatly influence the outcome of the crime – even if it will be considered a crime.

In the case of a fourteen-year-old student in Michigan, for instance, she pressed charges against her alleged rapist, which resulted in her being cyberstalked and cyberbullied by fellow students. After her suicide in 2010 all charges were dropped against the man who allegedly raped her, on the basis that the only witness was dead. This is the despite the fact that statutory rape charges could have been pressed.

In another case of cyberstalking, college student Dharun Ravi secretly filmed his roommate's sexual liaison with another man, then posted it online. After the victim committed suicide, Ravi was convicted in of bias intimidation and invasion of privacy in *New Jersey v. Dharun Ravi*. In 2012 he was sentenced to 30 days in jail, more than $11,000 in restitution and three years of probation. The judge ruled that he believes Ravi acted out of "colossal insensitivity, not hatred."

Europe

- Poland – Stalking, including cyberstalking, was made a criminal offence under the Polish Criminal Code on 6 June 2011.

- Spain – In Spain, it is possible to provide information about cyber-crime in an anonymous way to four safety bodies: Grupo de Delitos Telemáticos of the Civil Guard (Spain) (Spanish), Brigada de Investigación Tecnológica of the National Police Corps of Spain (Spanish), Mossos d'Esquadra in Catalonia, and Ertzaintza in Euskadi. It is also possible to provide information to a non-governmental organization.

- United Kingdom – In the United Kingdom, the Protection from Harassment Act 1997 contains an offence of stalking covering cyber-stalking, which was introduced into the act through the Protection of Freedoms Act 2012.

Cyberstalking Legislation

Cyberstalking and cyberbullying are relatively new phenomena, but that does not mean that crimes committed through the network are not punishable under legislation drafted for that purpose. Although there are often existing laws that prohibit stalking or harassment in a general sense, legislators sometimes believe that such laws are inadequate or do not go far enough, and thus bring forward new legislation to address this perceived shortcoming. In the United States, for example, nearly every state has laws that address cyberstalking, cyberbullying, or both.

Issues at Stake

Cyberbullying and cyberstalking, by their nature, define adversarial relationships. One person (or group), the provocateur, is exerting a view or opinion that the other person (or group), the target, finds offensive, hurtful, or damaging in some way. In a general sense, it would seem simple to legislate this type of behavior; slander and libel laws exist to tackle these situations. However, just as with slander and libel, it is important to balance the protection of freedom of speech of both parties with the need for protection of the target. Thus, something that may be deemed cyberbullying at first glance may, in fact, be more akin to something like parody or similar.

A 2006 National Crime Prevention Council survey found that some 40% of teens had experienced cyberbullying at some point in their lives, making the problem particularly widespread. Not only is the issue of cyberbullying extensive, it has adverse effects on adolescents: increased depression, suicidal behavior, anxiety, and increased susceptibility of drug use and aggressive behavior.

Legislation by Country

Australia

Australia does not have specific cyberbullying legislation, although the scope of existing laws can be extended to deal with cyberbullying.

State laws can deal with some forms of cyberbullying, such as documents containing threats, and threats to destroy and damage property.

Commonwealth offences that criminalise the misuse of telecommunication services are also relevant when technology is used to communicate harassment or threats.

The Family Law Act 1975 (Cth) protects individuals from harassment, including harassment that occurs via electronic communications. However, this is limited to the victims of family violence.

The Australian government has proposed specific cyberbullying laws to protect children.

United States

"Cyberbullying" versus "Cyberstalking"

In the US, in practice, there is little legislative difference between the concepts of "cyberbullying" and "cyberstalking." The primary distinction is one of age; if adults are involved, the act is usually termed *cyberstalking,* while among children it is usually referred to as *cyberbullying.* However, this distinction is one of semantics, and many laws treat *bullying* and *stalking* as much the same issue.

Freedom of Speech Issues

First Amendment concerns often arise when questionable speech is uttered or posted online. This is equally true when dealing with cyberbullying. Particularly in instances where there are no laws explicitly against cyberbullying, it is not uncommon for defendants to argue that their conduct amounts to an exercise of their freedom of speech.

The courts have variously come down on either side of that debate, even within the same state. For example, a student in California who was suspended from school based on cyberbullying claims took the school district to court, citing a breach of her First Amendment rights; the court agreed with the student and found the school district had overstepped its authority. In another California case, in which a student was harassed after posting personal information online, the court found that threatening posts were *not* protected speech.

That said, *true* threats are not considered to be protected speech.

Organizations such as the American Civil Liberties Union have taken the view that cyberbullying is an overly expansive term, and that the First Amendment protects all speech, even the reprehensible; this protection would extend to the Internet.

In general, such organizations argue that while the need for legislation against cyberbullying may exist, legislators must take a cautious, reasoned approach to enacting laws, and not rush into creating laws that would curtail speech too much.

Internet free speech issues have certainly made their way through the court systems, even as far back as cases from the mid-90s. In the case of United States v. Baker, for example, an undergraduate at the University of Michigan was charged with crimes related to snuff stories he had posted on Internet newsgroups, stories that named one of his fellow students. After progressing through the courts, the charges against Baker were dismissed primarily on grounds that there was no evidence that Baker would actually act out the fantasies contained in those stories. This case is now considered a landmark in the realm of First Amendment issues on the Internet.

The Need for New Laws

The focus on legislating cyberbullying and cyberstalking has largely come about as a result of the perceived inadequacy, generally by legislators and parents of bullying victims, of existing laws, whether those existing laws cover stalking, unauthorized use of computer resources, or the like. The motivation behind the bill in 1990 where 50 U.S. states and the federal government passed a bill to "criminalize" stalking was due to the cases of stalking against celebrities (Spitzberg & Hoobler, 2002).

For example, in the case of *United States v. Lori Drew*, in which Megan Meier had committed suicide after being bullied on MySpace, three of the four charges against the defendant (Drew) were actually in response to alleged violations of the Computer Fraud and Abuse Act, since specific statues against cyberbullying were not on the books. The jury eventually found Drew innocent of the charges (but guilty of a misdemeanor), a verdict that was later set aside by the judge. In this situation, legislators in Missouri, at the urging of the public and Meier's parents, passed "Megan's Law", primarily aimed at the crime of a person over 21 years of age bullying a person under 18 years of age.

In addition, prosecutors will sometimes use other legal avenues to prosecute offenders. In the case of Tyler Clementi, who killed himself after video of his homosexual encounter was broadcast on the Internet, prosecutors charged the defendants with invasion of privacy and computer crimes. Like the Meier case, the Clementi case spurred legislators (this time, in New Jersey) to pass a law specifically aimed at bullying, an "Anti-bullying Bill of Rights".

While some laws are written such that the focus on cyberbullying is the set of acts that occur within a school, others are more general, targeting cyberbullying no matter where it occurs. In addition, some of these newly written laws (like one in Connecticut) put more of an onus on the school system, mandating that the school's administration must intervene at the first sign of bullying.

Finally, it's not uncommon for cyberbullying to be coupled with "traditional", in-person bullying, for example, in the suicide of Phoebe Prince. Students at her school had bullied her for months in school, and that harassment eventually moved online as well. As in Connecticut, New Jersey, and Missouri, the Prince case led to stricter anti-bullying legislation in Massachusetts.

Legislation at the State Level

Some U.S. states have begun to address the problem of cyberbullying. States that have passed legislation have done so generally in response to incidents within that state, to address what they believe to be shortcomings in federal laws, or to expand protection to victims above and beyond existing statutes.

There are laws that only address online harassment of children or focus on child predators as well as laws that protect adult cyberstalking victims, or victims of any age. While some sites specialize in laws that protect victims age 18 and under, Working to Halt Online Abuse is a help resource listing current and pending cyberstalking-related United States federal and state laws. It also lists those states that do not have laws yet and related laws from other countries.

California

California passed the first cyberstalking law in 1999. (646.9 of the California Penal Code.) Its first use resulted in a six-year sentence for a man who harassed a woman who could identify him. After sending hundreds of threatening e-mails to an actress, another male convicted after spending months in jail waiting for trial was sentenced in 2001 to five years probation, forbidden access to computers and forced to attend mental health counseling. In 2011 a man was ordered to undergo psychiatric evaluation before sentencing for cyberstalking. On January 1, 2009, a California law became effective that allows schools to suspend or expel students who harass other students online. It also mandates that schools develop policies to address the problem. In addition, Section 1708.7 of the California Civil Code outlines grounds for an individual suing their cyberstalker and any accomplices for general damages, special damages, and punitive damages for cyberstalking.

Florida

Under Florida Statute 784.048, "cyberstalking," defined as *to engage in a course of conduct to communicate, or to cause to be communicated, words, images, or language by or through the use of electronic mail or electronic communication, directed at a specific person, causing substantial emotional distress to that person and serving no legitimate purpose,* is classified as a first degree misdemeanor. Cyberstalking a child under the age of 16 or a person of any age for which the offender has been ordered by the courts not to contact is considered "aggravated stalking," a third degree felony under Florida law. Cyberstalking in conjunction with a credible threat is also considered aggravated stalking.

In 2008, Florida passed the "Jeffrey Johnston Stand Up For All Students Act" in response to the suicide of 15-year-old Jeffrey Johnston, who had suffered cyberbullying over a long period of time. Unusual among state laws regarding cyberbullying is a provision that withholds funding for schools who are not in compliance with the provision that they must inform parents of those involved in cyberbullying—both the bully and the target.

Illinois

According to "Who@: Working to Halt Online Abuse":

Sec. 1-2. Harassment through electronic communications.

(a) Harassment through electronic communications is the use of electronic communication for any of the following purposes:

1. Making any comment, request, suggestion or proposal which is obscene with an intent to offend;

2. Interrupting, with the intent to harass, the telephone service or the electronic communication service of any person;

3. Transmitting to any person, with the intent to harass and regardless of whether the communication is read in its entirety or at all, any file, document, or other communication which prevents that person from using his or her telephone service or electronic communications device;

    i. Transmitting an electronic communication or knowingly inducing a person to transmit an electronic communication for the purpose of harassing another person who is under 13 years of age, regardless of whether the person under 13 years of age consents to the harassment, if the defendant is at least 16 years of age at the time of the commission of the offense;

4. Threatening injury to the person or to the property of the person to whom an electronic communication is directed or to any of his or her family or household members; or

5. Knowingly permitting any electronic communications device to be used for any of the purposes mentioned in this subsection (a).

(b) As used in this Act:

1. "Electronic communication" means any transfer of signs, signals, writings, images, sounds, data or intelligence of any nature transmitted in whole or in part by a wire, radio, electromagnetic, photoelectric or photo-optical system. "Electronic communication" includes transmissions by a computer through the Internet to another computer.

2. "Family or household member" includes spouses, former spouses, parents, children, step-

children and other persons related by blood or by present or prior marriage, persons who share or formerly shared a common dwelling, persons who have or allegedly share a blood relationship through a child, persons who have or have had a dating or engagement relationship, and persons with disabilities and their personal assistants. For purposes of this Act, neither a casual acquaintanceship nor ordinary fraternization between 2 individuals in business or social contexts shall be deemed to constitute a dating relationship.

(c) Telecommunications carriers, commercial mobile service providers, and providers of information services, including, but not limited to, Internet service providers and hosting service providers, are not liable under this Section, except for willful and wanton misconduct, by virtue of the transmission, storage, or caching of electronic communications or messages of others or by virtue of the provision of other related telecommunications, commercial mobile services, or information services used by others in violation of this Section.

Massachusetts

In response to Phoebe Prince's suicide, as well as that of Carl Walker—both of whom had been bullied before taking their lives—the Massachusetts legislature in 2010 passed what advocates call one of the toughest anti-bullying laws in the nation. The law prohibits both online taunting and physical or emotional abuse, and mandates training for faculty and students at schools. It further mandates that school administrators inform parents of bullying that occurs within the schools themselves.

Missouri

As noted previously, in 2008 Missouri revised its statutes on harassment to include harassment and stalking through electronic and telephonic communications and cyber-bullying after the suicide of Megan Meier.

New York

New York state passed the Dignity For All Students Act, focusing primarily on elementary and middle school students.

Texas

Texas enacted the Stalking by Electronic Communications Act in 2001.

Washington State

Washington takes the approach of putting the focus on cyberbullying prevention and response directly on the schools. The law also requires schools to create policies to address bullying in a general sense.

Legislation at the Federal Level

Attempts at legislating cyberbullying have been tried at the federal level, primarily because the Commerce Clause of the U.S. Constitution specifically provides that only the federal government can regulate commerce between the states; this includes electronic communication over the Internet. An early example, the Violence Against Women Act, passed in 2000, included cyberbullying in a part of interstate status on harassment.

Megan Meier Cyberbullying Prevention Act

In 2009, Representative Linda Sánchez (D-CA) brought legislation titled the "Megan Meier Cyberbullying Prevention Act" before the U.S. House of Representatives. Her efforts were met with little enthusiasm, however, as Representatives from both the Republican and Democratic parties were concerned with the bill's impact on the freedom of speech. One of the oft-cited arguments against the bill comes from talk radio, with the concern expressed being that the law would be used to silence political opponents who use the airwaves to espouse divergent viewpoints. Another issue is that would make violation of the law a felony, rather than a misdemeanor as has been done in most states. Opponents of the bill argue that since the target of such legislation is nominally teenagers, this would put an undue burden on the prison system—since there are no long-term facilities for teenage offenders at the federal level. In addition, opponents call the proposed sentences (up to two years incarceration) excessive.

While Sánchez' bill was discussed in committee, it has not passed that stage as of 2012.

Tyler Clementi Higher Education Anti-Harassment Act

In early March 2011, U.S. Senator Frank Lautenberg (D-NJ) and Representative Rush D. Holt, Jr. (D-NJ-12) introduced the "Tyler Clementi Higher Education Anti-Harassment Act", which would mandate that colleges and universities that receive federal funding have policies in place to address harassment—including cyberbullying. Universities would be required to address harassment that focuses on real or perceived race, color, national origin, sex, disability, sexual orientation, gender identity, or religion. The bill would also enable the U.S. Department of Education to provide training to institutes of higher education to prevent or address harassment. Furthermore, the bill addresses not just student-to-student harassment, but also harassment of students by faculty or staff as well.

However, like the Megan Meier Cyberbullying Prevention Act, this bill also has its detractors. Opponents point out that harassment on college campuses is already prohibited under existing laws; furthermore, they point out that harassment based on sexual orientation is also covered under existing statutes. In addition, as with the Sánchez bill, there are questions as to the free speech implications.

India

Prior to February 2013, there were no laws that directly regulate cyberstalking in India. India's Information Technology Act of 2000 (IT Act) was a set of laws to regulate the cyberspace. However, it merely focused on financial crimes and neglected interpersonal criminal behaviours such as cyberstalking (Behera, 2010; Halder & Jaishankar, 2008; Nappinai, 2010). In 2013, Indian Parliament made amendments to the Indian Penal Code, introducing cyberstalking as a criminal offence. Stalking has been defined as a man or woman who follows or contacts a man or woman, despite clear indication of disinterest to such contact by the man or woman, or monitoring of use of internet or electronic communication of a man or a woman. A man or a woman committing the offence of stalking would be liable for imprisonment up to three years for the first offence, and shall also be liable to fine and for any subsequent conviction would be liable for imprisonment up to five years and with fine.

Poland

Cyberstalking has been illegal since 2011.

New Zealand

New Zealand Minister of Justice Judith Collins plans to introduce a law that would make it an offence to incite people to commit suicide, or post material that is grossly offensive by the end of 2013.

International Law

Convention on Cybercrime

International law emphasizes a supranational concept related to cybercrime. This is the Convention on Cybercrime, signed by the Council of Europe in Budapest on November 23, 2001.

The Global Cyber Law Database (GCLD) aims to become the most comprehensive and authoritative source of cyber laws for all countries.

Universal Declaration of Human Rights

- Article 5 of the Universal Declaration of Human Rights.

No one shall be subjected to torture or to cruel, inhuman or degrading treatment.

Internet Troll

In Internet slang, a troll is a person who sows discord on the Internet by starting arguments or upsetting people, by posting inflammatory, extraneous, or off-topic messages in an online community (such as a newsgroup, forum, chat room, or blog) with the intent of provoking readers into an emotional response or of otherwise disrupting normal, on-topic discussion, often for the troll's amusement.

This sense of both the noun and the verb "troll" is associated with Internet discourse, but also has been used more widely. Media attention in recent years has equated trolling with online harassment. For example, the mass media have used "troll" to mean "a person who defaces Internet tribute sites with the aim of causing grief to families." In addition, depictions of trolling have been included in popular fictional works, such as the HBO television program *The Newsroom*, in which a main character encounters harassing persons online and tries to infiltrate their circles by posting negative sexual comments.

Usage

The advice to ignore rather than engage with a troll is sometimes phrased as "Please do not feed the trolls."

Application of the term *troll* is subjective. Some readers may characterize a post as *trolling*, while others may regard the same post as a legitimate contribution to the discussion, even if controversial. Like any pejorative term, it can be used as an *ad hominem* attack, suggesting a negative motivation.

As noted in an *OS News* article titled "Why People Troll and How to Stop Them" (25 January 2012), "The traditional definition of trolling includes intent. That is, trolls purposely disrupt forums. This definition is too narrow. Whether someone intends to disrupt a thread or not, the results are the same if they do." Others have addressed the same issue, e.g., Claire Hardaker, in her Ph.D. thesis "Trolling in asynchronous computer-mediated communication: From user discussions to academic definitions." Popular recognition of the existence (and prevalence) of non-deliberate, "accidental trolls", has been documented widely, in sources as diverse as Nicole Sullivan's keynote speech at the 2012 Fluent Conference, titled "Don't Feed the Trolls" Gizmodo, online opinions on the subject written by Silicon Valley executives and comics.

Regardless of the circumstances, controversial posts may attract a particularly strong response from those unfamiliar with the robust dialogue found in some online, rather than physical, communities. Experienced participants in online forums know that the most effective way to discourage a troll is usually to ignore it, because responding tends to encourage trolls to continue disruptive posts – hence the often-seen warning: "Please do not feed the trolls".

The "trollface" is an image occasionally used to indicate trolling in Internet culture.

At times, the word can be abused to refer to anyone with controversial opinions they disagree with. Such usages goes against the ordinary meaning of troll in multiple ways. While psychologists have determined that the dark triad traits are common among internet trolls, some observers claim trolls don't actually believe the controversial views they claim. Farhad Manjoo criticises this view, noting that if the person really is trolling, they are a lot more intelligent than their critics would believe.

There are competing theories of where and when "troll" was first used in Internet slang, with numerous unattested accounts of BBS and UseNet origins in the early 1980s or before.

The English noun "troll" in the standard sense of ugly dwarf or giant dates to 1610 and comes from the Old Norse word "troll" meaning giant or demon. The word evokes the trolls of Scandinavian folklore and children's tales: antisocial, quarrelsome and slow-witted creatures which make life difficult for travellers.

In modern English usage, "trolling" may describe the fishing technique of slowly dragging a lure or baited hook from a moving boat whereas *trawling* describes the generally commercial act of dragging a fishing net. Early non-Internet slang use of "trolling" can be found in the military: by 1972 the term "trolling for MiGs" was documented in use by US Navy pilots in Vietnam. It referred to use of "...decoys, with the mission of drawing...fire away..."

The contemporary use of the term is alleged to have appeared on the Internet in the late 1980s, but the earliest known attestation according to the *Oxford English Dictionary* is in 1992.

The context of the quote cited in the *Oxford English Dictionary* sets the origin in Usenet in the early 1990s as in the phrase "trolling for newbies", as used in *alt.folklore.urban* (AFU). Commonly, what is meant is a relatively gentle inside joke by veteran users, presenting questions or topics that had been so overdone that only a new user would respond to them earnestly. For example, a veteran of the group might make a post on the common misconception that glass flows over time. Long-time readers would both recognize the poster's name and know that the topic had been discussed a lot, but new subscribers to the group would not realize, and would thus respond. These types of trolls served as a practice to identify group insiders. This definition of trolling, considerably narrower than the modern understanding of the term, was considered a positive contribution. One of the most notorious AFU trollers, David Mikkelson, went on to create the urban folklore website Snopes.com.

By the late 1990s, *alt.folklore.urban* had such heavy traffic and participation that trolling of this sort was frowned upon. Others expanded the term to include the practice of playing a seriously misinformed or deluded user, even in newsgroups where one was not a regular; these were often attempts at humor rather than provocation. The noun *troll* usually referred to an act of trolling – or to the resulting discussion – rather than to the author, though some posts punned on the dual meaning of *troll*.

In Other Languages

In Chinese, trolling is referred to as *bái mù* (Chinese; literally: "white eye"), which can be straightforwardly explained as "eyes without pupils", in the sense that whilst the pupil of the eye is used for vision, the white section of the eye cannot see, and trolling involves blindly talking nonsense over the internet, having total disregard to sensitivities or being oblivious to the situation at hand, akin to having eyes without pupils. An alternative term is *bái làn* (Chinese; literally: "white rot"), which describes a post completely nonsensical and full of folly made to upset others, and derives from a Taiwanese slang term for the male genitalia, where genitalia that is pale white in colour represents that someone is young, and thus foolish. Both terms originate from Taiwan, and are also used in Hong Kong and mainland China. Another term, *xiǎo bái* (Chinese; literally: "little white") is a derogatory term that refers to both *bái mù* and *bái làn* that is used on anonymous posting internet forums. Another common term for a troll used in mainland China is *pēn zi* (Chinese; literally: "sprayer, spurter").

In Japanese, *tsuri* means "fishing" and refers to intentionally misleading posts whose only purpose is to get the readers to react, i.e. get trolled. *arashi* means "laying waste" and can also be used to refer to simple spamming.

In Icelandic, *þurs* (a thurs) or *tröll* (a troll) may refer to trolls, the verbs *þursa* (to troll) or *þursast* (to be trolling, to troll about) may be used.

In Korean, *nak-si* means "fishing", and is used to refer to Internet trolling attempts, as well as purposefully misleading post titles. A person who recognizes the troll after having responded (or, in case of a post title *nak-si*, having read the actual post) would often refer to himself as a caught fish.

In Portuguese, more commonly in its Brazilian variant, troll is the usual term to denote internet trolls (examples of common derivate terms are *trollismo* or *trollagem*, "trolling", and the verb *trollar*, "to troll", which entered popular use), but an older expression, used by those which want to avoid anglicisms or slangs, is *complexo do pombo enxadrista* to denote trolling behavior, and *pombos enxadristas* (literally, "chessplayer pigeons") or simply *pombos* are the terms used to name the trolls. The terms are explained by an adage or popular saying: "Arguing with *fulano* (i.e., John Doe) is the same as playing chess with a pigeon: the pigeon defecates on the table, drop the pieces and simply fly, claiming victory."

In Thai, the term *krian* has been adopted to address Internet trolls. According to the Royal Institute of Thailand, the term, which literally refers to a closely cropped hairstyle worn by schoolboys in Thailand, is from the behaviour of these schoolboys who usually gather to play online games and, during which, make annoying, disruptive, impolite, or unreasonable expressions. The term *top krian* ("slap a cropped head") refers to the act of posting intellectual replies to refute and cause the messages of Internet trolls to be perceived as unintelligent.

In the Sinhala language, this is called *ala kireema*, which means "Turning it into Potatoes (Sabotage)". Sometimes it is used as *ala vagaa kireema* – "Planting Potatoes". People/Profiles who does trolling often are called "Potato Planters" – *ala vagaakaruvan*. This seems to be originated from university slang *ala væda* which means "Potato business" is used for breaking the laws/codes of the university.

Trolling, Identity, and Anonymity

Early incidents of trolling were considered to be the same as flaming, but this has changed with modern usage by the news media to refer to the creation of any content that targets another person. The Internet dictionary NetLingo suggests there are four grades of trolling: playtime trolling, tactical trolling, strategic trolling, and domination trolling. The relationship between trolling and flaming was observed in open-access forums in California, on a series of modem-linked computers. *CommuniTree* was begun in 1978 but was closed in 1982 when accessed by high school teenagers, becoming a ground for trashing and abuse. Some psychologists have suggested that flaming would be caused by deindividuation or decreased self-evaluation: the anonymity of online postings would lead to disinhibition amongst individuals Others have suggested that although flaming and trolling is often unpleasant, it may be a form of normative behavior that expresses the social identity of a certain user group According to Tom Postmes, a professor of social and organisational psychology at the universities of Exeter, England, and Groningen, The Netherlands, and the author of *Individuality and the Group*, who has studied online behavior for 20 years, "Trolls aspire to violence, to the level of trouble they can cause in an environment. They want it to kick off. They want to promote antipathetic emotions of disgust and outrage, which morbidly gives them a sense of pleasure."

The practice of trolling has been documented by a number of academics as early as the 1990s. This included Steven Johnson in 1997 in the book, Interface Culture, and Judith Donath in 1999. Donath's paper outlines the ambiguity of identity in a disembodied "virtual community" such as Usenet:

> In the physical world there is an inherent unity to the self, for the body provides a compelling and convenient definition of identity. The norm is: one body, one identity ... The virtual world is different. It is composed of information rather than matter.

Donath provides a concise overview of identity deception games which trade on the confusion between physical and epistemic community:

Trolling is a game about identity deception, albeit one that is played without the consent of most of the players. The troll attempts to pass as a legitimate participant, sharing the group's common interests and concerns; the newsgroups members, if they are cognizant of trolls and other identity deceptions, attempt to both distinguish real from trolling postings, and upon judging a poster a troll, make the offending poster leave the group. Their success at the former depends on how well they – and the troll – understand identity cues; their success at the latter depends on whether the troll's enjoyment is sufficiently diminished or outweighed by the costs imposed by the group.

Trolls can be costly in several ways. A troll can disrupt the discussion on a newsgroup, disseminate bad advice, and damage the feeling of trust in the newsgroup community. Furthermore, in a group that has become sensitized to trolling – where the rate of deception is high – many honestly naïve questions may be quickly rejected as trollings. This can be quite off-putting to the new user who upon venturing a first posting is immediately bombarded with angry accusations. Even if the accusation is unfounded, being branded a troll is quite damaging to one's online reputation.

Susan Herring and colleagues in "Searching for Safety Online: Managing 'Trolling' in a Feminist Forum" point out the difficulty inherent in monitoring trolling and maintaining freedom of speech in online communities: "harassment often arises in spaces known for their freedom, lack of censure, and experimental nature". Free speech may lead to tolerance of trolling behavior, complicating the members' efforts to maintain an open, yet supportive discussion area, especially for sensitive topics such as race, gender, and sexuality.

In an effort to reduce uncivil behavior by increasing accountability, many web sites (e.g. Reuters, Facebook, and Gizmodo) now require commenters to register their names and e-mail addresses.

Corporate, Political, and Special Interest Sponsored Trolls

Investigative journalist Sharyl Attkisson is one of several in the media who has reported on the increasing trend for organizations to utilize trolls to manipulate public opinion as part and parcel of an Astroturfing initiative. Teams of sponsored trolls, sometimes referred to as sockpuppet armies, swarm a site to overwhelm any honest discourse and denigrate any who disagree with them. A 2012 Pew Center on the States presentation on *Effective Messaging* included two examples of social media posts by a recently launched "rapid response team" dedicated to promoting fluoridation of community water supplies. That same presentation also emphasized changing the topic of conversation as a winning strategy.

A 2016 study by Harvard political scientist Gary King reported that the Chinese government's 50 Cent Party creates 440 million pro-government social media posts per year. The report said that government employees were paid to create pro-government posts around the time of national holidays to avoid mass political protests. The Chinese Government ran an editorial in the state-funded *Global Times* defending censorship and 50c party trolls.

A 2016 study for the NATO Strategic Communications Centre of Excellence (NATO StratCom COE) on hybrid warfare notes that the Russian military intervention in Ukraine "demonstrated how fake identities and accounts were used to disseminate narratives through social media, blogs, and web commentaries in order to manipulate, harass, or deceive opponents."

Psychological Characteristics

Researcher Ben Radford wrote about the phenomenon of clowns in history and modern day in his book *Bad Clowns* and found that bad clowns have evolved into Internet trolls. They do not dress up as traditional clowns but, for their own amusement, they tease and exploit "human foibles" in order to speak the "truth" and gain a reaction. Like clowns in make-up, Internet trolls hide behind "anonymous accounts and fake usernames." In their eyes they are the trickster and are performing for a nameless audience via the Internet.

Concern Troll

A *concern troll* is a false flag pseudonym created by a user whose actual point of view is opposed to the one that the troll claims to hold. The concern troll posts in Web forums devoted to its declared point of view and attempts to sway the group's actions or opinions while claiming to share their goals, but with professed "concerns". The goal is to sow fear, uncertainty and doubt within the group. This is a particular case of sockpuppeting.

An example of this occurred in 2006 when Tad Furtado, a staffer for then-Congressman Charles Bass (R-NH), was caught posing as a "concerned" supporter of Bass' opponent, Democrat Paul Hodes, on several liberal New Hampshire blogs, using the pseudonyms "IndieNH" or "IndyNH". "IndyNH" expressed concern that Democrats might just be wasting their time or money on Hodes, because Bass was unbeatable. Hodes eventually won the election.

Although the term "concern troll" originated in discussions of online behavior, it now sees increasing use to describe similar behaviors that take place offline. For example, James Wolcott of *Vanity Fair* accused a conservative *New York Daily News* columnist of "concern troll" behavior in his efforts to downplay the Mark Foley scandal. Wolcott links what he calls concern trolls to what Saul Alinsky calls "Do-Nothings", giving a long quote from Alinsky on the Do-Nothings' method and effects:

These Do-Nothings profess a commitment to social change for ideals of justice, equality, and opportunity, and then abstain from and discourage all effective action for change. They are known by their brand, 'I agree with your ends but not your means'.

The Hill published an op-ed piece by Markos Moulitsas of the liberal blog Daily Kos titled "Dems: Ignore 'Concern Trolls'". The concern trolls in question were not Internet participants but rather Republicans offering public advice and warnings to the Democrats. The author defines "concern trolling" as "offering a poisoned apple in the form of advice to political opponents that, if taken, would harm the recipient".

Troll Sites

While many webmasters and forum administrators consider trolls a scourge on their sites, some websites welcome them. For example, a *New York Times* article discussed troll activity at 4chan and at Encyclopedia Dramatica, which it described as "an online compendium of troll humor and troll lore". 4chan's /b/ board is recognized as "one of the Internet's most infamous and active trolling hotspots." This site and others are often used as a base to troll against sites that their members can not normally post on. These trolls feed off the reactions of their victims because "their agenda is to take delight in causing trouble".

Another site, NationStates, while not a troll site, has been known to have a unknown number of self-proclaimed 'professional trolls', who claim to be paid by the administrators and moderators of the site to harass people speaking out against them over cases of cyber-bullying on the site by the admins and mods.

Media Coverage and Controversy

Mainstream media outlets have focused their attention on the willingness of some Internet users to go to extreme lengths to participate in organized psychological harassment.

Australia

In February 2010, the Australian government became involved after users defaced the Facebook tribute pages of murdered children Trinity Bates and Elliott Fletcher. Australian communications minister Stephen Conroy decried the attacks, committed mainly by 4chan users, as evidence of the need for greater Internet regulation, stating, "This argument that the Internet is some mystical creation that no laws should apply to, that is a recipe for anarchy and the wild west." Facebook responded by strongly urging administrators to be aware of ways to ban users and remove inappropriate content from Facebook pages. In 2012, the *Daily Telegraph* started a campaign to take action against "Twitter trolls", who abuse and threaten users. Several high-profile Australians including Charlotte Dawson, Robbie Farah, Laura Dundovic, and Ray Hadley have been victims of this phenomenon.

United Kingdom

In the United Kingdom, contributions made to the Internet are covered by the Malicious Communications Act 1988 as well as Section 127 of the Communications Act 2003, under which jail sentences were, until 2015, limited to a maximum of six months. In October 2014, the UK's Justice Secretary, Chris Grayling, said that "internet trolls" would face up to two years in jail, under measures in the Criminal Justice and Courts Bill that extend the maximum sentence and time limits for bringing prosecutions. The House of Lords Select Committee on Communications had earlier recommended against creating a specific offence of trolling. Sending messages which are "grossly offensive or of an indecent, obscene or menacing character" is an offence whether they are received by the intended recipient or not. Several people have been imprisoned in the UK for online harassment.

Trolls of the testimonial page of Georgia Varley faced no prosecution due to misunderstandings of the legal system in the wake of the term trolling being popularized. In October 2012, a twenty-year-old man was jailed for twelve weeks for posting offensive jokes to a support group for friends and family of April Jones.

United States

On 31 March 2010, the *Today Show* ran a segment detailing the deaths of three separate adolescent girls and trolls' subsequent reactions to their deaths. Shortly after the suicide of high school student Alexis Pilkington, anonymous posters began performing organized psychological harassment across various message boards, referring to Pilkington as a "suicidal slut", and posting graphic images on her Facebook memorial page. The segment also included an exposé of a 2006 accident, in which an eighteen-year-old fatally crashed her father's car into a highway pylon; trolls emailed her grieving family the leaked pictures of her mutilated corpse.

In 2007, the media was fooled by trollers into believing that students were consuming a drug called Jenkem, purportedly made of human waste. A user named Pickwick on TOTSE posted pictures implying that he was inhaling this drug. Major news corporations such as Fox News Channel reported the story and urged parents to warn their children about this drug. Pickwick's pictures of Jenkem were fake and the pictures did not actually feature human waste.

In August 2012, the subject of trolling was featured on the HBO television series *The Newsroom*. The character of Neal Sampat encounters harassing individuals online, particularly looking at 4chan, and he ends up choosing to post negative comments himself on an economics related forum. The attempt by the character to infiltrate trolls' inner circles attracted debate from media reviewers critiquing the series.

The publication of the 2015 non-fiction book *The Dark Net: Inside the Digital Underworld* by Jamie Bartlett, a journalist and a representative of the British think tank Demos, attracted some attention for its depiction of misunderstood sections of the internet, describing interactions on encrypted sites such as those accessible with the software Tor. Detailing trolling-related groups and the harassment created by them, Bartlett advocated for greater awareness of them and monitoring of their activities. Professor Matthew Wisnioski wrote for *The Washington Post* that a "league of trolls, anarchists, perverts and drug dealers is at work building a digital world beyond the Silicon Valley offices where our era's best and brightest have designed a Facebook-friendly" surface and agreed with Bartlett that the activities of trolls go back decades to the Usenet 'flame wars' of the 1990s and even earlier.

India

Newslaundry covered the phenomenon of "Twitter Trolling" in its Criticles. It has also been characterising Twitter trolls in its weekly podcasts.

Examples

As reported on 8 April 1999, investors became victims of trolling via an online financial discussion regarding PairGain, a telephone equipment company based in California. Trolls operating in the stock's Yahoo Finance chat room posted a fabricated Bloomberg News article stating that an Israeli telecom company could potentially acquire PairGain. As a result, PairGain's stock jumped by 31%. However, the stock promptly crashed after the reports were identified as false.

So-called Gold Membership trolling originated in 2007 on 4chan boards, when users posted fake images claiming to offer upgraded 4chan account privileges; without a "Gold" account, one could not view certain content. This turned out to be a hoax designed to fool board members, especially newcomers. It was copied and became an Internet meme. In some cases, this type of troll has been used as a scam, most notably on Facebook, where fake Facebook Gold Account upgrade ads have proliferated in order to link users to dubious websites and other content.

The case of *Zeran v. America Online, Inc.* resulted primarily from trolling. Six days after the Oklahoma City bombing, anonymous users posted advertisements for shirts celebrating the bombing on AOL message boards, claiming that the shirts could be obtained by contacting Mr. Kenneth Zeran. The posts listed Zeran's address and home phone number. Zeran was subsequently harassed.

Anti-Scientology protests by Anonymous, commonly known as Project Chanology, are sometimes labeled as "trolling" by media such as *Wired*, and the participants sometimes explicitly self-identify as "trolls".

Neo-Nazi website *The Daily Stormer* orchestrates what it calls a "Troll Army", and has encouraged trolling of Jewish MP Luciana Berger and Muslim activist Mariam Veiszadeh.

Gamergate Controversy

The Gamergate controversy concerns issues of sexism and progressivism in video game culture, stemming from a harassment campaign conducted primarily through the use of the hashtag #GamerGate. *Gamergate* is used as a blanket term for the controversy, the harassment campaign and actions of those participating in it, and the loosely organized movement that emerged around the hashtag.

Beginning in August 2014, supporters of the Gamergate movement targeted several women in the video game industry, including game developers Zoë Quinn and Brianna Wu, as well as feminist media critic Anita Sarkeesian. After Eron Gjoni, Quinn's former boyfriend, wrote a disparaging blog post about her, other people falsely accused her of entering a relationship with a journalist in exchange for positive coverage. Harassment campaigns against Quinn and others included doxing, threats of rape, and death threats. Gamergate supporters claimed unethical collusion between the press and feminists, progressives, and social critics. These concerns have been dismissed by commentators as trivial, conspiracy theories, groundless, or unrelated to actual issues of ethics.

Gamergate supporters typically organized on online platforms which allow anonymous or pseudonymous communication; these platforms include 4chan, Internet Relay Chat, Twitter and Reddit. Gamergate has no official leaders, spokespeople, or manifesto. Statements claiming to represent Gamergate have been inconsistent and contradictory, making it difficult for commentators to identify goals and motives. As a result, Gamergate has often been defined by the harassment its supporters committed. Some Gamergate supporters attempted to dissociate themselves from misogyny and harassment, but their attempts have often been dismissed as insincere and self-serving.

The controversy has been described as a manifestation of a culture war over cultural diversification, artistic recognition, and social criticism in video games, and over the social identity of gamers. Many supporters of Gamergate oppose what they view as the increasing influence of feminism on video game culture; as a result, Gamergate is often viewed as a right-wing backlash against progressivism.

Industry responses to Gamergate have been predominantly negative. Gamergate has led figures both inside and outside the industry to focus on better methods of tackling online harassment.

History

In February 2013, Zoë Quinn, an independent game developer, released *Depression Quest*, an interactive fiction browser game. The game was met with positive reviews in the gaming media, but some backlash developed among those who believed that it had received undue attention. Quinn began to receive hate mail upon its release, leading her to change her phone number and screen her calls. By August 2014 Quinn had been the target of eighteen months of increasing harassment, which had created what *The New Yorker* characterized as "an ambient hum of menace in her life, albeit one that she [had] mostly been able to ignore".

Game developer Zoë Quinn, the initial target of the harassment campaign

In August 2014, Eron Gjoni, Quinn's former boyfriend, published the "Zoe Post", a 9,425-word blog post that quoted from personal chat logs, emails, and text messages to describe their relationship. The post, described as "a rambling online essay" in *The New York Times*, complained, among other things, that Quinn entered a romantic relationship with Nathan Grayson, a journalist for the Gawker Media video game website *Kotaku*. The post was linked on 4chan, where some erroneously claimed the relationship had induced Grayson to publish a favorable review of *Depression Quest*. Grayson had never reviewed Quinn's games and Grayson's only article for *Kotaku* mentioning her was published before their relationship began. Gjoni later updated his blog post to acknowledge this.

After Gjoni's blog post, Quinn and her family were subjected to a virulent and often misogynistic harassment campaign. The people behind this campaign initially referred to it as the "quinnspiracy", but adopted the Twitter hashtag "Gamergate" after it was coined by actor Adam Baldwin near the end of August. Baldwin has described Gamergate as a backlash against political correctness, saying it has started a discussion "about culture, about ethics, and about freedom". Journalists who did not cover the examination into Quinn's private life were accused of conspiracy, and a blacklist circulated by Gamergate supporters. The accusations and harassment were coordinated by 4chan users over Internet Relay Chat (IRC), spreading rapidly over imageboards and forums like 4chan and Reddit.

Commentators both inside and outside the video game industry condemned the attacks against Quinn. The attacks included doxing (researching and broadcasting personally identifiable information about an individual) and hacking of her Tumblr, Dropbox, and Skype accounts; she was also subjected to rape and death threats. The release of personal information forced Quinn to flee her home; she explained that "I can't go home because they have been posting around my home address, often with threats attached to it".

At a conference Quinn said, "I used to go to game events and feel like I was going home ... Now it's just like... are any of the people I'm currently in the room with ones that said they wanted to beat me to death?". One such threat, reported in *The New Yorker*, proposed that: "Next time she shows up at a conference we... give her a crippling injury that's never going to fully heal... a good solid injury to the knees. I'd say a brain damage, but we don't want to make it so she ends up too retarded to fear us."

Further Harassment

Gamergate supporters subjected others to similar harassment, doxing, and death threats. Those who came to the victims' defense were ridiculed as "white knights", or "social justice warriors" (SJW); this characterization was intended, according to Heron, Belford and Goker, to neutralize any opposition by questioning their motives. Shortly after the Gamergate hashtag was coined, video game developer Phil Fish had his personal information, including various accounts and passwords, hacked and publicly posted in retaliation for defending Quinn and attacking her detractors. The hacks and doxing also exposed documents relating to Fish's company, Polytron. As a result, Fish left the gaming industry and put Polytron up for sale, calling the situation "unacceptable" and saying, "it's not worth it".

Feminist and media critic Anita Sarkeesian faced death threats after releasing a *Tropes vs. Women in Video Games* video.

The campaign expanded to include renewed harassment of prominent feminist media critic Anita Sarkeesian, who had previously been a target of online harassment due in part to her YouTube video series *Tropes vs. Women in Video Games*, which analyzes sexist stereotypes in video games. Sarkeesian's attackers took her critical commentary as unfair and unwarranted, and considered her an interloper. After a new episode of *Tropes vs. Women* was released on August 24, 2014, Sarkeesian received rape and death threats, and private information including her home address was leaked; she was compelled to flee her home. At the XOXO arts and technology conference in Portland, Oregon, she said, in regard to the accusations that high-profile women were making up the threats against them, that "one of the most radical things you can do is to actually believe women when they talk about their experiences". "The perpetrators", Sarkeesian went on to say, "do not see themselves as perpetrators at all... They see themselves as noble warriors".

Sarkeesian canceled an October 2014 speaking appearance at Utah State University (USU) after the school received three anonymous threats, the second of which claimed affiliation with Gamergate. The initial threat proposed that "a Montreal Massacre style attack will be carried out against the attendees, as well as the students and staff at the nearby Women's Center", alluding to the École Polytechnique massacre, a 1989 mass shooting motivated by antifeminism. USU's President and Provost released a joint statement saying that USU, in consultation with state and federal law enforcement agencies, had assessed that there was no credible threat to students, staff or the speaker. Requests for additional security measures were declined because of Utah's open carry laws, leading to the cancellation. The threats drew the attention of mainstream media to the Gamergate situation. Wingfield of *The New York Times* referred to the threat as "the most noxious example of a weeks long campaign to discredit or intimidate outspoken critics of the male-dominated gaming industry and its culture". The Federal Bureau of Investigation (FBI) investigated the threat to attack Sarkeesian and other Gamergate-related threats. The investigations, which were plagued with jurisdictional issues, ultimately closed with the FBI failing to identify the perpetrators of some threats and declining to prosecute others.

Video game developer Brianna Wu suffered Gamergate-related harassment beginning in late 2014.

In mid-October Brianna Wu, another independent game developer and co-founder of video game studio Giant Spacekat, saw her home address and other identifying information posted on 8chan as retaliation for mocking Gamergate. Wu then became the target of rape and death threats on Twitter and elsewhere. After contacting police, Wu fled her home with her husband, saying she would not allow the threats to intimidate her into silence. Wu later announced an US$11,000 reward for any information leading to a conviction for those involved in her harassment, and set up a legal fund to help other game developers who have been harassed online. As of April 2016, Wu was still receiving threats in such volume that she employed full-time staff to document them.

Harassment related to Gamergate continued for several months after the onset of the controversy. Two critics of Gamergate were targets of attempted "swatting"—hoaxed reports to emergency services intended to provoke a SWAT team response at the target's home. *The Guardian* reported that both swatting attempts were coordinated through the "baphomet" subforum of 8chan. Since the initial rush of threats that caused her to flee her home, Wu documented receiving roughly 45 death threats by April 2015; Silicon Valley investor Marc Andreessen has offered up to a $10,000 reward for information leading to the conviction of those who have issued these threats. Wu's studio, Giant Spacekat, withdrew from the Expo Hall of PAX East 2015. Wu cited security concerns, lack of confidence in the management and their failure to return calls.

Actress and gamer Felicia Day wrote a blog post about her concerns over Gamergate and her fear of retaliation if she spoke against it. Almost immediately her home address and phone number were posted online, leading to harassing letters and phone calls. Actor Wil Wheaton and former NFL player Chris Kluwe also posted criticisms of Gamergate. Inasmuch as the latter is widely noted for his use of creative insults, Stephen Colbert questioned why men like Kluwe had not been threatened by Gamergate, noting that "it's almost entirely women being threatened in Gamergate".

Some people who have identified as supporters of Gamergate said that they have been harassed. YouTube personality Steven "Boogie2988" Williams, remarked that a comment on one of his videos included his address and a threat to his wife's life. In an interview with BBC Three, Gamergate supporter John Bain, known by his YouTube moniker "TotalBiscuit," said he has been the target of death threats and harassment from anonymous people who opposed his view on Gamergate. Mike Diver wrote in *Vice* that threats against Gamergate supporters had been neglected in press coverage. Misogynist abuse and vitriolic messages were targeted at many people involved.

Bomb threats have also been made towards events attended by Gamergate supporters. A May 2015 meeting in Washington D.C. arranged by writer Christina Hoff Sommers and journalist Milo Yiannopoulos was the target of a bomb threat made over Twitter, according to local police responding to information supplied by the FBI. During "Airplay", an event run by the Society of Professional Journalists in August 2015, multiple bomb threats were made. This led to the evacuation of the building and the surrounding neighborhood.

Coordination of Harassment

Ars Technica reported that a series of 4chan discussion logs suggests that Twitter sockpuppet accounts were used to popularize the Gamergate hashtag. Heron, Belford, and Goker, analyzing the logs, said that early Gamergate IRC discussions focused on coordinating the harassment of Quinn by using astroturf campaigns to push attacks against her into mainstream view. They also describe how initial organizers deliberately attempted to cultivate a palpable narrative for public consumption while internally focusing on personal grudges against Quinn and aggressive sexual imagery. Mortensen wrote in *Games and Culture* that Gamergate's structure as an anonymous swarm allowed it to create an environment where anyone who criticized it or became its target was at risk, while allowing them to avoid individual responsibility for harassment.

There has been considerable discussion of self-policing and the responsibility supporters of Gamergate share when the hashtag is used for harassment. A number of websites have blocked users, removed posts, and created policies to prevent their users from threatening Quinn and others with doxing, assault, rape and murder, and planning and coordinating such threats. 4chan's founder, Christopher Poole, banned all discussion of Gamergate on the site as more attacks occurred, leading to Gamergate supporters using 8chan as their central hub.

Gamergate supporters have responded to accusations of harassment in a variety of ways. Many have denied that the harassment came from Gamergate, or falsely accused victims of fabricating the evidence. Gamergate supporters have used the term "Literally Who" to refer to victims of harassment such as Quinn, saying they are not relevant to Gamergate's goals and purposes. Commentators have decried the use of such terminology as dehumanizing, and said that discussions on Gamergate forums often center around those referred to as "Literally Who". Some Gamergate supporters have denounced the harassment, arguing that the perpetrators are in the minority and do not represent them. Gamergate supporters have also reported threatening or hateful comments.

By September 24, 2014, over one million Twitter messages incorporating the Gamergate hashtag had been sent. A *Newsweek* and Brandwatch analysis found more than two million Twitter messages between September and October 2014. Software developer Andy Baio also produced an analysis of #Gamergate tweets showing a discussion that was polarized between pro- and anti-Gamergate factions. One quarter of the tweets sampled were produced by users new to Twitter, most of whom were pro-Gamergate. While the number of Gamergate supporters is unclear, in October 2014 *Deadspin* estimated 10,000 supporters based on the number of users discussing Gamergate on Reddit.

In an interview with NPR's *Marketplace*, voice actress Jennifer Hale called on the gaming community to improve the self-policing of its small and vicious fringe, and said race and gender barriers persist in the industry. Developer Peter Molyneux considered that the Internet's instant accessibility of social media allows for people to express of-the-moment opinions without thinking about their consequences, leading to a "whole Pandora's Box" of both good and bad issues that society must consider in terms of freedom of speech. Todd VanDerWerff wrote that the Gamergate supporters' message was lost in the vitriolic harassment, frequently directed at women.

Gamergate Activities

Following the accusations against Quinn, proponents of Gamergate began to use the "KotakuIn-Action" subreddit and boards on 8chan to organize. Because of its anonymous membership, lack of organization and leaderless nature, sources differ as to the goals or mission of Gamergate and defining it has been difficult. As the threats expanded, international media focused on Gamergate's violent, misogynistic element and its inability to present a coherent message. Bob Stuart, in *The Daily Telegraph,* reported that: "Gamergate has since swelled into an unwieldy movement with no apparent leaders, mission statement, or aims beyond calling out "social justice warriors". ... When members of the games industry are being driven from their houses and jobs, threatened, or abused, it makes Gamergate's claim that it is engaged in an ethical campaign appear laughable."

Jesse Singal, in *New York* (magazine), stated that he had spoken to several Gamergate supporters to try to understand their concerns, but found conflicting ideals and incoherent messages. Singal observed Gamergate supporters making a constant series of attacks on Quinn, Sarkeesian, and other women, while frequently stating that Gamergate "is not about [Quinn, et al]". The *Columbia Journalism Review's* Chris Ip said any legitimate message from Gamergate supporters regarding ethics in journalism was being lost in the noise created by harassment, sexism, and misogyny. With anyone able to tweet under the hashtag and no single person willing or able to represent the hashtag and take responsibility for its actions, Ip said it is not possible for journalists to neatly separate abusers from those seeking reasonable debate.

University of Oxford research fellow Anders Sandberg observed that the Gamergate debate "has been a train wreck hard to look away from". He argues that the vituperative nature of the discourse is the result of its origins in imageboard subculture, which values anonymity and promotes the kind of mob behavior where any publicly stated claim could justifiably result in a wave of hostility. Noting that those rules are "radically different" from other subcultures, and that the differences in discourse could lead to misunderstanding and conflict.

Jon Stone wrote, "[Gamergate] readjusts and reinvents itself in response to attempts to disarm and disperse its noxiousness, subsuming disaffected voices in an act of continual regeneration, cycling through targets, pretexts, manifestoes, and moralisms". Christopher Grant, editor-in-chief of *Polygon*, said that Gamergate has remained amorphous and leaderless so that the harassment can be conducted without any culpability. Grant said that meant that "ultimately Gamergate will be defined—I think has been defined—by some of its basest elements".

The Gamergate movement's focus broadened from video games into an aggressive campaign against both the news media and what they call "social justice warriors," such as with Hulk Hogan's lawsuit against Gawker Media.

Efforts to Impact Public Perceptions

Early in the controversy, posters on 4chan focused on donating to a self-described radical feminist group called The Fine Young Capitalists (TFYC), who had been embroiled in a dispute with Quinn over a female-only game development contest they had organized. Advocating donations to help TFYC create the game, posters on 4chan's politics board argued that such donations would make them "look really good" and would make them "PR-untouchable".

To respond to widespread criticism of Gamergate as misogynistic, Gamergate supporters adopted a second Twitter hashtag, #NotYourShield, intended to show that some women and minorities in the gaming community were supportive of #Gamergate and critical of Quinn and Sarkeesian. In the 4chan post that *Ars Technica* said may have coined the hashtag, this was framed as a way to "demand the SJWs stop using you as a shield to deflect genuine criticism".

Ars Technica and *The Daily Dot* reported that a series of logs from 4chan chat rooms and discussion boards indicated that the #NotYourShield hashtag was created on 4chan. *Ars Technica* said that many of the avatars for accounts used to tweet the tag seemed to be sockpuppets that had been copied from elsewhere on the internet, and compared the hashtag to #EndFathersDay, a hoax manufactured on 4chan using similar methods. Quinn said that in light of Gamergate's exclusive targeting of women or those who stood up for women, "#notyourshield was, ironically, solely designed to be a shield for this campaign once people started calling it misogynistic". Arthur Chu wrote that the hashtag was an attempt to leverage white guilt and to prevent allies from supporting the people being attacked by Gamergate. Members of 4chan have said that most of the information was taken out of context or misrepresented.

Targeting Advertisers

Gamergate supporters were critical of the wave of articles calling for diversity that followed the initial outbreak of the controversy; interpreting them as an attack on games and gamer culture. Gamergaters responded with a coordinated email campaign that demanded advertisers drop several involved publications; in a five-step 'war plan' against organizations that offended them, a

Gamergate posting described how they would choose from a list of target organizations, pick a grievance from a list others had compiled, and send a form letter containing it to an advertiser. Intel reacted to this by withdrawing an ad campaign from Gamasutra in October 2014. After a number of game developers criticized Intel for this, arguing that it could have a chilling effect on free speech and that it amounted to supporting harassment, Intel apologized for appearing to take sides in the controversy and resumed advertising on Gamasutra in mid-November.

Debate Over Ethics Allegations

Some Gamergate supporters contend that their actions are driven by concern for ethics in videogame journalism, arguing that the close relationships between journalists and developers provide evidence of an unethical conspiracy among reviewers to focus on progressive social issues, leading to conflicts of interest. As evidence of this, they point to what they consider as disproportionate praise that video game journalism has given broadly towards recent games such as *Depression Quest* and *Gone Home*, which offer little conventional gameplay, require minimal skill to complete, and relate stories with social implications, while traditional AAA titles are downplayed. Some commentators have argued that harassment and misogyny within Gamergate has prevented those with valid ethics concerns from being heard. Many of Gamergate's claims have been rejected as ill-founded and unsupported. *The Week*, *Vox*, and *Wired*, among others, stated that discussions of gender equality, sexism and other social issues in game reviews present no ethical issue. An analysis of a week's worth of public posts tagged with the hashtag said that issue publics were not primarily about ethics in gaming journalism.

In mid-September 2014, Milo Yiannopoulos published leaked discussions from a mailing list for gaming journalists called GameJournoPros on the Breitbart News website, which included discussion of events related to Gamergate. Yiannopoulos and Gamergate supporters saw the mailing list as evidence of collusion among journalists, drawing comparisons between it and JournoList. In an interview with *Vice*, one Gamergate supporter said "GameJournoPros exemplifies every single major ethical problem with modern games journalism". The list's founder acknowledged suggesting that journalists write an open letter of support to Quinn in response to the harassment she was facing, but said other members of the list had rejected his suggestion and helped him understand why his idea was inappropriate. Commentators did not consider the list to represent collusion, observing that it is a standard practice across professions to adopt informal venues for discussing matters of professional interest. Following the leak, the mailing list was closed.

Researchers at the Berkman Center for Internet & Society at Harvard University described Gamergate as a "vitriolic campaign against Quinn that quickly morph[ed] into a broader crusade against alleged corruption in games journalism" which involved considerable abuse and harassment of female developers and game critics. Other commentators argued that Gamergate had the potential to raise significant issues in gaming journalism, but that the wave of misogynistic harassment and abuse associated with the hashtag had poisoned the well, making it impossible to separate honest criticism from sexist trolling. The authors of "Sexism in the Circuitry" argued that some Gamergate supporters were "genuinely motivated by a desire to uncover these issues and improve the quality of journalism, such as it is, within the game industry", but said that viable discussion was obscured by the harassment and misogyny. Concerns have also been raised when juxtaposing the behavior of Gamergate supporters with their claimed message: Dr. Kathleen Bartzen Culver, a professor and media ethics expert at the University of Wisconsin–Madison, wrote that while Gamergate supporters claimed to be interested in journalism ethics, their "misogynistic and threatening" behavior belied this claim. "Much of the conversation—if I can even call it that—has been a toxic sludge of rumor, invective, and gender bias. The irony comes from people who claim to be challenging the ethics of game journalists through patently unethical behavior."

In an interview with Anita Sarkeesian in *The Guardian*, Jessica Valenti said that "the movement's much-mocked mantra, 'It's about ethics in journalism'" was seen by others as "a natural extension of sexist harassment and the fear of female encroachment on a traditionally male space". Sarkeesian asked, "if this 'movement' was about journalism, why wasn't it journalists who had to deal with a barrage of rape and death threats?". Writing in *Vox*, Todd VanDerWerff said that "[e]very single question of journalistic ethics Gamergate has brought up has either been debunked or dealt with". Similarly, Leigh Alexander, then editor-at-large of *Gamasutra*, described the ethics concerns as deeply sincere but based on conspiracy theories, saying that there is nothing unethical about journalists being acquainted with those they cover and that meaningful reporting requires journalists to develop professional relationships with sources.

Journalists who have attempted to understand Gamergate's motivations have concluded that, rather than relating to ethics, they are part of a culture war to suppress views with which Gamergate supporters disagree. *The Verge*'s Chris Plante wrote that under the guise of ethics concerns, Gamergate supporters repeatedly attacked him for criticizing mainstream video games from the point of view of his social convictions. *Columbia Journalism Review* writer Chris Ip said "many criticisms of press coverage by people who identify with Gamergate ... have been debunked" and concluded that "at core, the movement is a classic culture war". Alyssa Rosenberg of *The Washington Post* said that some of the ostensible concerns about video game reviews are actually rooted in Gamergate supporters' belief that video games are appliances rather than art and that they should be reviewed based on feature checklists rather than traditional artistic criteria. Chris Suellentrop of *The New York Times* criticized resistance to innovative uses of the gaming medium, and the belief that increased coverage and praise of artistic games like *Gone Home* would negatively affect blockbuster games such as *Grand Theft Auto V*. After analyzing a sample of tweets related to Gamergate, *Newsweek* concluded that it was primarily about harassment rather than ethics, stating that the sample "suggests that ... contrary to its stated goal, Gamergate spends more time tweeting negatively at game developers than at game journalists". *Ars Technica*, analyzing logs from the 4chan users who initially pushed Gamergate into the spotlight, wrote that the goal behind the hashtag campaign was to "perpetuate misogynistic attacks by wrapping them in a debate about ethics in gaming journalism".

Gamergate has been criticized for focusing on women, especially female developers, while ignoring many large-scale journalistic ethics issues. Alex Goldman of NPR's *On the Media* criticized Gamergate for targeting female indie developers rather than AAA games publishers, and said claims of unethical behavior by Quinn and Sarkeesian were unfounded. In *Wired*, Laura Hudson found it telling that Gamergate supporters concentrated on impoverished independent creators and critics, and nearly exclusively women, rather than the large game companies whose work they enjoyed. *Vox* writer Todd VanDerWerff highlighted an essay written by game developer David Hill, who said that corruption, nepotism, and excessive commercialism existed in the gaming industry, but that Gamergate was not addressing those issues. Adi Robertson, of *The Verge*, commented on the

long-standing ethical issues gaming journalism has dealt with, but that most Gamergate supporters did not seem interested in "addressing problems that don't directly relate to feminist criticism
or the tiny indie games scene".

Social and Cultural Implications

Observers have generally described Gamergate as part of a long-running culture war against efforts to diversify the traditionally male video gaming community, particularly targeting outspoken
women. They cite Gamergate supporters' frequent harassment of female figures in the gaming
industry and its overt hostility toward people involved in social criticism and analysis of video
games. *Vox* said that Gamergate supporters were less interested in criticizing ethical issues than in
opposition to social criticism and analysis of video games and in harassment of prominent women.
Ars Technica quoted early members as saying that they had no interest in videogames and were
primarily interested in attacking Quinn. In *First Things*, Nathaniel Givens described Gamergate as
a reaction to the aggressive promotion of a progressive environment in video game culture, while
Carter Dotson blamed progressives themselves for the backlash, which he believed to be a reaction
to their negative mode of engagement.

Gamergate has been described as being driven by anti-feminist ideologies. Some supporters have
denied this, but acknowledge that there are misogynistic voices within Gamergate. Jon Stone, in
The Guardian, called it a "swelling of vicious right-wing sentiment" and compared it to the men's
rights movement. Commentators such as Jon Stone, Liana Kerzner and Ryan Cooper have said
that the controversy is being exploited by right-wing voices and by conservative pundits who had
little interest in gaming. Chrisella Herzog states that in addition to violent sexism, Gamergate has
virulent strains and violent sentiments of homophobia, transphobia, anti-Semitism, racism, and
neo-Nazism Some in the gamergate movement went on to be part of the alt-right.

Quinn said the campaign had "roped well-meaning people who cared about ethics and transparency into a pre-existing hate mob", and urged industry publishers and developers to condemn the
hashtag. She further asked those Gamergate supporters who had any earnest discussion about
ethics to move away from the "Gamergate" tag. In *Der Bund*, Jan Rothenberger wrote that a majority of gamers were distancing themselves from the hate campaigns, and that some supporters
were seeking a new banner because "Gamergate" is now indelibly associated with such campaigns.

Nathaniel Givens said that, regardless of their actions, Gamergate supporters were painted in a
negative light due to associating themselves with Gamergate, which was now a toxic term. Alex
Goldman from *On the Media* wrote that Gamergate's involvement in harassment had caused it to
lose mainstream credibility, and advised its supporters to adopt a self-identifier other than gamer
as a way of distancing themselves from their worst representatives.

Gamer Identity

The Gamergate situation is often considered to be a reaction to the changing cultural identity of
the "gamer". The notion of a gamer identity emerged in video game magazines catering to the
interests of an audience that was predominantly young and male. These publications were seen
by industry leaders as a means of promoting their products, and the close relationship between
gaming journalists and major gaming companies drew criticism. Over the years, the growing pop-

ularity of games expanded their audience to include many who did not fit the traditional gamer demographic. Games with artistic and cultural themes grew in popularity, and independent video game development made these games more common, while mobile and casual games expanded the scope of the industry beyond the traditional gamer identity.

A 2014 annual survey by the Entertainment Software Association showed that nearly as many women played video games (48%) as men, and this broader audience began to question some assumptions and tropes that had been common in games. Shira Chess and Adrienne Shaw wrote that concern over these changes is integral to Gamergate, especially a fear that sexualized games aimed primarily at young men might eventually be replaced by less sexualized games marketed to broader audiences.

Critics became interested in issues of gender representation and identity in video games. One prominent feminist critic of the representation of women in gaming is Anita Sarkeesian, whose *Tropes vs. Women in Video Games* project is devoted to female stereotypes in games. Her fund-raising campaign and videos were met with hostility and harassment by some gamers. Further incidents raised concerns about sexism in video gaming. Prior to August 2014, escalating harassment prompted the International Game Developers Association (IGDA) to provide support groups for harassed developers and to begin discussions with the FBI to help investigate online harassment of game developers. In an interview on Comedy Central's program *The Colbert Report*, Sarkeesian said she believes women are targeted because they are "challenging the status quo of gaming as a male-dominated space".

In late August 2014, shortly after the initial accusations against Grayson and harassment of Quinn, several gaming sites published op-eds on the controversy focused on the growing diversity of gaming and the mainstreaming of the medium, some of which included criticism of sexism within gamer culture. The timing and number of articles published on or around August 28 was seen by Gamergate supporters as evidence of a conspiracy to declare the death of the gamer identity, according to Chess and Shaw. *Slate's* David Auerbach and *The Sentinel's* David Elks criticized these articles for alienating their publications' audience by attacking the gamer identity. Writing for *Paste*, L. Rhodes said the antagonism in the Gamergate controversy was a result of the industry seeking to widen its customer demographic instead of focusing on core gamers, which Rhodes says "is precisely what videogames needed". Brendan Keogh of *Overland* stated that Gamergate "does not represent a marginalised, discriminated identity under attack so much as a hegemonic and normative mainstream being forced to redistribute some of its power".

Misogyny and Sexism

Gamergate has been associated with sexism, misogyny, and criticism of both feminism and those it labels as "social justice warriors". According to Sarah Kaplan of *The Washington Post*, "sexism in gaming is a long-documented, much-debated but seemingly intractable problem", and became the crux of the Gamergate controversy. Jaime Weinman writing in *Maclean's* said, "[w]hether it was supposed to be or not, GamerGate is largely about women". Discussing Gamergate on her ESPN blog, Jane McManus compared the misogyny that women in the gaming industry experience to that faced by the first women entering sporting communities. Canadian Prime Minister Justin Trudeau has described Gamergate as "something that we need to stand clearly against".

Sexism and misogyny had been identified as problems in the video game industry and online community prior to the events of Gamergate. Sarkeesian considered that the Internet has a "boys'-locker-room feel" to it, with male users trying to show off to each other which causes escalating cases of harassment in situations like Gamergate. In March 2014, game designer Cliff Bleszinski wrote a blog post commenting on the "latent racism, homophobia and misogyny" that existed within the online gaming community. In a November 2014 interview with *Develop*, Wu said the game industry "has been a boys' club for 30 years", and that the common portrayal of women as "sex symbols and damsels in distress" in video games has led to the players taking the same attitudes. Brendan Sinclair, writing for *GamesIndustry.biz*, stated that the events of the Gamergate controversy were "reprehensible and saddening" and "this industry has some profound issues in the way it treats women".

Many commentators have said that the harassment associated with Gamergate springs from this existing well of deep-seated misogyny, and that it was merely brought to the fore by the anonymity of the Internet. Regarding the false allegations against Quinn, Amanda Marcotte in an article for *The Daily Beast* accused the video game world of being "thick with misogynists who are aching to swarm" with hate on any "random woman held up for them to hate, no matter what the pretext". She related these attacks to harassment sent to a woman who criticized a *Teen Titans* cover and to a community manager of the *Mighty No. 9* game because she drew a feminine Mega Man, and virtual rapes committed against women's player avatars in *Grand Theft Auto V* and *DayZ*. In an interview with the BBC, Quinn stated that "Before [Gamergate] had a name, it was nothing but trying to get me to kill myself, trying to get people to hurt me, going after my family. ... There is no mention of ethics in journalism at all outside of making the same accusation everybody makes towards any successful woman; that clearly she got to where she is because she had sex with someone." Danielle Citron of the University of Maryland wrote that the intent of this type of harassment is to demean the victim, make them doubt their own integrity, and to redefine the victim's identity in order to "fundamentally distort who she is".

Targets of Gamergate supporters have overwhelmingly been women, even when men were responsible for the supposed wrongdoings. Writing in *The New Yorker*, Simon Parkin observed that Quinn was attacked while the male journalist who was falsely accused of reviewing her work favorably largely escaped, revealing the campaign as "a pretense to make further harassment of women in the industry permissible". In *The New York Times*, Chris Suellentrop said that a petition sought to have a female colleague fired for criticizing the portrayal of women in *Grand Theft Auto V*, while he and many other male critics raised similar concerns but did not face similar reprisals. Most commentators have described Gamergate as consisting largely of white males, though some supporters have said that the movement includes a notable percentage of women, minorities and LGBT members.

Writing in *The Week*, Ryan Cooper called the harassment campaign "an online form of terrorism" intended to reverse a trend in gaming culture toward increasing acceptance of women, and stated that social media platforms need to tighten their policies and protections against threats and abuse. Speaking on Iowa Public Radio, academic Cindy Tekobbe said the harassment campaign was intended to drive women from public spaces and intimidate them into silence.

Prof. Joanne St. Lewis of the University of Ottawa stated that Gamergate's harassment and threats should be considered acts of terrorism as the perpetrators seek to harm women and to prevent them from speaking back or defending others.

Law Enforcement

Katherine Clark, the U.S. Congresswoman from Massachusetts' 5th District, sought to expand the FBI's ability to take action against cyberharassment similar to that faced by Wu.

Though *Newsweek* reported that the FBI had a file regarding Gamergate, no arrests have been made nor charges filed, and parts of the FBI investigation into the threats had been closed in September 2015 due to a lack of leads. Former FBI supervisory special agent for cybercrimes, Tim Ryan, stated that cyberharassment cases are a low priority for authorities because it is difficult to track down the perpetrator and they have lower penalties compared to other crimes they are tasked to enforce. In June 2015, the US Supreme Court ruled in *Elonis v. United States* that harassing messages sent online are not necessarily true threats that would be prosecutable under criminal law and, according to *Pacific Standard*, this poses a further challenge in policing Gamergate-related harassment. However, the Court's decision also suggested that if threats made over social media were found to be true threats, they should be treated the same as threats made in other forms of communication.

Wu has expressed her frustration over how law enforcement agencies have responded to the threats that she and other women in the game industry have received. On public release of the FBI's case files on Gamergate, Wu said she was "livid", and that "Only a fraction of information we gave the FBI was looked into. They failed on all levels." The lack of legal enforcement contributes towards the harassers' ability to maintain these activities without any risk of punishment, according to Chrisella Herzog of *The Diplomatic Courier*; at worst, harassers would see their social media accounts suspended but are able to turn around to register new accounts to continue to engage.

U.S. Representative Katherine Clark from Massachusetts wrote a letter to the House Appropriations Committee asking it to call on the Justice Department to crack down on the harassment of women on the internet, saying the campaign of intimidation associated with Gamergate had highlighted the problem. Clark also hosted a Congressional briefing on March 15, 2015, along with the Congressional Victims' Rights Caucus to review issues of cyberstalking and online threats; during the briefing, Quinn spoke to her experience with Gamergate, which an executive director of the National Coalition

Against Domestic Violence described during the hearing as "an online hate group ... which was started by an ex-boyfriend to ruin [Quinn's] life". On May 27, 2015, the United States House of Representatives formally supported Clark's request for increased measures to combat online abuse against women, explicitly pressing for more investigations and prosecutions by the Department of Justice. On June 2, 2015, Rep. Clark introduced H.R. 2602, the "Prioritizing Online Threat Enforcement Act of 2015" to Congress. The bill would allocate more funding for the FBI to employ additional agents to enforce laws against cyberstalking, online criminal harassment, and threats.

Gaming Industry Response

The harassment of Quinn, Sarkeesian, Wu, and others led prominent industry professionals to condemn the Gamergate attacks for damaging the video gaming community and the public perception of the industry. *Vanity Fair*'s Laura Parker stated that the Gamergate situation led those outside of the video game industry to be "flooded with evidence of the video-game community as a poisonous and unwelcoming place", furthering any negative views they may have had of video games. Independent game developer Andreas Zecher wrote an open letter calling upon the community to take a stand against the attacks, attracting the signatures of more than two thousand professionals within the gaming industry. Many in the industry saw the signatures "as proof that the people sending vicious attacks at Quinn and Sarkeesian weren't representative of the video game industry overall". Writing for *The Guardian*, Jenn Frank described the tactics used in the harassment campaign and the climate of fear it generated through its attacks on women and their allies, concluding that this alienating and abusive environment would harm not only women but also the industry as a whole. Frank herself received significant harassment for writing this article, and announced an intention to quit games journalism as a result. Games designer Damion Schubert said that Gamergate was "an unprecedented catastrof**k [*sic*]", and that silencing critiques of games harms games developers by depriving them of feedback. Several video game developers, journalists, and gamers from across various gender, racial, and social backgrounds adopted new Twitter hashtags, such as #INeedDiverseGames, #StopGamergate2014 and #GamersAgainstGamergate, to show solidarity with the people targeted by the harassment and their opposition to the reactionary messages from Gamergate supporters.

The Electronic Frontier Foundation characterized Gamergate as a "magnet for harassment", and notes the possible financial risk for companies dealing with it on social media platforms. The Entertainment Software Association (ESA) issued a statement condemning the harassment, stating that "[t]here is no place in the video game community—or our society—for personal attacks and threats". ESA president Mike Gallagher, speaking at the June 2015 Electronic Entertainment Expo, clarified that the ESA did not become more involved as they felt it was an argument that was outside their industry and their involvement would have been disruptive, but praised the efforts to counter harassment that will benefit the industry in the future. At BlizzCon 2014, Blizzard Entertainment president and co-founder Mike Morhaime denounced recent harassment; blaming a "small group of people [who] have been doing really awful things" and "tarnishing our reputation" as gamers. He called on attendees to treat each other with kindness and demonstrate to the world that the community rejects harassment. His statements were widely interpreted as referring to Gamergate. CEOs of both the American and European branches of Sony Computer Entertainment, Shawn Layden and Jim Ryan respectively, said the harassment and bullying were absolutely horrific and that such inappropriate behavior would not be tolerated at Sony. The Swedish Games Industry issued a statement denouncing the harassment and sexism from Gamergate supporters.

In January 2015, Quinn and Alex Lifschitz created the Crash Override Network, a private group of experts who provide free support and counsel to those that have been harassed online, including as a result of Gamergate, and to work with law authorities and social media sites in response to such threats. Software developer Randi Harper founded a similar group, the Online Abuse Prevention Initiative, a non-profit organization that also seeks to provide aid to those harassed online.

Responses to Gamergate have encouraged the video game industry to review its treatment of women and minorities, and to make changes to support them. Intel, following its accidental involvement in Gamergate, pledged more than $300 million to help support a "Diversity in Technology" program with partners including Sarkeesian's Feminist Frequency organization and the IGDA, aimed at increasing the number of women and minorities in the industry. Intel CEO Brian Krzanich stated in announcing the program that "it's not good enough to say we value diversity, and then have our industry not fully represent". Electronic Arts (EA) COO Peter Moore said the controversy made EA pay more attention to diversity and inclusion, telling *Fortune* "[i]f there's been any benefit to Gamergate, ... I think it just makes us think twice at times". Speaking about Gamergate harassment to the *Seattle Times*, IGDA executive director Kate Edwards said, "Gaming culture has been pretty misogynistic for a long time now. There's ample evidence of that over and over again... What we're finally seeing is that it became so egregious that now companies are starting to wake up and say, "We need to stop this. This has got to change."

In response to a perceived conflict of interest between game developers and journalists, *Kotaku* and *Polygon* adopted policies of prohibiting or disclosing Patreon contributions to game developers respectively.

The Electronic Entertainment Expo 2015, which is used by the major video game publishers to reveal new titles in development, included markedly more female protagonists in these new games, as well as more visible presence by women at the event overall. Some commentators characterized this as a response to Gamergate and a rejection of the misogynistic harassment Gamergate had perpetrated.

The game *Batman: Arkham Knight* references Gamergate with hashtag, #CrusaderGate, which the Riddler used to unsuccessfully try to rally the Internet against Batman; bemoaning its failure, the Riddler describes those who use the hashtag as "idiotic and easily roused rabble".

Wider Reception

Anita Sarkeesian was named as one of *Time* magazine's list of the 30 most influential people on the Internet in March 2015, and later in the magazine's Top 100 Most Influential People of 2015, citing her role in highlighting sexism in the video game community in the wake of the Gamergate controversy. She was also highlighted as one of *Cosmopolitan*'s fifty "Internet's Most Fascinating" in a 2015 list due to her efforts to curb online harassment.

"Intimidation Game", an episode of the American crime drama television series *Law & Order: Special Victims Unit*, first broadcast on February 11, 2015, portrays a fictionalized version of the Gamergate controversy, including a character some observers said resembled Sarkeesian and whose story seemed based on those of women involved in the controversy.

In the run up to the 2015 Hugo Awards for science fiction writing, organized groups voting in bloc (the "Sad Puppies" and a Gamergate-affiliated splinter group led by Vox Day, calling themselves "Rabid Puppies") completely filled the nominations for five categories with white male authors who wrote action-oriented stories without social commentary. The *Los Angeles Times*, *Wired*, *The Atlantic*, and other reports described the campaign as a backlash against the increasing racial, ethnic, and gender diversity in science fiction, while members of the bloc gave a variety of reasons for their actions, saying that they sought to counteract what they saw as a focus on giving awards based on the race, ethnicity, or gender of the author or characters rather than quality, and bemoaning the increasing prominence of what they described as 'message' fiction with fewer traditional "zap gun" sci-fi trappings. Ultimately, vote tallies suggest around 19% of voters followed these groups' suggestions, though except *Guardians of the Galaxy*, none of the works nominated by these groups won an award. Convention members preferred "no award" to any nominee in the five categories filled by these groups.

The 2015 documentary film *GTFO* analyzed issues of sexism and harassment in video gaming. Already in production prior to the events of Gamergate the film's director, Shannon Sun-Higginson, addressed the controversy in a post-script to the film. Sun-Higginson stated Gamergate was "a terrible, terrible thing, but it's actually symptomatic of a wider, cultural, systemic problem". The Gamergate situation was covered as part of a larger topic of online harassment towards women in the June 21, 2015, episode of *Last Week Tonight with John Oliver*, while the impact of the Gamergate controversy on Brianna Wu was the subject of the March 16, 2016, episode of the *The Internet Ruined My Life*.

An on-line abuse panel (itself the subject of controversy) at the 2016 SXSW festival said that there was no technological solution to the problem of harassment given human nature; although policy changes have been made, the larger issue is more societal than platform-specific. Also, the sheer volume of the material to be vetted was described as being problematic by the corporations involved.

Referring to this discussion in a speech for Women's History Month, President of the United States Barack Obama said that "We know that women gamers face harassment and stalking and threats of violence from other players. When they speak out about their experiences, they're attacked on Twitter and other social media outlets, even threatened in their homes." Obama urged targets of harassment to speak out, praising the courage of those who had resisted online harassment. "And what's brought these issues to light is that there are a lot of women out there, especially young women, who are speaking out bravely about their experiences, even when they know they'll be attacked for it".

Gamergate has since become a notable cultural component of the so-called alt-right in the 2016 American presidential election.

Social Media

Twitter was criticized for its inability to respond quickly and prevent harassment over the service. Within the United States, Twitter and other social media sites are not liable for content posted by third-parties of their service under Section 230 of the Communications Decency Act (1996), and this removes any legal pressure for these sites to police malicious content such as harassment and threats. Brianna Wu, shortly after becoming a target of harassment, stated that Twitter facilitated harassment by the ease with which anyone could make a new account even after having an earlier account blocked, and challenged the service to improve its responsiveness to complaints. Robinson Meyer of *The Atlantic* said Gamergate is an "identity crisis" for Twitter, as, by not dealing with harassing users as Facebook has, the platform is failing to protect victims and losing readers. Early in the Gamergate controversy, software developer Randi Harper started the "Good Game Auto Blocker" or "ggautoblocker", an expanding list of known Twitter accounts that were tied to the Gamergate hashtag which could be automatically blocked, therefore reducing the degree of harassment received. In November 2014, Twitter announced a collaboration with the non-profit group "Women, Action & the Media" (WAM), in which users of Twitter can report harassment to a tool monitored by WAM members, who would forward affirmed issues to Twitter within 24 hours. The move, while in the wake of the Gamergate harassment, was due to general issues of the harassment of women on the Internet. The report, released in May 2015, determined that of 512 reported harassment instances by the tool during the month of November 2014, 12% of those were tied to the Gamergate controversy based on the ggautoblocker list, with most harassment occurring from single-instance accounts targeting a single person.

Online Shaming

In 2015, an American dentist and recreational big-game hunter received a flood
of negative messages and online reviews after killing Cecil the lion.

Online shaming is a form of Internet vigilantism in which targets are publicly humiliated using technology like social and new media. Proponents of shaming see it as a form of online participation that allows hacktivists and cyber-dissidents to right injustices. Critics see it as a tool that encourages online mobs to destroy the reputation and careers of people or organizations who made perceived slights.

Online shaming frequently involves the publication of private information on the Internet (called doxing), which can frequently lead to hate messages and death threats being used to intimidate that person. The ethics of public humiliation has been a source of debate over privacy and ethics.

Public Shaming

The social networking tools of the Internet have been used as a tool to easily and widely publicize instances of perceived anti-social behavior.

Jon Ronson has compared modern online shaming to medieval pillories.

David Furlow, chairman of the Media, Privacy and Defamation Committee of the American Bar Association, has identified the potential privacy concerns raised by websites facilitating the distribution of information that is not part of the public record (documents filed with a government agency), and has said that such websites "just [give] a forum to people whose statements may not reflect truth."

After some controversial incidents of public shaming, the popular link-sharing and discussion website Reddit introduced a strict rule against the publication of non-public personally-identifying information via the site (colloquially known on Reddit and elsewhere as "doxing"). Those who break the rule are subject to a site-wide ban, and their posts and even entire communities may be removed for breaking the rule.

In 2015, online shaming was the subject of the book *So You've Been Publicly Shamed* by Jon Ronson. Ronson documented how people had become agoraphobic due to humiliation online for misinterpreted jokes, and says people should think twice before gleefully condemning someone for doing almost nothing wrong.

Types

Doxing

Doxing involves researching and broadcasting personally identifiable information about an individual, often with the intention of harming that person. This can often lead to extortion, coercion, harassment and other forms of abuse. On February 1, 2017, Reddit, a social news website, has banned two alt-right communities, r/altright and r/alternativeright for doxing and violating Reddit community guidelines.

Revenge Porn

Nonconsensual pornography is a form of sexually explicit recording publicized on the Internet in order to humiliate a person, frequently distributed by computer hackers or ex-partners (called revenge porn). Images and video of sexual acts are often combined with doxing of a person's private details, such as their home addresses and workplaces. Victims' lives can be ruined as a result, the victims exposed to cyber-stalking and physical attack as well as facing difficulties in their workplace should their images become known as a result of routine checks by employers. Some have lost their jobs, while others have been unable to find work at all.

Negative Reviews

Products frequently attract negative reviews on Goodreads, Amazon and other online commerce websites.

In many cases, users of Yelp write reviews in order to lash out at corporate interests or businesses they dislike. During the Chick-fil-A same-sex marriage controversy, activists encouraged a consumer boycott of Chick-fil-A and left negative reviews of the site's locations on restaurant rating websites after the founder declared that corporate profits would be donated to political causes opposing same-sex marriage in the United States. In 2015 an Indiana pizzeria was swarmed with negative Yelp reviews after the owner said it wouldn't cater gay weddings. Similar reactions have frequently followed bakers refusing to make cakes for gay weddings. After Cecil the lion was shot by an American recreational big-game hunter, his business was flooded with negative reviews.

Government Shaming

Various governments have used "name and shame" policies to punish tax evasion, environmental violations and minor crimes like littering.

Notable Examples

Ashley Madison Data Breach

Public humiliation of Ashley Madison users has been argued to be a form of "flogging in the virtual town square".

In July 2015, a group hacked the user data of Ashley Madison, a commercial dating website marketed as helping people have extramarital affairs. In August 2015, over 30 million user account details, including names and email addresses were released publicly.

A variety of security researchers and Internet privacy activists debated the ethics of the release.

Clinical psychologists argued that dealing with an affair in a particularly public way increases the hurt for spouses and children. Carolyn Gregoire argued "[s]ocial media has created an aggressive culture of public shaming in which individuals take it upon themselves to inflict psychological damage" and more often than not, "the punishment goes beyond the scope of the crime." Charles J. Orlando, who had joined the site to conduct research concerning women who cheat, said he felt users of the site were anxious the release of sexually explicit messages would humiliate their spouses and children. He wrote it is alarming "the mob that is the Internet is more than willing to serve as judge, jury, and executioner" and members of the site "don't deserve a flogging in the virtual town square with millions of onlookers."

Political

Justine Sacco Incident

In December 2013, Justine Sacco, a woman with 170 Twitter followers, tweeted acerbic jokes during a plane trip from New York to Cape Town, such as "Weird German dude get some deodorant" and, in Heathrow; "Going to Africa. Hope I don't get AIDS. Just Kidding. I'm white!" Sacco, a South African herself, intended the tweet to mock American ignorance of South Africa, and in a later interview expressed that her intention was to "mimic—and mock what an actual racist, ignorant person would say." Sacco slept during her 11-hour plane trip, and woke up to find out that she had lost her job and was the number one Twitter topic worldwide, with celebrities and new media bloggers all over the globe denouncing her and encouraging all their followers to do the same. Sacco's employer, New York internet firm IAC, declared that she had lost her job as Director of Corporate Communications. People began tweeting "Has Justine landed yet?", expressing schadenfreude at the loss of her career. Sam Biddle, the Gawker Media blogger who promoted the #HasJustineLandedYet hashtag, later apologised for his role, admitting that he did so for Internet traffic to his blog, and noting that "it's easy and thrilling to hate a stranger online."

According to Ronson, the public does not understand that a vigilante campaign of public shaming, undertaken with the ostensible intention of defending the underdog, may create a mob mentality capable of destroying the lives and careers of the public figures singled out for shaming. Ronson argued that in the early days of Twitter, people used the platform to share intimate details of their lives, and not as a vehicle of shaming. Brooke Gladstone argued that the Sacco affair may deter people from expressing themselves online due to a fear of being misinterpreted. Kelly McBride argues that journalists play a key role in expanding the shame and humiliation of targets of the campaigns by relaying claims to a larger audience, while justifying their actions as simply documenting an event in an impartial manner. She writes: "Because of the mob mentality that accompanies public shaming events, often there is very little information about the target, sometimes only a single tweet. Yet there is a presumption of guilt and swift move toward justice, with no process for ascertaining facts." McBride further notes "If newspapers ran front-page photos of adulterers in the Middle East being stripped naked and whipped in order to further their shame, we would criticize them as part of a backward system of justice." Ben Adler compared the Sacco incident to a number of Twitter hoaxes, and argued that the media needs to be more careful to fact-check articles and evaluate context.

Adria Richards Incident

In March 2013, at a PyCon technology conference, Adria Richards took offense at a private discussion between two male attendees seated nearby using the word "dongle" in what she perceived as a sexual joke. Richards photographed the attendees with their faces visible, then published the photograph on Twitter including a shaming statement in her tweet. The following day, the employer of one of the photographed individuals, a software developer, terminated his employment because of the joke.

In response to Richards' public shaming of the developers, Internet users who were uninvolved launched a DDoS Attack on her employer, SendGrid, and according to an article by Jon Ronson in *The New York Times Magazine* "told the employer the attacks would stop if Richards was fired".

SendGrid subsequently terminated her employment later the same day citing Richards' dividing the very community she was hired to unite, and the male anatomy joke she had posted a few days earlier on the employer website. Following the incident, PyCon updated its attendee rules stating, "Public shaming can be counter-productive to building a strong community. PyCon does not condone nor participate in such actions out of respect."

In a 2014 interview, Richards – still unemployed – speculated whether the developer was responsible for instigating the Internet backlash against her. The developer, who was offered a new job "right away", said he had not engaged with those who sent him messages of support, and had posted a short statement on Hacker News the same night after he was fired saying in part that Richards had "every right to report me to staff, and I defend her position".

Australian Racist Bus Passengers Incident

In November 2012, an Australian man filmed several passengers on a Melbourne bus verbally abusing and threatening a woman who had begun singing a song in French. A video alerting viewers of their racist and sexist comments was uploaded to YouTube and quickly attracted national and international media attention. The two male perpetrators who were most prominent in the video were later jailed, with Magistrate Jennifer Goldsbrough describing their threats as "offensive to the entire population".

Conduct on Public Transportation

A woman taking up empty seats on the London Underground

Starting as a turn of phrase by feminists on Tumblr, manspreading is a critique of men who take up more than one seat with their legs widely spread. In New York, actor Tom Hanks was photographed on the subway, taking up two seats, and then criticized for it. He responded on a talk show, "Hey Internet, you idiot! The train was half empty! It was scattered – there was plenty of room!" The controversy surrounding manspreading have been described by libertarian feminist Cathy Young as "pseudo feminism – preoccupied with male misbehavior, no matter how trivial". The practice of posting pictures of manspreading taken on subways, buses, and other modes of transportation online has been described as a form public shaming. The criticism and campaigns against manspreading have been counter-criticized for not addressing similar behavior by women, such as taking up adjacent seats with bags, or "she-bagging". Twitter campaigns with the hashtag #manspreading have also been accompanied by hashtags like #she-bagging.

Hypatia Transracialism Controversy

The feminist philosophy journal *Hypatia* became involved in a dispute in April 2017 that led to the online shaming of one of their authors. The journal published an article by Rebecca Tuvel, an assistant professor of philosophy, comparing the situation of Caitlin Jenner, a trans woman, to that of Rachel Dolezal, a white woman who identifies as black. The article was criticized on Facebook and Twitter as a source of "epistemic violence", and the author became the subject of personal attacks.

Academics associated with *Hypatia* joined in the criticism. A member of the journal's editorial board, Alexis Shotwell, became the point of contact for an open letter demanding that the article be retracted, and the journal's board of associate editors issued an apology, ostensibly on behalf of the journal, saying the article should never have been published. The editor-in-chief, Sally Scholz, later stood by the author, saying that the associate editors had acted independently. Rogers Brubaker described the episode in the *New York Times* as an example of "internet shaming". Jesse Singal of *New York* magazine referred to it as a "massive internet witch-hunt", while Glen Greenwald called it a "hideous smear campaign".

Animal Abuse

YouTube Cat Abuse Incident

In February 2009, an incident occurred involving the posting on YouTube of a video clip in which a domestic cat, named Dusty, was beaten and tortured by a 14-year-old boy calling himself "Timmy". After about 30,000 viewings, this clip and the account were removed by YouTube as a violation of their terms of service. Members of the 4chan imageboard investigated the incident, and by extrapolating from the poster's YouTube user name and the background in the video, they identified the abuser. As a result of these complaints, the Comanche County Sheriff's Department investigated the incident, and two suspects were arrested. Dusty survived the abuse, and was placed in the care of a local veterinarian. Both the assailant and the cameraman were charged with animal cruelty; as both were juveniles, possible punishments included "psychological counseling, court monitoring until they turn 18, community service to provide restitution for treatment of animals, and/or placement in court custody."

The Kitten Killer of Hangzhou

In 2006, Wang-Jue, a Chinese nurse appearing in an Internet crush video stomping a helpless kitten with her stilettos, gave herself up to authorities after bloggers and some print media started a campaign to trace back the recording. In the beginning, she was labeled as the kitten killer of Hangzhou, because it was believed she was from there; but some internauts recognized an island in northern Heilongjiang province. Upon discovery of her identity, Wang Jue received death threats from many angry animal lovers.

Wang posted an apology on the Luobei city government official website. She said she was recently divorced and did not know what to do with her life. The cameraman, a provincial TV employee, and she lost their jobs when internauts discovered their identities.

Cat Dumped in Wheelie Bin

In August 2010, a passer-by in Coventry, England, later identified as Mary Bale by 4chan's members, was caught on a private security camera stroking a cat, named Lola, then looking around and dumping her in a wheelie bin, where she was found by her owners 15 hours later. The owners posted the video on the Internet in a bid to identify the woman, who was later interviewed by the RSPCA about her conduct. Outrage was sparked among animal lovers, and a Facebook group called "Death to Mary Bale" was created, and later removed. Police said they were speaking to the 45-year-old about her personal safety.

The woman, who at first downplayed her actions ("I thought it would be funny", "it's just a cat" and "didn't see what all the buzz was about") eventually apologised "profusely for the upset and distress".

Bale was convicted under the Animal Welfare Act of 2006 with causing unnecessary suffering to a cat. An additional charge of failing to provide the cat with a suitable environment was dropped. She was fined £250 and ordered to pay costs, totaling £1,436.04.

Rabbit Gate

In 2010, a case was publicized involving a young female, from Sichuan under the alias name Huang siu siu torturing and crushing rabbits. The group that financially sponsor the making of these videos was later revealed to be called "Crushfetish" who pay young girls to crush fish, insects, rabbits and other small animals. The girl was paid 100 yuan for each attempt, and she has been participating since 2007. Police said the group makes videos to sell overseas, and the company has allegedly made 279 animal abuse videos with a subscription fee. Because of the concurrent hosting of the 2010 Asian Games, the animal videos were only limited to hosting just a few hours a day on some websites.

Operation Dogfight

On February 9, 2011, a man supposedly located in Spain posted a video of himself torturing a Pomeranian dog. Within two days, Anonymous picked up on the incident, and began searching for the man. After attention was brought locally by Spanish Anonymous members, a news website carried an article asking local people to remain calm, and confirming that the IP address had identified Badajoz as the location of the blogger who uploaded the video.

General

The Goblin Valley Rock-toppling Incident

In October 2013, a delicately balanced hoodoo in Goblin Valley State Park was intentionally knocked over by three Boy Scout leaders who had been camping in the area. The men claimed that the hoodoo appeared ready to fall, and that they knocked it over to prevent park visitors from being hurt. They recorded the illegal act and posted it to Facebook, but subsequently admitted that they should have told a park ranger. The two scouts leaders were targeted by death threats and Internet vigilantes encouraged the prosecution to charge the two with felony charges.

China's Watch Brother Incident

On August 26, 2012, Yang Dacai, chief of the Shanxi provincial work safety administration, was caught grinning widely amid the wreckage of a long-distance bus that killed 36 passengers when it collided with a tanker loaded with highly flammable methanol on a Chinese highway in Shanxi Province. Pictures of the accident began to circulate on Sina Weibo, the most popular micro-blogging site in China which led to a meme dubbing him as the "Smiling Brother". Searches on the Human flesh search engine followed leading to pictures surfacing on Weibo, showing Yang wearing luxury watches such as a $10,000 Rolex initiating another meme calling him "Watch Brother". On Sept. 21, Yang was relieved of his position and accused of serious discipline violations. He was subsequently jailed for 14 years after being found guilty of taking bribes.

Dog Poop Girl

In 2005 in South Korea, bloggers targeted a woman who refused to clean up when her dog defecated on the floor of a Seoul subway car, labeling her "Dog Poop Girl" . Another commuter had taken a photograph of the woman and her dog, and posted it on a popular South Korean website. Within days, she had been identified by Internet vigilantes, and much of her personal information was leaked onto the Internet in an attempt to punish her for the offense. The story received mainstream attention when it was widely reported in South Korean media. The public humiliation led the woman to drop out of her university, according to reports.

The reaction by the South Korean public to the incident prompted several newspapers in South Korea to run editorials voicing concern over Internet vigilantism. One paper quoted Daniel Solove as saying that the woman was the victim of a "cyber-posse, tracking down norm violators and branding them with digital Scarlet Letters." Another called it an "Internet witch-hunt," and went on to say that "the Internet is turning the whole society into a kangaroo court."

Evan Guttman and the Stolen Sidekick

Other notable instances also include the case of Evan Guttman and his friend's stolen Sidekick II smartphone, and the case of Jesse McPherson and his stolen Xbox 360, PowerBook, and TV.

Rocky Mountain Chocolate Factory

In 2008, a 5-year-old girl asked to use the bathroom at the Rocky Mountain Chocolate Factory at Bella Terra/Huntington Beach. "I [The mother of the girl] explained she had diarrhea and couldn't hold it and told [the store owners] she was about to go on the floor. They refused again and never offered me any alternatives. I begged them to have a heart and that she was 5 but by that time she had lost it all over herself and me." The story then spread to sites like digg.com where contact information for the owner of the store was released in message boards.

Zhang Ya & Sichuan Earthquake

In 2008, a girl called Zhang Ya from Liaoning province, Northeast China, posted a 4-minute video of herself complaining about the amount of attention the Sichuan earthquake victims were receiving on television. An intense response from Internet vigilantes resulted in the girl's personal details (even including her blood type) being made available online, as well as dozens of abusive video responses on Chinese websites and blogs. The girl was taken into police custody for three days as protection from vigilante death threats.

Stephen Fowler and *Wife Swap*

Stephen Fowler, a British expatriate and venture capitalist businessman, gained notoriety after his performance on ABC's *Wife Swap* (originally aired Friday January 30, 2009) when his wife exchanged positions in his family with a woman from Missouri for a two-week period. In response to her rule changes (standard procedure for the second week in the show) he insulted his guest and, in doing so, groups including the lower classes, soldiers, and the overweight. Several websites were made in protest against his behaviour. After the show, and after watching the *Wife Swap* video, his wife, a professional life coach, reported that she had encouraged him to attend professional behaviour counselling. Businesses with only tangential connection to Fowler publicly disclaimed any association with him due to the negative publicity. He resigned positions on the boards of two environmental charities to avoid attracting negative press.

Cyclist Abuser Incident

In 2008, video of Patrick Pogan, a rookie police officer, body-slamming Christopher Long, a cyclist, surfaced on the Internet. The altercation happened when members of Critical Mass conducted a bicycling advocacy event at Times Square. The officer claimed the cyclist had veered into him, and so the biker was charged with assault, disorderly conduct and resisting arrest.

The charges against the cyclist were later dropped and Pogan was convicted of lying about the confrontation with the cyclist.

Vigilante Group Targets Mother

In 2009, a Facebook group was started, accusing a single mother for the death of a 13-month-old child in her foster care. It was the mother's then common-law husband who pleaded guilty to manslaughter and the mother was not formally accused of any wrongdoing. However, the members of the group, such as the boy's biological mother, accuse her of knowing what was going on and doing nothing to stop it.

Cooks Source Incident

The food magazine *Cooks Source* printed an article by Monica Gaudio without her permission in their October 2010 issue. Learning of the copyright violation, Gaudio emailed Judith Griggs, managing editor of *Cooks Source Magazine*, requesting that the magazine both apologize and also donate $130 to the Columbia School of Journalism as payment for using her work. Instead she received a very unapologetic letter stating that she (Griggs) herself should be thanked for making the piece better and that Gaudio should be glad that she didn't give someone else credit for writing the article. During the ensuing public outcry, online vigilantes took it upon themselves to avenge Gaudio. The *Cooks Source* Facebook page was flooded with thousands of contemptuous comments, forcing the magazine's staff to create new pages in an attempt to escape the protest and accuse 'hackers' of taking control of the original page. The magazine's website was stripped of all content by the staff and shut down a week later.

Bullied Bus Monitor Karen Klein

An elderly bus monitor, Karen Klein, was taunted, picked on, and threatened by four seventh-graders. The act was caught on video and uploaded to the Internet which in turn caused an act of kindness from complete strangers. $703,833 was raised for Klein in donations from concerned strangers who were outraged after viewing a video that captured her torment.

Doxing

Doxing (from *dox*, abbreviation of *documents*), or doxxing, is the Internet-based practice of researching and broadcasting private or identifiable information (especially personally identifiable information) about an individual or organization.

The methods employed to acquire this information include searching publicly available databases and social media websites (like Facebook), hacking, and social engineering. It is closely related to internet vigilantism and hacktivism.

Doxing may be carried out for various reasons, including to aid law enforcement, business analysis, extortion, coercion, harassment, online shaming, and vigilante justice.

"Doxing" is a neologism that has evolved over its brief history. It comes from a spelling alteration of the abbreviation "docs" (for "documents") and refers to "compiling and releasing a dossier of personal information on someone". Essentially, doxing is openly revealing and publicizing records of an individual, which were previously private or difficult to obtain.

The term dox derives from the slang "dropping dox", which, according to *Wired* writer Mat Honan, was "an old-school revenge tactic that emerged from hacker culture in 1990s". Hackers operating outside the law in that era used the breach of an opponent's anonymity as a means to expose opponents to harassment or legal repercussions.

As such, doxing often comes with a negative connotation, because it can be a vehicle for revenge via the violation of privacy.

History

Doxware is a cryptovirology attack invented by Adam Young and further developed with Moti Yung that carries out doxing extortion via malware. It was first presented at West Point in 2003. The attack is rooted in game theory and was originally dubbed "non-zero sum games and survivable malware". The attack is summarized in the book Malicious Cryptography as follows, "The attack differs from the extortion attack in the following way. In the extortion attack, the victim is denied access to its own valuable information and has to pay to get it back, where in the attack that is presented here the victim retains access to the information but its disclosure is at the discretion of the computer virus". Doxware is the converse of ransomware. In a ransomware attack (originally called cryptoviral extortion) the malware encrypts the victim's data and demands payment to provide the needed decryption key. In the doxware cryptovirology attack, the attacker or malware steals the victim's data and threatens to publish it unless a fee is paid.

Common Techniques

Hackers, police officers and amateur detectives alike can harvest the information from the internet about individuals. There is no particular structure in place for doxing, meaning a hacker may seek out any kind of information related to the target.

A basic Web search can yield results. Social media platforms like Facebook, Twitter, MySpace, and Linkedin offer a wealth of private information, because many users have high levels of self-disclosure (i.e. sharing their photos, place of employment, phone number, email address), but low levels of security. It is also possible to derive a person's name and home address from a cell-phone number, through such services as reverse phone lookup. Social engineering has been used to extract information from government sources or phone companies.

In addition to these, a hacker may use other methods to harvest information. These include information search by domain name and location searching based on an individual's IP address.

Once people have been exposed through doxing, they may be targeted for harassment through methods such as harassment in person, fake signups for mail and pizza deliveries, or through swatting (dispatching armed police to their house through spoofed tips).

It is important to note that a hacker may obtain an individual's dox without making the information public. A hacker may harvest a victim's information in order to break into their internet accounts, or to take over their social media accounts.

The victim may also be shown their details as proof that they have been doxed in order to intimidate them. Doxing is therefore a standard tactic of online harassment, and has been used by people associated with 4chan, the Gamergate controversy and anti-vaccine activists.

The ethics of doxing by journalists, on matters that they assert are issues of public interest, is an area of much controversy. Many authors have argued that doxing in journalism blurs the line between revealing information in the interest of the public and releasing information about an individual's private life against their wishes.

Notable Examples

Boston Marathon

Following the 2013 Boston Marathon bombing, vigilantes on Reddit wrongly identified a number of people as suspects. Notable among misidentified bombing suspects was Sunil Tripathi, a student reported missing before the bombings took place. A body reported to be Tripathi's was found in Rhode Island's Providence River on April 25, 2013, as reported by the Rhode Island Health Department. The cause of death was not immediately known, but authorities said they did not suspect foul play. The family later confirmed Tripathi's death was a result of suicide. Reddit general manager Martin later issued an apology for this behavior, criticizing the "online witch hunts and dangerous speculation" that took place on the website.

Hit Lists of Abortion Providers

In the 1990s anti-abortion terrorists secured abortion providers' personal information, such as their home addresses, phone numbers, and photographs, and posted them as a hit list, ruled by the courts to be in immediate incitement to violence. The site's legend explained: "Black font (working); Greyed-out Name (wounded); Strikethrough (fatality)." The website included blood-dripping graphics, celebrated providers' deaths and incited others to kill or injure the remaining providers on the list. Between 1993 and 2016, eight abortion providers were killed by anti-abortion terrorists.

Anonymous

The term "dox" entered mainstream public awareness through media attention attracted by Anonymous, the Internet-based group of hacktivists and pranksters who make frequent use of doxing, as well as related groups like AntiSec and LulzSec. *The Washington Post* has described the consequences for innocent people incorrectly accused of wrongdoing and doxed as "nightmarish".

In December 2011, Anonymous exposed detailed information of 7,000 members of law enforcement in response to investigations into hacking activities.

In November 2014, Anonymous began releasing the identities of members of the Ku Klux Klan. This was in relation to local Klan members in Ferguson, Missouri, making threats to shoot anyone who provoked them while protesting the shooting of Michael Brown. Anonymous also hijacked the group's Twitter page, and this resulted in veiled threats of violence against members of Anonymous. In November 2015, a major release of information about the KKK was planned. Discredited information was released prematurely and Anonymous denied involvement. On November 5, 2015 (Guy Fawkes Night) Anonymous released an official list of supposed but currently unverified KKK members and sympathizers.

Human Flesh Search Engine

The Chinese Internet phenomenon of the "Human flesh search engine" shares much in common with doxing. Specifically, it refers to distributed, sometimes deliberately crowdsourced searches for similar kinds of information through use of digital media.

Journalists

Journalists with *The Journal News* of Westchester County, New York, were accused of doxing gun owners in the region in a story the paper published in December 2012.

Newsweek came under fire when writer Leah McGrath Goodman claimed to have revealed the identity of the anonymous creator of Bitcoin, Satoshi Nakamoto. Though the source of her sleuthing was primarily the public record, she was heavily criticized for her doxing by users on Reddit.

The Satoshi Nakamoto case brought doxing to greater attention, particularly on platforms such as Twitter, where users questioned the ethics of doxing in journalism. Many Twitter users condemned doxing in journalism, wherein they argued that the practice was seemingly acceptable for professional journalists but wrong for anyone else. Other users discussed the effect the popularization that the concept of doxing could have on journalism in public interest, raising questions over journalism concerning public and private figures. Many users have argued that doxing in journalism blurs the line between revealing information in the interest of the public and releasing information about an individual's private life against their wishes.

Curt Schilling

In March 2015, former Major League Baseball (MLB) pitcher Curt Schilling used doxing to identify several people responsible for "Twitter troll" posts with obscene, sexually explicit comments about his teenaged daughter. One person was suspended from his community college, and another lost a part-time job with the New York Yankees.

Alondra Cano

In December 2015, Minneapolis city councilwoman Alondra Cano used her Twitter account to publish private cellphone numbers and e-mail addresses of critics who wrote about her involvement in a Black Lives Matter rally.

Lou Dobbs

In 2016, Fox Business news anchor Lou Dobbs revealed the address and phone number of Jessica Leeds, one of the women who accused American presidential candidate Donald Trump of inappropriate sexual advances; Dobbs later apologized.

Erdogan Emails

In July 2016, Wikileaks released 300,000 e-mails called the Erdogan emails, initially thought to be damaging to Turkish President Recep Tayyip Erdogan. Included in the leak was Michael Best, who uploaded Turkish citizens' personal information databases that WikiLeaks promoted, who came forward to say that doing so was a mistake after the site where he uploaded the information took it down. The files were removed due to privacy concerns, as they included spreadsheets of private, sensitive information of what appears to be every female voter in 79 out of 81 provinces in Turkey, including their home addresses and other private information, sometimes including their cellphone numbers.

Michael Hirsh

In November 2016, Politico editor Michael Hirsh resigned after publishing the home address of white nationalist Richard B. Spencer on Facebook.

Cyber Defamation Law

Cyber defamation is not a specific criminal offense, misdemeanor or tort, but rather defamation or slander conducted via digital media, usually through the Internet.

Penalties for "cyber defamation" vary from country to country, but the fundamental rights covered in the UN Declaration of Human Rights and European Union Fundamental Human Rights.

Stopping or addressing defamation can be difficult. If the person has no serious grudge, then a cease and desist letter may stop the behavior and get the statements removed from the Internet. On the other hand, if the person is acting out of spite, it may be necessary to file a report with the police depending on local law.

South Korea

The cyber defamation law that the Korean government pursues allows police to crack down on hateful comments without any reports from victims. The only country where such cyber defamation law is being implemented is China. South Korea is the first democratic country in the process of introducing the law.

The Korea Communications Commission (KCC), South Korea's telecommunications and broadcasting regulator, has been considering revising the current Telecommunications Law and put more regulations and deeper scrutiny on major Internet portals.

Controversies

There have been talks about introducing the stricter laws in cyberspace. A famous celebrity's suicide in South Korea, triggered the controversies once again as to whether such law is necessary. The law supported by the governing Grand National Party (GNP), if implemented, will allow police to investigate the cyber defamation cases without any complaints of the victims. The opposition Democratic Party has been against the introduction of such law.

Advocate Views

- The current laws have failed to prevent the number of the victims from increasing at an escalating rate.

- Freedom of speech comes with responsibility.

- Because information and rumors can travel in a matter of seconds across the Internet, cyber-bullying and cyber defamation could take a significant toll on each victim without such strict regulations by authorities.

Opposing Views

- There are already ways to regulate the cyberspace with the current laws.

- It is potentially possible for the law to be exploited by authorities in an attempt to crack down on people who express opposite views.

- Such law might cause a harmful effect on freedom of speech.

- "Defamation" is too ambiguous to be defined by a third party, other than the victims.

Survey

A Research & Research survey of 800 Korean people conducted on Jan. 14, 2009 showed that 60% supported the GNP-led bill dealing with cyber defamation, and 32.1% opposed it.

Celebrities' Suicide

Some Korean celebrities have suffered from severe depression, caused in part by malicious online comments, before committing suicide.

- Lee Eun-ju

- Jung Da Bin

- U;Nee

- Choi Jin-sil

References

- Diaz, Fernando L. (2016). "Trolling & the First Amendment: Protecting Internet Speech in the Era of Cyberbullies & Internet Defamation". University of Illinois Journal of Law, Technology & Policy: 135–160

- Hu, Winnie (1 October 2010). "Legal Debate Swirls Over Charges in a Student's Suicide". New York Times. Nate Schweber. Retrieved 1 December 2016

- Görzig, Anke; Lara A. Frumkin (2013). "Cyberbullying experiences on-the-go: When social media can become distressing". Cyberpsychology: Journal of Psychosocial Research on Cyberspace

- Bocij, Paul (2004). Cyberstalking: Harassment in the Internet Age and how to Protect Your Family. Greenwood Publishing Group. pp. 12–13. ISBN 978-0-275-98118-1

- Topping, Alexandra. "Cyberbullying on social networks spawning form of self-harm". Guardian News and Media Limited. Retrieved 6 August 2013

- Fung, Annis L. C. "The Phenomenon Of Cyberbullying: Its Aetiology And Intervention." Journal Of Youth Studies (10297847) 13.2 (2010): 31–42. Academic Search Complete. Web. 28 Oct. 2016

- "What Parents Need to Know About Cyberbullying". ABC News Primetime. ABC News Internet Ventures. 2006-09-12. Retrieved 2015-02-03

- Callaghan, Mary; Kelly, Colette; Molcho, Michal (2014). "360 Link". International Journal of Public Health. 60 (2): 199. doi:10.1007/s00038-014-0638-7&rft.externaldbid=n/a&rft.externaldocid=601082949&paramdict=en-us

- Hertz, M. F.; David-Ferdon, C. (2008). Electronic Media and Youth Violence: A CDC Issue Brief for Educators and Caregivers (PDF). Atlanta (GA): Centers for Disease Control. p. 9. Retrieved 2015-02-03

- Hinduja, S. & Patchin, J. W. (2007). Offline Consequences of Online Victimization: School Violence and Delinquency. Journal of School Violence, 6(3), 89–112

- Kowalski, Robin M.; Limber, Susan P. (December 2007). "Electronic bullying among middle school students". Journal of Adolescent Health. 41 (6 Suppl 1): S22–S30. doi:10.1016/j.jadohealth.2007.08.017

- Opsahl, Kevin (December 13, 2014). "USU awaits FBI report on Sarkeesian death threat". The Herald Journal. Logan, Utah. Archived from the original on December 22, 2014. Retrieved January 5, 2014

- Ip, Chris (October 23, 2014). "How do we know what we know about #Gamergate?". Columbia Journalism Review. Archived from the original on October 24, 2014. Retrieved October 24, 2014

- Citron, Danielle (2014). Hate Crimes in Cyberspace. Cambridge, Mass., USA & London, UK: Harvard University Press. ISBN 978-0-674-36829-3

- Culver, Kathleen Bartzen (January 3, 2015). "A Magical Putter and the Year in Media Ethics". Center for Journalism Ethics. University of Wisconsin–Madison. Archived from the original on January 14, 2015

- Auerbach, David (September 9, 2014). "Gaming Journalism Is Over". Slate. Archived from the original on September 13, 2014. Retrieved September 14, 2014

- Chan, Terry (8 October 1992). "Post the FAQ". Newsgroup: alt.folklore.urban. Usenet: 26717@dog.ee.lbl.gov. Retrieved 21 July 2016. Maybe after I post it, we could go trolling some more and see what happens

- Fitzgerald, Brian (November 7, 2014). "New Online Tool Lets Twitter Users Report Harassment". The Wall Street Journal. Archived from the original on November 7, 2014. Retrieved November 7, 2014

4

Digital Forensic Science: An Overview

Digital forensics is the method of interpreting electronic data. It is mainly used in courts to approve or disapprove a hypothesis. There are several sub-branches of the subject like network forensics, mobile device forensics, computer forensics and mobile device forensics. The topics discussed in the chapter are of great importance to broaden the existing knowledge on cybercrime and digital forensics.

Digital Forensics

Aerial photo of FLETC, where US digital forensics standards were developed in the 1980s and '90s

Digital forensics (sometimes known as digital forensic science) is a branch of forensic science encompassing the recovery and investigation of material found in digital devices, often in relation to computer crime. The term digital forensics was originally used as a synonym for computer forensics but has expanded to cover investigation of all devices capable of storing digital data. With roots in the personal computing revolution of the late 1970s and early 1980s, the discipline evolved in a haphazard manner during the 1990s, and it was not until the early 21st century that national policies emerged.

Digital forensics investigations have a variety of applications. The most common is to support or refute a hypothesis before criminal or civil (as part of the electronic discovery process) courts. Forensics may also feature in the private sector; such as during internal corporate investigations or intrusion investigation (a specialist probe into the nature and extent of an unauthorized network intrusion).

The technical aspect of an investigation is divided into several sub-branches, relating to the type of digital devices involved; computer forensics, network forensics, forensic data analysis and mobile device forensics. The typical forensic process encompasses the seizure, forensic imaging (acquisition) and analysis of digital media and the production of a report into collected evidence.

As well as identifying direct evidence of a crime, digital forensics can be used to attribute evidence to specific suspects, confirm alibis or statements, determine intent, identify sources (for example, in copyright cases), or authenticate documents. Investigations are much broader in scope than other areas of forensic analysis (where the usual aim is to provide answers to a series of simpler questions) often involving complex time-lines or hypotheses.

History

Prior to the 1980s crimes involving computers were dealt with using existing laws. The first computer crimes were recognized in the 1978 Florida Computer Crimes Act, which included legislation against the unauthorized modification or deletion of data on a computer system. Over the next few years the range of computer crimes being committed increased, and laws were passed to deal with issues of copyright, privacy/harassment (e.g., cyber bullying, cyber stalking, and online predators) and child pornography. It was not until the 1980s that federal laws began to incorporate computer offences. Canada was the first country to pass legislation in 1983. This was followed by the US Federal *Computer Fraud and Abuse Act* in 1986, Australian amendments to their crimes acts in 1989 and the British *Computer Misuse Act* in 1990.

1980s–1990s: Growth of the Field

The growth in computer crime during the 1980s and 1990s caused law enforcement agencies to begin establishing specialized groups, usually at the national level, to handle the technical aspects of investigations. For example, in 1984 the FBI launched a *Computer Analysis and Response Team* and the following year a computer crime department was set up within the British Metropolitan Police fraud squad. As well as being law enforcement professionals, many of the early members of these groups were also computer hobbyists and became responsible for the field's initial research and direction.

One of the first practical (or at least publicized) examples of digital forensics was Cliff Stoll's pursuit of hacker Markus Hess in 1986. Stoll, whose investigation made use of computer and network forensic techniques, was not a specialized examiner. Many of the earliest forensic examinations followed the same profile.

Throughout the 1990s there was high demand for these new, and basic, investigative resources. The strain on central units lead to the creation of regional, and even local, level groups to help handle the load. For example, the British National Hi-Tech Crime Unit was set up in 2001 to provide a national infrastructure for computer crime; with personnel located both centrally in London and with the various regional police forces (the unit was folded into the Serious Organised Crime Agency (SOCA) in 2006).

During this period the science of digital forensics grew from the ad-hoc tools and techniques developed by these hobbyist practitioners. This is in contrast to other forensics disciplines which developed from work by the scientific community. It was not until 1992 that the term "computer forensics" was used in academic literature (although prior to this it had been in informal use); a paper by Collier and Spaul attempted to justify this new discipline to the forensic science world. This swift development resulted in a lack of standardization and training. In his 1995 book, "*High-Technology Crime: Investigating Cases Involving Computers*", K. Rosenblatt wrote:

Seizing, preserving, and analyzing evidence stored on a computer is the greatest forensic challenge facing law enforcement in the 1990s. Although most forensic tests, such as fingerprinting and DNA testing, are performed by specially trained experts the task of collecting and analyzing computer evidence is often assigned to patrol officers and detectives.

2000s: Developing Standards

Since 2000, in response to the need for standardization, various bodies and agencies have published guidelines for digital forensics. The Scientific Working Group on Digital Evidence (SWGDE) produced a 2002 paper, *"Best practices for Computer Forensics"*, this was followed, in 2005, by the publication of an ISO standard (ISO 17025, *General requirements for the competence of testing and calibration laboratories*). A European lead international treaty, the Convention on Cybercrime, came into force in 2004 with the aim of reconciling national computer crime laws, investigative techniques and international co-operation. The treaty has been signed by 43 nations (including the US, Canada, Japan, South Africa, UK and other European nations) and ratified by 16.

The issue of training also received attention. Commercial companies (often forensic software developers) began to offer certification programs and digital forensic analysis was included as a topic at the UK specialist investigator training facility, Centrex.

Since the late 1990s mobile devices have become more widely available, advancing beyond simple communication devices, and have been found to be rich forms of information, even for crime not traditionally associated with digital forensics. Despite this, digital analysis of phones has lagged behind traditional computer media, largely due to problems over the proprietary nature of devices.

Focus has also shifted onto internet crime, particularly the risk of cyber warfare and cyberterrorism. A February 2010 report by the United States Joint Forces Command concluded:

Through cyberspace, enemies will target industry, academia, government, as well as the military in the air, land, maritime, and space domains. In much the same way that airpower transformed the battlefield of World War II, cyberspace has fractured the physical barriers that shield a nation from attacks on its commerce and communication.

The field of digital forensics still faces unresolved issues. A 2009 paper, "Digital Forensic Research: The Good, the Bad and the Unaddressed", by Peterson and Shenoi identified a bias towards Windows operating systems in digital forensics research. In 2010 Simson Garfinkel identified issues facing digital investigations in the future, including the increasing size of digital media, the wide availability of encryption to consumers, a growing variety of operating systems and file formats, an increasing number of individuals owning multiple devices, and legal limitations on investigators. The paper also identified continued training issues, as well as the prohibitively high cost of entering the field.

Development of Forensic Tools

During the 1980s very few specialized digital forensic tools existed, and consequently investigators often performed live analysis on media, examining computers from within the operating system using existing sysadmin tools to extract evidence. This practice carried the risk of modifying data on the disk, either inadvertently or otherwise, which led to claims of evidence tampering. A number of tools were created during the early 1990s to address the problem.

The need for such software was first recognized in 1989 at the Federal Law Enforcement Training Center, resulting in the creation of IMDUMP (by Michael White) and in 1990, SafeBack (developed by Sydex). Similar software was developed in other countries; DIBS (a hardware and software solution) was released commercially in the UK in 1991, and Rob McKemmish released *Fixed Disk Image* free to Australian law enforcement. These tools allowed examiners to create an exact copy of a piece of digital media to work on, leaving the original disk intact for verification. By the end of the 1990s, as demand for digital evidence grew more advanced commercial tools such as EnCase and FTK were developed, allowing analysts to examine copies of media without using any live forensics. More recently, a trend towards "live memory forensics" has grown resulting in the availability of tools such as WindowsSCOPE.

More recently, the same progression of tool development has occurred for mobile devices; initially investigators accessed data directly on the device, but soon specialist tools such as XRY or Radio Tactics Aceso appeared.

Forensic Process

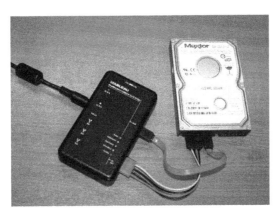

A portable Tableau write-blocker attached to a hard drive

A digital forensic investigation commonly consists of 3 stages: acquisition or imaging of exhibits, analysis, and reporting. Ideally acquisition involves capturing an image of the computer's volatile memory (RAM) and creating an exact sector level duplicate (or "forensic duplicate") of the media, often using a write blocking device to prevent modification of the original. However, the growth in size of storage media and developments such as cloud computing have led to more use of 'live' acquisitions whereby a 'logical' copy of the data is acquired rather than a complete image of the physical storage device. Both acquired image (or logical copy) and original media/data are hashed (using an algorithm such as SHA-1 or MD5) and the values compared to verify the copy is accurate.

During the analysis phase an investigator recovers evidence material using a number of different methodologies and tools. In 2002, an article in the *International Journal of Digital Evidence* referred to this step as "an in-depth systematic search of evidence related to the suspected crime." In 2006, forensics researcher Brian Carrier described an "intuitive procedure" in which obvious evidence is first identified and then "exhaustive searches are conducted to start filling in the holes."

The actual process of analysis can vary between investigations, but common methodologies include conducting keyword searches across the digital media (within files as well as unallocated and slack space), recovering deleted files and extraction of registry information (for example to list user accounts, or attached USB devices).

The evidence recovered is analysed to reconstruct events or actions and to reach conclusions, work that can often be performed by less specialised staff. When an investigation is complete the data is presented, usually in the form of a written report, in lay persons' terms.

Application

Camera manufacturer	Canon
Camera model	Canon EOS 400D DIGITAL
Exposure time	1/60 sec (0.016666666666667)
F-number	f/4.5
ISO speed rating	400
Date and time of data generation	11:06, August 27, 2010
Lens focal length	31 mm
Show extended details	

An example of an image's Exif metadata that might be used to prove its origin

Digital forensics is commonly used in both criminal law and private investigation. Traditionally it has been associated with criminal law, where evidence is collected to support or oppose a hypothesis before the courts. As with other areas of forensics this is often as part of a wider investigation spanning a number of disciplines. In some cases the collected evidence is used as a form of intelligence gathering, used for other purposes than court proceedings (for example to locate, identify or halt other crimes). As a result, intelligence gathering is sometimes held to a less strict forensic standard.

In civil litigation or corporate matters digital forensics forms part of the electronic discovery (or eDiscovery) process. Forensic procedures are similar to those used in criminal investigations, often with different legal requirements and limitations. Outside of the courts digital forensics can form a part of internal corporate investigations.

A common example might be following unauthorized network intrusion. A specialist forensic examination into the nature and extent of the attack is performed as a damage limitation exercise. Both to establish the extent of any intrusion and in an attempt to identify the attacker. Such attacks were commonly conducted over phone lines during the 1980s, but in the modern era are usually propagated over the Internet.

The main focus of digital forensics investigations is to recover objective evidence of a criminal activity (termed actus reus in legal parlance). However, the diverse range of data held in digital devices can help with other areas of inquiry.

Attribution

Meta data and other logs can be used to attribute actions to an individual. For example, personal documents on a computer drive might identify its owner.

Alibis and statements

> Information provided by those involved can be cross checked with digital evidence. For example, during the investigation into the Soham murders the offender's alibi was disproved when mobile phone records of the person he claimed to be with showed she was out of town at the time.

Intent

> As well as finding objective evidence of a crime being committed, investigations can also be used to prove the intent (known by the legal term mens rea). For example, the Internet history of convicted killer Neil Entwistle included references to a site discussing *How to kill people.*

Evaluation of source

> File artifacts and meta-data can be used to identify the origin of a particular piece of data; for example, older versions of Microsoft Word embedded a Global Unique Identifer into files which identified the computer it had been created on. Proving whether a file was produced on the digital device being examined or obtained from elsewhere (e.g., the Internet) can be very important.

Document authentication

> Related to "Evaluation of source," meta data associated with digital documents can be easily modified (for example, by changing the computer clock you can affect the creation date of a file). Document authentication relates to detecting and identifying falsification of such details.

Limitations

One major limitation to a forensic investigation is the use of encryption; this disrupts initial examination where pertinent evidence might be located using keywords. Laws to compel individuals to disclose encryption keys are still relatively new and controversial.

Legal Considerations

The examination of digital media is covered by national and international legislation. For civil investigations, in particular, laws may restrict the abilities of analysts to undertake examinations. Restrictions against network monitoring, or reading of personal communications often exist. During criminal investigation, national laws restrict how much information can be seized. For example, in the United Kingdom seizure of evidence by law enforcement is governed by the PACE act. During its existence early in the field, the "International Organization on Computer Evidence" (IOCE) was one agency that worked to establish compatible international standards for the seizure of evidence.

In the UK the same laws covering computer crime can also affect forensic investigators. The 1990 computer misuse act legislates against unauthorised access to computer material; this is a particular concern for civil investigators who have more limitations than law enforcement.

An individuals right to privacy is one area of digital forensics which is still largely undecided by courts. The US Electronic Communications Privacy Act places limitations on the ability of law enforcement or civil investigators to intercept and access evidence. The act makes a distinction between stored communication (e.g. email archives) and transmitted communication (such as VOIP). The latter, being considered more of a privacy invasion, is harder to obtain a warrant for. The ECPA also affects the ability of companies to investigate the computers and communications of their employees, an aspect that is still under debate as to the extent to which a company can perform such monitoring.

Article 5 of the European Convention on Human Rights asserts similar privacy limitations to the ECPA and limits the processing and sharing of personal data both within the EU and with external countries. The ability of UK law enforcement to conduct digital forensics investigations is legislated by the Regulation of Investigatory Powers Act.

Digital Evidence

Digital evidence can come in a number of forms

When used in a court of law digital evidence falls under the same legal guidelines as other forms of evidence; courts do not usually require more stringent guidelines. In the United States the Federal Rules of Evidence are used to evaluate the admissibility of digital evidence, the United Kingdom PACE and Civil Evidence acts have similar guidelines and many other countries have their own laws. US federal laws restrict seizures to items with only obvious evidential value. This is acknowledged as not always being possible to establish with digital media prior to an examination.

Laws dealing with digital evidence are concerned with two issues: integrity and authenticity. Integrity is ensuring that the act of seizing and acquiring digital media does not modify the evidence (either the original or the copy). Authenticity refers to the ability to confirm the integrity of information; for example that the imaged media matches the original evidence. The ease with which digital media can be modified means that documenting the chain of custody from the crime scene, through analysis and, ultimately, to the court, (a form of audit trail) is important to establish the authenticity of evidence.

Attorneys have argued that because digital evidence can theoretically be altered it undermines the reliability of the evidence. US judges are beginning to reject this theory, in the case *US v. Bonallo* the court ruled that "the fact that it is possible to alter data contained in a computer is plainly insufficient to establish untrustworthiness." In the United Kingdom guidelines such as those issued by ACPO are followed to help document the authenticity and integrity of evidence.

Digital investigators, particularly in criminal investigations, have to ensure that conclusions are based upon factual evidence and their own expert knowledge. In the US, for example, Federal Rules of Evidence state that a qualified expert may testify "in the form of an opinion or otherwise" so long as:

(1) the testimony is based upon sufficient facts or data, (2) the testimony is the product of reliable principles and methods, and (3) the witness has applied the principles and methods reliably to the facts of the case.

The sub-branches of digital forensics may each have their own specific guidelines for the conduct of investigations and the handling of evidence. For example, mobile phones may be required to be placed in a Faraday shield during seizure or acquisition to prevent further radio traffic to the device. In the UK forensic examination of computers in criminal matters is subject to ACPO guidelines. There are also international approaches to providing guidance on how to handle electronic evidence. The "Electronic Evidence Guide" by the Council of Europe offers a framework for law enforcement and judicial authorities in countries who seek to set up or enhance their own guidelines for the identification and handling of electronic evidence.

Investigative Tools

The admissibility of digital evidence relies on the tools used to extract it. In the US, forensic tools are subjected to the Daubert standard, where the judge is responsible for ensuring that the processes and software used were acceptable. In a 2003 paper Brian Carrier argued that the Daubert guidelines required the code of forensic tools to be published and peer reviewed. He concluded that "open source tools may more clearly and comprehensively meet the guideline requirements than would closed source tools." In a 2011 article Josh Brunty stated that the scientific validation of the technology and software associated with performing a digital forensic examination is critical to any laboratory process. He argued that "the science of digital forensics is founded on the principles of repeatable processes and quality evidence therefore knowing how to design and properly maintain a good validation process is a key requirement for any digital forensic examiner to defend their methods in court."

Branches

Digital forensics investigation is not restricted to retrieve data merely from the computer, as laws are breached by the criminals and small digital devices (e.g. PDAs, smart phones, flash sticks) are now extensively used. Some of these devices got volatile memory while some got non-volatile memory. Sufficient methodologies are available to retrieve data from volatile memory, however there is lack of detailed methodology or a framework for data retrieval from non-volatile memory sources. Depending on the type of devices, media or artifacts, digital forensics investigation is branched into various types.

Computer Forensics

The goal of computer forensics is to explain the current state of a digital artifact; such a computer system, storage medium or electronic document. The discipline usually covers computers, embedded systems (digital devices with rudimentary computing power and onboard memory) and static memory (such as USB pen drives).

Computer forensics can deal with a broad range of information; from logs (such as internet history) through to the actual files on the drive. In 2007 prosecutors used a spreadsheet recovered from the computer of Joseph E. Duncan III to show premeditation and secure the death penalty. Sharon Lopatka's killer was identified in 2006 after email messages from him detailing torture and death fantasies were found on her computer.

Mobile phones in a UK Evidence bag

Private Investigator & Certified Digital Forensics Examiner Imaging a hard drive in the field for forensic examination.

Mobile Device Forensics

Mobile device forensics is a sub-branch of digital forensics relating to recovery of digital evidence or data from a mobile device. It differs from Computer forensics in that a mobile device will have an inbuilt communication system (e.g. GSM) and, usually, proprietary storage mechanisms. Investigations usually focus on simple data such as call data and communications (SMS/Email) rather than in-depth recovery of deleted data. SMS data from a mobile device investigation helped to exonerate Patrick Lumumba in the murder of Meredith Kercher.

Mobile devices are also useful for providing location information; either from inbuilt gps/location tracking or via cell site logs, which track the devices within their range. Such information was used to track down the kidnappers of Thomas Onofri in 2006.

Network Forensics

Network forensics is concerned with the monitoring and analysis of computer network traffic, both local and WAN/internet, for the purposes of information gathering, evidence collection, or intrusion detection. Traffic is usually intercepted at the packet level, and either stored for later analysis or filtered in real-time. Unlike other areas of digital forensics network data is often volatile and rarely logged, making the discipline often reactionary.

In 2000 the FBI lured computer hackers Aleksey Ivanov and Gorshkov to the United States for a fake job interview. By monitoring network traffic from the pair's computers, the FBI identified passwords allowing them to collect evidence directly from Russian-based computers.

Forensic Data Analysis

Forensic Data Analysis is a branch of digital forensics. It examines structured data with the aim to discover and analyse patterns of fraudulent activities resulting from financial crime.

Database Forensics

Database forensics is a branch of digital forensics relating to the forensic study of databases and their metadata. Investigations use database contents, log files and in-RAM data to build a timeline or recover relevant information.

Education and Research

Academic centre of education and research in forensic sciences:

North America: Penn State University offers Security and Risk Analysis Major, Master of Professional Studies in Information Sciences, Master of Professional Studies in Homeland Security, and Ph.D. in Information Sciences and Technology in the digital forensics area.

Computer Forensics

Computer forensics (also known as computer forensic science) is a branch of digital forensic science pertaining to evidence found in computers and digital storage media. The goal of computer forensics is to examine digital media in a forensically sound manner with the aim of identifying, preserving, recovering, analyzing and presenting facts and opinions about the digital information.

Although it is most often associated with the investigation of a wide variety of computer crime, computer forensics may also be used in civil proceedings. The discipline involves similar techniques and principles to data recovery, but with additional guidelines and practices designed to create a legal audit trail.

Evidence from computer forensics investigations is usually subjected to the same guidelines and practices of other digital evidence. It has been used in a number of high-profile cases and is becoming widely accepted as reliable within U.S. and European court systems.

Overview

In the early 1980s personal computers became more accessible to consumers, leading to their increased use in criminal activity (for example, to help commit fraud). At the same time, several new "computer crimes" were recognized (such as hacking). The discipline of computer forensics emerged during this time as a method to recover and investigate digital evidence for use in court. Since then computer crime and computer related crime has grown, and has jumped 67% between 2002 and 2003. Today it is used to investigate a wide variety of crime, including child pornography, fraud, espionage, cyberstalking, murder and rape. The discipline also features in civil proceedings as a form of information gathering (for example, Electronic discovery).

Forensic techniques and expert knowledge are used to explain the current state of a *digital artifact*; such as a computer system, storage medium (e.g. hard disk or CD-ROM), an electronic document (e.g. an email message or JPEG image). The scope of a forensic analysis can vary from simple information retrieval to reconstructing a series of events. In a 2002 book *Computer Forensics* authors Kruse and Heiser define computer forensics as involving "the preservation, identification, extraction, documentation and interpretation of computer data". They go on to describe the discipline as "more of an art than a science", indicating that forensic methodology is backed by flexibility and extensive domain knowledge. However, while several methods can be used to extract evidence from a given computer the strategies used by law enforcement are fairly rigid and lacking the flexibility found in the civilian world.

Use as Evidence

In court, computer forensic evidence is subject to the usual requirements for digital evidence. This requires that information be authentic, reliably obtained, and admissible. Different countries have specific guidelines and practices for evidence recovery. In the United Kingdom, examiners often follow Association of Chief Police Officers guidelines that help ensure the authenticity and integrity of evidence. While voluntary, the guidelines are widely accepted in British courts.

Computer forensics has been used as evidence in criminal law since the mid-1980s, some notable examples include:

- BTK Killer: Dennis Rader was convicted of a string of serial killings that occurred over a period of sixteen years. Towards the end of this period, Rader sent letters to the police on a floppy disk. Metadata within the documents implicated an author named "Dennis" at "Christ Lutheran Church"; this evidence helped lead to Rader's arrest.

- Joseph E. Duncan III: A spreadsheet recovered from Duncan's computer contained evidence that showed him planning his crimes. Prosecutors used this to show premeditation and secure the death penalty.

- Sharon Lopatka: Hundreds of emails on Lopatka's computer lead investigators to her killer, Robert Glass.

- Corcoran Group: This case confirmed parties' duties to preserve digital evidence when litigation has commenced or is reasonably anticipated. Hard drives were analyzed by a computer forensics expert who could not find relevant emails the Defendants should have had. Though the expert found no evidence of deletion on the hard drives, evidence came out that the defendants were found to have intentionally destroyed emails, and misled and failed to disclose material facts to the plaintiffs and the court.

- Dr. Conrad Murray: Dr. Conrad Murray, the doctor of the deceased Michael Jackson, was convicted partially by digital evidence on his computer. This evidence included medical documentation showing lethal amounts of propofol.

Forensic Process

Computer forensic investigations usually follow the standard digital forensic process or phases: acquisition, examination, analysis and reporting. Investigations are performed on static data (i.e. acquired images) rather than "live" systems. This is a change from early forensic practices where a lack of specialist tools led to investigators commonly working on live data.

Techniques

A number of techniques are used during computer forensics investigations and much has been written on the many techniques used by law enforcement in particular. E.g., "Defending Child Pornography Cases".

Cross-drive analysis

> A forensic technique that correlates information found on multiple hard drives. The process, still being researched, can be used to identify social networks and to perform anomaly detection.

Live analysis

> The examination of computers from within the operating system using custom forensics or existing sysadmin tools to extract evidence. The practice is useful when dealing with Encrypting File Systems, for example, where the encryption keys may be collected and, in some instances, the logical hard drive volume may be imaged (known as a live acquisition) before the computer is shut down.

Deleted files

> A common technique used in computer forensics is the recovery of deleted files. Modern forensic software have their own tools for recovering or carving out deleted data. Most operating systems and file systems do not always erase physical file data, allowing investigators to reconstruct it from the physical disk sectors. File carving involves searching for known file headers within the disk image and reconstructing deleted materials.

Stochastic forensics

> A method which uses stochastic properties of the computer system to investigate activities lacking digital artifacts. Its chief use is to investigate data theft.

Steganography

> One of the techniques used to hide data is via steganography, the process of hiding data inside of a picture or digital image. An example would be to hide pornographic images of children or other information that a given criminal does not want to have discovered. Computer forensics professionals can fight this by looking at the hash of the file and comparing it to the original image (if available.) While the image appears exactly the same, the hash changes as the data changes.

Volatile Data

When seizing evidence, if the machine is still active, any information stored solely in RAM that is not recovered before powering down may be lost. One application of "live analysis" is to recover RAM data (for example, using Microsoft's COFEE tool, windd, WindowsSCOPE) prior to removing an exhibit. CaptureGUARD Gateway bypasses Windows login for locked computers, allowing for the analysis and acquisition of physical memory on a locked computer.

RAM can be analyzed for prior content after power loss, because the electrical charge stored in the memory cells takes time to dissipate, an effect exploited by the cold boot attack. The length of time that data is recoverable is increased by low temperatures and higher cell voltages. Holding unpowered RAM below −60 °C helps preserve residual data by an order of magnitude, improving the chances of successful recovery. However, it can be impractical to do this during a field examination.

Some of the tools needed to extract volatile data, however, require that a computer be in a forensic lab, both to maintain a legitimate chain of evidence, and to facilitate work on the machine. If necessary, law enforcement applies techniques to move a live, running desktop computer. These include a mouse jiggler, which moves the mouse rapidly in small movements and prevents the computer from going to sleep accidentally. Usually, an uninterruptible power supply (UPS) provides power during transit.

However, one of the easiest ways to capture data is by actually saving the RAM data to disk. Various file systems that have journaling features such as NTFS and ReiserFS keep a large portion of the RAM data on the main storage media during operation, and these page files can be reassembled to reconstruct what was in RAM at that time.

Analysis Tools

A number of open source and commercial tools exist for computer forensics investigation. Typical forensic analysis includes a manual review of material on the media, reviewing the Windows registry for suspect information, discovering and cracking passwords, keyword searches for topics related to the crime, and extracting e-mail and pictures for review.

Certifications

There are several computer forensics certifications available, such as the ISFCE Certified Computer Examiner, Digital Forensics Investigation Professional (DFIP) and IACRB Certified Computer Forensics Examiner.

IACIS (the International Association of Computer Investigative Specialists) offers the Certified Computer Forensic Examiner (CFCE) program.

Asian School of Cyber Laws offers international level certifications in Digital Evidence Analysis and in Digital Forensic Investigation. These Courses are available in online and class room mode.

Many commercial based forensic software companies are now also offering proprietary certifications on their products. For example, Guidance Software offering the (EnCE) certification on their tool EnCase, AccessData offering (ACE) certification on their tool FTK, PassMark Software offering (OCE) certification on their tool OSForensics, and X-Ways Software Technology offering (X-PERT) certification for their software, X-Ways Forensics.

Network Forensics

Network forensics is a sub-branch of digital forensics relating to the monitoring and analysis of computer network traffic for the purposes of information gathering, legal evidence, or intrusion detection. Unlike other areas of digital forensics, network investigations deal with volatile and dynamic information. Network traffic is transmitted and then lost, so network forensics is often a pro-active investigation.

Network forensics generally has two uses. The first, relating to security, involves monitoring a network for anomalous traffic and identifying intrusions. An attacker might be able to erase all log files on a compromised host; network-based evidence might therefore be the only evidence available for forensic analysis. The second form relates to law enforcement. In this case analysis of captured network traffic can include tasks such as reassembling transferred files, searching for keywords and parsing human communication such as emails or chat sessions.

Two systems are commonly used to collect network data; a brute force "catch it as you can" and a more intelligent "stop look listen" method.

Overview

Network forensics is a comparatively new field of forensic science. The growing popularity of the Internet in homes means that computing has become network-centric and data is now available outside of disk-based digital evidence. Network forensics can be performed as a standalone investigation or alongside a computer forensics analysis (where it is often used to reveal links between digital devices or reconstruct how a crime was committed).

Marcus Ranum is credited with defining Network forensics as "the capture, recording, and analysis of network events in order to discover the source of security attacks or other problem incidents".

Compared to computer forensics, where evidence is usually preserved on disk, network data is more volatile and unpredictable. Investigators often only have material to examine if packet filters, firewalls, and intrusion detection systems were set up to anticipate breaches of security.

Systems used to collect network data for forensics use usually come in two forms:

- "Catch-it-as-you-can" – This is where all packets passing through a certain traffic point are captured and written to storage with analysis being done subsequently in batch mode. This approach requires large amounts of storage.

- "Stop, look and listen" – This is where each packet is analyzed in a rudimentary way in memory and only certain information saved for future analysis. This approach requires a faster processor to keep up with incoming traffic.

Types

Ethernet

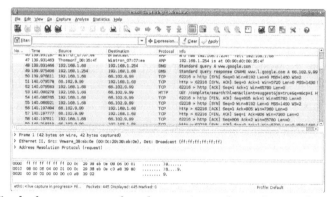

Wireshark, a common tool used to monitor and record network traffic

Applying forensic methods on the Ethernet layer is done by eavesdropping bit streams with tools called monitoring tools or sniffers. The most common tool on this layer is Wireshark (formerly known as Ethereal) and tcpdump where tcpdump works mostly on unix-like operating systems. These tools collect all data on this layer and allows the user to filter for different events. With these tools, website pages, email attachments, and other network traffic can be reconstructed only if they are transmitted or received unencrypted. An advantage of collecting this data is that it is directly connected to a host. If, for example the IP address or the MAC address of a host at a certain time is known, all data sent to or from this IP or MAC address can be filtered.

To establish the connection between IP and MAC address, it is useful to take a closer look at auxiliary network protocols. The Address Resolution Protocol (ARP) tables list the MAC addresses with the corresponding IP addresses.

To collect data on this layer, the network interface card (NIC) of a host can be put into "promiscuous mode". In so doing, all traffic will be passed to the CPU, not only the traffic meant for the host.

However, if an intruder or attacker is aware that his connection might be eavesdropped, he might use encryption to secure his connection. It is almost impossible nowadays to break encryption but the fact that a suspect's connection to another host is encrypted all the time might indicate that the other host is an accomplice of the suspect.

TCP/IP

On the network layer the Internet Protocol (IP) is responsible for directing the packets generated by TCP through the network (e.g., the Internet) by adding source and destination information which can be interpreted by routers all over the network. Cellular digital packet networks, like GPRS, use similar protocols like IP, so the methods described for IP work with them as well.

For the correct routing, every intermediate router must have a routing table to know where to send the packet next. These routing tables are one of the best sources of information if investigating a digital crime and trying to track down an attacker. To do this, it is necessary to follow the packets of the attacker, reverse the sending route and find the computer the packet came from (i.e., the attacker).

The Internet

The internet can be a rich source of digital evidence including web browsing, email, newsgroup, synchronous chat and peer-to-peer traffic. For example, web server logs can be used to show when (or if) a suspect accessed information related to criminal activity. Email accounts can often contain useful evidence; but email headers are easily faked and, so, network forensics may be used to prove the exact origin of incriminating material. Network forensics can also be used in order to find out who is using a particular computer by extracting user account information from the network traffic.

Wireless Forensics

Wireless forensics is a sub-discipline of network forensics. The main goal of wireless forensics is to provide the methodology and tools required to collect and analyze (wireless) network traffic that can be presented as valid digital evidence in a court of law. The evidence collected can correspond to plain data or, with the broad usage of Voice-over-IP (VoIP) technologies, especially over wireless, can include voice conversations.

Analysis of wireless network traffic is similar to that on wired networks, however there may be the added consideration of wireless security measures.

Forensic Data Analysis

Forensic Data Analysis (FDA) is a branch of Digital forensics. It examines structured data with regard to incidents of financial crime. The aim is to discover and analyse patterns of fraudulent activities. Data from application systems or from their underlying databases is referred to as structured data.

Unstructured data in contrast is taken from communication and office applications or from mobile devices. This data has no overarching structure and analysis thereof means applying keywords or mapping communication patterns. Analysis of unstructered data is usually referred to as Computer forensics.

Methodology

The analysis of large volumes of data is typically performed in a separate database system run by the analysis team. Live systems are usually not dimensioned to run extensive individual analysis without affecting the regular users. On the other hand, it is methodically preferable to analyze data copies on separate systems and protect the analysis teams against the accusation of altering original data.

Due to the nature of the data, the analysis focuses more often on the content of data than on the database it is contained in. If the database itself is of interest then Database forensics are applied.

In order to analyze large structured data sets with the intention of detecting financial crime it takes at least three types of expertise in the team: A data analyst to perform the technical steps and write the queries, a team member with extensive experience of the processes and internal controls in the relevant area of the investigated company and a forensic scientist who is familiar with patterns of fraudulent behaviour.

After an initial analysis phase using methods of explorative data analysis the following phase is usually highly iterative. Starting with a hypothesis on how the perpetrator might have created a personal advantage the data is analyzed for supporting evidence. Following that the hypothesis is refined or discarded.

The combination of different databases, in particular data from different systems or sources is highly effective. These data sources are either unknown to the perpetrator or he/she can not manipulate them afterwards.

Data Visualization is often used to display the results.

Mobile Device Forensics

Mobile device forensics is a branch of digital forensics relating to recovery of digital evidence or data from a mobile device under forensically sound conditions. The phrase *mobile device* usually refers to mobile phones; however, it can also relate to any digital device that has both internal memory and communication ability, including PDA devices, GPS devices and tablet computers.

The use of phones in crime was widely recognised for some years, but the forensic study of mobile devices is a relatively new field, dating from the early 2000s and late 1990s. A proliferation of phones (particularly smartphones) and other digital devices on the consumer market caused a demand for forensic examination of the devices, which could not be met by existing computer forensics techniques.

Mobile devices can be used to save several types of personal information such as contacts, photos, calendars and notes, SMS and MMS messages. Smartphones may additionally contain video, email, web browsing information, location information, and social networking messages and contacts.

There is growing need for mobile forensics due to several reasons and some of the prominent reasons are:

- Use of mobile phones to store and transmit personal and corporate information

- Use of mobile phones in online transactions

- Law enforcement, criminals and mobile phone devices

Mobile device forensics can be particularly challenging on a number of levels:

Evidential and technical challenges exist. for example, cell site analysis following from the use of a mobile phone usage coverage, is not an exact science. Consequently, whilst it is possible to determine roughly the cell site zone from which a call was made or received, it is not yet possible to say with any degree of certainty, that a mobile phone call emanated from a specific location e.g. a residential address.

- To remain competitive, original equipment manufacturers frequently change mobile phone form factors, operating system file structures, data storage, services, peripherals, and even pin connectors and cables. As a result, forensic examiners must use a different forensic process compared to computer forensics.

- Storage capacity continues to grow thanks to demand for more powerful "mini computer" type devices.

- Not only the types of data but also the way mobile devices are used constantly evolve.

- Hibernation behaviour in which processes are suspended when the device is powered off or idle but at the same time, remaining active.

As a result of these challenges, a wide variety of tools exist to extract evidence from mobile devices; no one tool or method can acquire all the evidence from all devices. It is therefore recommended that forensic examiners, especially those wishing to qualify as expert witnesses in court, undergo extensive training in order to understand how each tool and method acquires evidence; how it maintains standards for forensic soundness; and how it meets legal requirements such as the Daubert standard or Frye standard.

History

As a field of study forensic examination of mobile devices dates from the late 1990s and early 2000s. The role of mobile phones in crime had long been recognized by law enforcement. With the increased availability of such devices on the consumer market and the wider array of communication platforms they support (e.g. email, web browsing) demand for forensic examination grew.

Early efforts to examine mobile devices used similar techniques to the first computer forensics investigations: analysing phone contents directly via the screen and photographing important content. However, this proved to be a time-consuming process, and as the number of mobile devices began to increase, investigators called for more efficient means of extracting data. Enterprising mobile forensic examiners sometimes used cell phone or PDA synchronization software to "back up" device data to a forensic computer for imaging, or sometimes, simply performed computer forensics on the hard drive of a suspect computer where data had been synchronized. However, this type of software could write to the phone as well as reading it, and could not retrieve deleted data.

Some forensic examiners found that they could retrieve even deleted data using "flasher" or "twister" boxes, tools developed by OEMs to "flash" a phone's memory for debugging or updating. However, flasher boxes are invasive and can change data; can be complicated to use; and, because they are not developed as forensic tools, perform neither hash verifications nor (in most cases) audit trails. For physical forensic examinations, therefore, better alternatives remained necessary.

To meet these demands, commercial tools appeared which allowed examiners to recover phone memory with minimal disruption and analyse it separately. Over time these commercial techniques have developed further and the recovery of deleted data from proprietary mobile devices has become possible with some specialist tools. Moreover, commercial tools have even automated much of the extraction process, rendering it possible even for minimally trained first responders—who currently are much more likely to encounter suspects with mobile devices in their possession, compared to computers—to perform basic extractions for triage and data preview purposes.

Professional Applications

Mobile device forensics is best known for its application to law enforcement investigations, but it is also useful for military intelligence, corporate investigations, private investigations, criminal and civil defense, and electronic discovery.

Types of Evidence

As mobile device technology advances, the amount and types of data that can be found on a mobile device is constantly increasing. Evidence that can be potentially recovered from a mobile phone may come from several different sources, including handset memory, SIM card, and attached memory cards such as SD cards.

Traditionally mobile phone forensics has been associated with recovering SMS and MMS messaging, as well as call logs, contact lists and phone IMEI/ESN information. However, newer generations of smartphones also include wider varieties of information; from web browsing, Wireless network settings, geolocation information (including geotags contained within image metadata), e-mail and other forms of rich internet media, including important data—such as social networking service posts and contacts—now retained on smartphone 'apps'.

Internal Memory

Nowadays mostly flash memory consisting of NAND or NOR types are used for mobile devices.

External Memory

External memory devices are SIM cards, SD cards (commonly found within GPS devices as well as mobile phones), MMC cards, CF cards, and the Memory Stick.

Service Provider Logs

Although not technically part of mobile device forensics, the call detail records (and occasionally, text messages) from wireless carriers often serve as "back up" evidence obtained after the mobile phone has been seized. These are useful when the call history and/or text messages have been deleted from the phone, or when location-based services are not turned on. Call detail records and cell site (tower) dumps can show the phone owner's location, and whether they were stationary or moving (i.e., whether the phone's signal bounced off the same side of a single tower, or different sides of multiple towers along a particular path of travel). Carrier data and device data together can be used to corroborate information from other sources, for instance, video surveillance footage or eyewitness accounts; or to determine the general location where a non-geotagged image or video was taken.

The European Union requires its member countries to retain certain telecommunications data for use in investigations. This includes data on calls made and retrieved. The location of a mobile phone can be determined and this geographical data must also be retained. In the United States, however, no such requirement exists, and no standards govern how long carriers should retain data or even what they must retain. For example, text messages may be retained only for a week or two, while call logs may be retained anywhere from a few weeks to several months. To reduce the risk of evidence being lost, law enforcement agents must submit a preservation letter to the carrier, which they then must back up with a search warrant.

Forensic Process

The forensics process for mobile devices broadly matches other branches of digital forensics; however, some particular concerns apply. Generally, the process can be broken down into three main categories: seizure, acquisition, and examination/analysis. Other aspects of the computer forensic process, such as intake, validation, documentation/reporting, and archiving still apply.

Seizure

Seizing mobile devices is covered by the same legal considerations as other digital media. Mobiles will often be recovered switched on; as the aim of seizure is to preserve evidence, the device will often be transported in the same state to avoid a shutdown, which would change files. In addition, the investigator or first responder would risk user lock activation.

However, leaving the phone on carries another risk: the device can still make a network/cellular connection. This may bring in new data, overwriting evidence. To prevent a connection, mobile devices will often be transported and examined from within a Faraday cage (or bag). Even so, there are two disadvantages to this method. First, it renders the device unusable, as its touch screen or keypad cannot be used. Second, a device's search for a network connection will drain its battery more quickly. While devices and their batteries can often be recharged, again, the investigator risks that the phone's user lock will have activated. Therefore, network isolation is advisable either through placing the device in Airplane Mode, or cloning its SIM card (a technique which can also be useful when the device is missing its SIM card entirely).

Acquisition

iPhone in an RF shield bag

The second step in the forensic process is acquisition, in this case usually referring to retrieval of material from a device (as compared to the bit-copy imaging used in computer forensics).

Due to the proprietary nature of mobiles it is often not possible to acquire data with it powered down; most mobile device acquisition is performed live. With more advanced smartphones using advanced memory management, connecting it to a recharger and putting it into a faraday cage may not be good practice. The mobile device would recognize the network disconnection and therefore it would change its status information that can trigger the memory manager to write data.

RTL Aceso, a mobile device acquisition unit

Most acquisition tools for mobile devices are commercial in nature and consist of a hardware and software component, often automated.

Examination and Analysis

As an increasing number of mobile devices use high-level file systems, similar to the file systems of computers, methods and tools can be taken over from hard disk forensics or only need slight changes.

The FAT file system is generally used on NAND memory. A difference is the block size used, which is larger than 512 bytes for hard disks and depends on the used memory type, e.g., NOR type 64, 128, 256 and NAND memory 16, 128, 256, or 512 kilobyte.

Different software tools can extract the data from the memory image. One could use specialized and automated forensic software products or generic file viewers such as any hex editor to search for characteristics of file headers. The advantage of the hex editor is the deeper insight into the memory management, but working with a hex editor means a lot of handwork and file system as well as file header knowledge. In contrast, specialized forensic software simplifies the search and extracts the data but may not find everything. AccessData, Sleuthkit, and EnCase, to mention only some, are forensic software products to analyze memory images. Since there is no tool that extracts all possible information, it is advisable to use two or more tools for examination. There is currently (February 2010) no software solution to get all evidences from flash memories.

Data Acquisition Types

Mobile device data extraction can be classified according to a continuum, along which methods become more technical and "forensically sound," tools become more expensive, analysis takes longer, examiners need more training, and some methods can even become more invasive.

Manual Acquisition

The examiner utilizes the user interface to investigate the content of the phone's memory. Therefore, the device is used as normal, with the examiner taking pictures of each screen's contents. This method has an advantage in that the operating system makes it unnecessary to use specialized tools or equipment to transform raw data into human interpretable information. In practice this method is applied to cell phones, PDAs and navigation systems. Disadvantages are that only data visible to the operating system can be recovered; that all data are only available in form of pictures; and the process itself is time-consuming.

Logical Acquisition

Logical acquisition implies a bit-by-bit copy of logical storage objects (e.g., directories and files) that reside on a logical storage (e.g., a file system partition). Logical acquisition has the advantage that system data structures are easier for a tool to extract and organize. Logical extraction acquires information from the device using the original equipment manufacturer application programming interface for synchronizing the phone's contents with a personal computer. A logical extraction is generally easier to work with as it does not produce a large binary blob. However, a skilled forensic examiner will be able to extract far more information from a physical extraction.

File System Acquisition

Logical extraction usually does not produce any deleted information, due to it normally being re-moved from the phone's file system. However, in some cases—particularly with platforms built on SQLite, such as iOS and Android—the phone may keep a database file of information which does not overwrite the information but simply marks it as deleted and available for later overwriting. In such cases, if the device allows file system access through its synchronization interface, it is possible to recover deleted information. File system extraction is useful for understanding the file structure, web browsing history, or app usage, as well as providing the examiner with the ability to perform an analysis with traditional computer forensic tools.

Physical Acquisition

Physical acquisition implies a bit-for-bit copy of an entire physical store (e.g. flash memory); therefore, it is the method most similar to the examination of a personal computer. A physical acquisition has the advantage of allowing deleted files and data remnants to be examined. Physical extraction acquires information from the device by direct access to the flash memories.

Generally this is harder to achieve because the device original equipment manufacturer needs to se-cure against arbitrary reading of memory; therefore, a device may be locked to a certain operator. To get around this security, mobile forensics tool vendors often develop their own boot loaders, enabling the forensic tool to access the memory (and often, also to bypass user passcodes or pattern locks).

Generally the physical extraction is split into two steps, the dumping phase and the decoding phase.

Brute Force Acquisition

Brute force acquisition can be performed by 3rd party passcode brute force tools that send a series of passcodes / passwords to the mobile device. This is a time consuming method, but effective nonetheless. Brute forcing tools are connected to the device and will physically send codes on iOS devices starting from 0000 to 9999 in sequence until the correct code is successfully entered. Once the code entry has been successful, full access to the device is given and data extraction can commence.

Tools

Early investigations consisted of live manual analysis of mobile devices; with examiners photographing or writing down useful material for use as evidence. Without forensic photography equipment such as Fernico ZRT, EDEC Eclipse, or Project-a-Phone, this had the disadvantage of risking the modification of the device content, as well as leaving many parts of the proprietary operating system inaccessible.

In recent years a number of hardware/software tools have emerged to recover logical and physical evidence from mobile devices. Most tools consist of both hardware and software portions. The hardware includes a number of cables to connect the phone to the acquisition machine; the software exists to extract the evidence and, occasionally even to analyse it.

Most recently, mobile device forensic tools have been developed for the field. This is in response both to military units' demand for fast and accurate anti-terrorism intelligence, and to law enforcement demand for forensic previewing capabilities at a crime scene, search warrant execution, or exigent circumstances. Such mobile forensic tools are often ruggedized for harsh environments (e.g. the battlefield) and rough treatment (e.g. being dropped or submerged in water).

Generally, because it is impossible for any one tool to capture all evidence from all mobile devices, mobile forensic professionals recommend that examiners establish entire toolkits consisting of a mix of commercial, open source, broad support, and narrow support forensic tools, together with accessories such as battery chargers, Faraday bags or other signal disruption equipment, and so forth.

Commercial Forensic Tools

Some current tools include Cellebrite UFED, Susteen Secure View and Micro Systemation XRY.

Some tools have additionally been developed to address increasing criminal usage of phones manufactured with Chinese chipsets, which include MediaTek (MTK), Spreadtrum and MStar. Such tools include Cellebrite's CHINEX, and XRY PinPoint.

Open Source

Most open source mobile forensics tools are platform-specific and geared toward smartphone analysis. Though not originally designed to be a forensics tool, BitPim has been widely used on CDMA phones as well as LG VX4400/VX6000 and many Sanyo Sprint cell phones.

Physical Tools

Forensic Desoldering

Commonly referred to as a "Chip-Off" technique within the industry, the last and most intrusive method to get a memory image is to desolder the non-volatile memory chip and connect it to a memory chip reader. This method contains the potential danger of total data destruction: it is possible to destroy the chip and its content because of the heat required during desoldering. Before the invention of the BGA technology it was possible to attach probes to the pins of the memory chip and to recover the memory through these probes. The BGA technique bonds the chips directly onto the PCB through molten solder balls, such that it is no longer possible to attach probes.

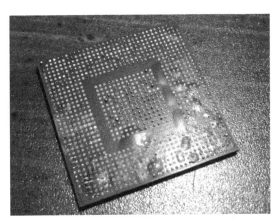

Here you can see that moisture in the circuit board turned to steam when it was
subjected to intense heat. This produces the so-called "popcorn effect."

Desoldering the chips is done carefully and slowly, so that the heat does not destroy the chip or
data. Before the chip is desoldered the PCB is baked in an oven to eliminate remaining water. This
prevents the so-called popcorn effect, at which the remaining water would blow the chip package
at desoldering.

There are mainly three methods to melt the solder: hot air, infrared light, and steam-phasing. The
infrared light technology works with a focused infrared light beam onto a specific integrated circuit
and is used for small chips. The hot air and steam methods cannot focus as much as the infrared
technique.

Chip Re-balling

After desoldering the chip a re-balling process cleans the chip and adds new tin balls to the chip.
Re-balling can be done in two different ways.

- The first is to use a stencil. The stencil is chip-dependent and must fit exactly. Then the
  tin-solder is put on the stencil. After cooling the tin the stencil is removed and if necessary
  a second cleaning step is done.

- The second method is laser re-balling. Here the stencil is programmed into the re-balling
  unit. A bondhead (looks like a tube/needle) is automatically loaded with one tin ball from
  a solder ball singulation tank. The ball is then heated by a laser, such that the tin-solder
  ball becomes fluid and flows onto the cleaned chip. Instantly after melting the ball the laser turns off and a new ball falls into the bondhead. While reloading the bondhead of the
  re-balling unit changes the position to the next pin.

A third method makes the entire re-balling process unnecessary. The chip is connected to an
adapter with Y-shaped springs or spring-loaded pogo pins. The Y-shaped springs need to have a
ball onto the pin to establish an electric connection, but the pogo pins can be used directly on the
pads on the chip without the balls.

The advantage of forensic desoldering is that the device does not need to be functional and that a
copy without any changes to the original data can be made. The disadvantage is that the re-balling devices are expensive, so this process is very costly and there are some risks of total data loss.
Hence, forensic desoldering should only be done by experienced laboratories.

JTAG

Existing standardized interfaces for reading data are built into several mobile devices, e.g., to get position data from GPS equipment (NMEA) or to get deceleration information from airbag units.

Not all mobile devices provide such a standardized interface nor does there exist a standard interface for all mobile devices, but all manufacturers have one problem in common. The miniaturizing of device parts opens the question how to automatically test the functionality and quality of the soldered integrated components. For this problem an industry group, the Joint Test Action Group (JTAG), developed a test technology called boundary scan.

Despite the standardization there are four tasks before the JTAG device interface can be used to recover the memory. To find the correct bits in the boundary scan register one must know which processor and memory circuits are used and how they are connected to the system bus. When not accessible from outside one must find the test points for the JTAG interface on the printed circuit board and determine which test point is used for which signal. The JTAG port is not always soldered with connectors, such that it is sometimes necessary to open the device and re-solder the access port. The protocol for reading the memory must be known and finally the correct voltage must be determined to prevent damage to the circuit.

The boundary scan produces a complete forensic image of the volatile and non-volatile memory. The risk of data change is minimized and the memory chip doesn't have to be desoldered. Generating the image can be slow and not all mobile devices are JTAG enabled. Also, it can be difficult to find the test access port.

Command Line Tools

System Commands

Mobile devices do not provide the possibility to run or boot from a CD, connecting to a network share or another device with clean tools. Therefore, system commands could be the only way to save the volatile memory of a mobile device. With the risk of modified system commands it must be estimated if the volatile memory is really important. A similar problem arises when no network connection is available and no secondary memory can be connected to a mobile device because the volatile memory image must be saved on the internal non-volatile memory, where the user data is stored and most likely deleted important data will be lost. System commands are the cheapest method, but imply some risks of data loss. Every command usage with options and output must be documented.

AT Commands

AT commands are old modem commands, e.g., Hayes command set and Motorola phone AT commands, and can therefore only be used on a device that has modem support. Using these commands one can only obtain information through the operating system, such that no deleted data can be extracted.

dd

For external memory and the USB flash drive, appropriate software, e.g., the Unix command *dd*, is needed to make the bit-level copy. Furthermore, USB flash drives with memory protection do not need special hardware and can be connected to any computer. Many USB drives and memory cards have a write-lock switch that can be used to prevent data changes, while making a copy.

If the USB drive has no protection switch, a blocker can be used to mount the drive in a read-only mode or, in an exceptional case, the memory chip can be desoldered. The SIM and memory cards need a card reader to make the copy. The SIM card is soundly analyzed, such that it is possible to recover (deleted) data like contacts or text messages.

The Android operating system includes the dd command. In a blog post on Android forensic techniques, a method to live image an Android device using the dd command is demonstrated.

Non-forensic Commercial Tools

Flasher Tools

A flasher tool is programming hardware and/or software that can be used to program (flash) the device memory, e.g., EEPROM or flash memory. These tools mainly originate from the manufacturer or service centers for debugging, repair, or upgrade services. They can overwrite the non-volatile memory and some, depending on the manufacturer or device, can also read the memory to make a copy, originally intended as a backup. The memory can be protected from reading, e.g., by software command or destruction of fuses in the read circuit.

This would not prevent writing or using the memory internally by the CPU. The flasher tools are easy to connect and use, but some can change the data and have other dangerous options or do not make a complete copy.

Controversies

In general there exists no standard for what constitutes a supported device in a specific product. This has led to the situation where different vendors define a supported device differently. A situation such as this makes it much harder to compare products based on vendor provided lists of supported devices. For instance a device where logical extraction using one product only produces a list of calls made by the device may be listed as supported by that vendor while another vendor can produce much more information.

Furthermore, different products extract different amounts of information from different devices. This leads to a very complex landscape when trying to overview the products. In general this leads to a situation where testing a product extensively before purchase is strongly recommended. It is quite common to use at least two products which complement each other.

Mobile phone technology is evolving at a rapid pace. Digital forensics relating to mobile devices seems to be at a stand still or evolving slowly. For mobile phone forensics to catch up with release cycles of mobile phones, more comprehensive and in depth framework for evaluating mobile forensic toolkits should be developed and data on appropriate tools and techniques for each type of phone should be made available a timely manner.

Anti-forensics

Anti-computer forensics is more difficult because of the small size of the devices and the user's restricted data accessibility. Nevertheless, there are developments to secure the memory in hardware with security circuits in the CPU and memory chip, such that the memory chip cannot be read even after desoldering.

Digital Forensic Process

A Tableau forensic write blocker

The digital forensic process is a recognized scientific and forensic process used in digital forensics investigations. Forensics researcher Eoghan Casey defines it as a number of steps from the original incident alert through to reporting of findings. The process is predominantly used in computer and mobile forensic investigations and consists of three steps: *acquisition*, *analysis* and *reporting*.

Digital media seized for investigation is usually referred to as an "exhibit" in legal terminology. Investigators employ the scientific method to recover digital evidence to support or disprove a hypothesis, either for a court of law or in civil proceedings.

Personnel

The stages of the digital forensics process require differing specialist training and knowledge, there are two rough levels of personnel:

Digital forensic technician

> Technicians may gather or process evidence at crime scenes, in the field of digital forensics training is needed on the correct handling of technology (for example to preserve the evidence). Technicians may be required to carry out "Live analysis" of evidence - various tools to simplify this procedure have been produced, most notably Microsoft's COFEE.

Digital Evidence Examiners

> Examiners specialize in one area of digital evidence; either at a broad level (i.e. computer or network forensics etc.) or as a sub-specialist (i.e. image analysis)

Process Models

There have been many attempts to develop a process model but so far none have been universally accepted. Part of the reason for this may be due to the fact that many of the process models were designed for a specific environment, such as law enforcement, and they therefore could not be readily applied in other environments such as incident response. This is a list of the main models since 2001 in chronological order:

The Abstract Digital Forensic Model (Reith, et al., 2002)

The Integrated Digital Investigative Process (Carrier & Spafford, 2003)

An Extended Model of Cybercrime Investigations (Ciardhuain, 2004)

The Enhanced Digital Investigation Process Model (Baryamureeba & Tushabe, 2004)

The Digital Crime Scene Analysis Model (Rogers, 2004)

A Hierarchical, Objectives-Based Framework for the Digital Investigations Process (Beebe & Clark, 2004)

Framework for a Digital Investigation (Kohn, et al., 2006)

The Four Step Forensic Process (Kent, et al., 2006)

FORZA - Digital forensics investigation framework (Ieong, 2006)

Process Flows for Cyber Forensics Training and Operations (Venter, 2006)

The Common Process Model (Freiling & Schwittay, (2007)

The Two-Dimensional Evidence Reliability Amplification Process Model (Khatir, et al., 2008)

The Digital Forensic Investigations Framework (Selamat, et al., 2008)

The Systematic Digital Forensic Investigation Model (SRDFIM) (Agarwal, et al., 2011)

The Advanced Data Acquisition Model (ADAM): A process model for digital forensic practice (Adams, 2012)

Seizure

Prior to the actual examination digital media will be seized. In criminal cases this will often be performed by law enforcement personnel trained as technicians to ensure the preservation of evidence. In civil matters it will usually be a company officer, often untrained. Various laws cover the seizure of material. In criminal matters law related to search warrants is applicable. In civil proceedings the assumption is that a company is able to investigate their own equipment without a warrant, so long as the privacy and human rights of employees are observed.

Acquisition

Once exhibits have been seized an exact sector level duplicate (or "forensic duplicate") of the media is created, usually via a write blocking device, a process referred to as *Imaging* or *Acquisition*. The duplicate is created using a hard-drive duplicator or software imaging tools such as DCFLdd,

IXimager, Guymager, TrueBack, EnCase, FTK Imager or FDAS. The original drive is then returned to secure storage to prevent tampering.

Example of a portable disk imaging device

The acquired image is verified by using the SHA-1 or MD5 hash functions. At critical points throughout the analysis, the media is verified again, known as "hashing", to ensure that the evidence is still in its original state.

Analysis

After acquisition the contents of (the HDD) image files are analysed to identify evidence that either supports or contradicts a hypothesis or for signs of tampering (to hide data). In 2002 the *International Journal of Digital Evidence* referred to this stage as "an in-depth systematic search of evidence related to the suspected crime". By contrast Brian Carrier, in 2006, describes a more "intuitive procedure" in which obvious evidence is first identified after which "exhaustive searches are conducted to start filling in the holes"

During the analysis an investigator usually recovers evidence material using a number of different methodologies (and tools), often beginning with recovery of deleted material. Examiners use specialist tools (EnCase, ILOOKIX, FTK, etc.) to aid with viewing and recovering data. The type of data recovered varies depending on the investigation; but examples include email, chat logs, images, internet history or documents. The data can be recovered from accessible disk space, deleted (unallocated) space or from within operating system cache files.

Various types of techniques are used to recover evidence, usually involving some form of keyword searching within the acquired image file; either to identify matches to relevant phrases or to parse out known file types. Certain files (such as graphic images) have a specific set of bytes which identify the start and end of a file, if identified a deleted file can be reconstructed. Many forensic tools use hash signatures to identify notable files or to exclude known (benign) ones; acquired data is hashed and compared to pre-compiled lists such as the *Reference Data Set* (RDS) from the National Software Reference Library

On most media types including standard magnetic hard disks, once data has been securely deleted it can never be recovered.

Once evidence is recovered the information is analysed to reconstruct events or actions and to reach conclusions, work that can often be performed by less specialist staff. Digital investigators, particularly in criminal investigations, have to ensure that conclusions are based upon data and their own expert knowledge. In the US, for example, Federal Rules of Evidence state that a qualified expert may testify "in the form of an opinion or otherwise" so long as:

(1) the testimony is based upon sufficient facts or data, (2) the testimony is the product of reliable principles and methods, and (3) the witness has applied the principles and methods reliably to the facts of the case.

Reporting

When an investigation is completed the information is often reported in a form suitable for non-technical individuals. Reports may also include audit information and other meta-documentation.

When completed reports are usually passed to those commissioning the investigation, such as law enforcement (for criminal cases) or the employing company (in civil cases), who will then decide whether to use the evidence in court. Generally, for a criminal court, the report package will consist of a written expert conclusion of the evidence as well as the evidence itself (often presented on digital media).

List of Digital Forensics Tools

During the 1980s, most digital forensic investigations consisted of "live analysis", examining digital media directly using non-specialist tools. In the 1990s, several freeware and other proprietary tools (both hardware and software) were created to allow investigations to take place without modifying media. This first set of tools mainly focused on computer forensics, although in recent years similar tools have evolved for the field of mobile device forensics. This list includes notable examples of digital; forensic tools.

Computer Forensics

(Alphabetical)

Name	Platform	License	Version	Description
COFEE	Windows	proprietary	n/a	A suite of tools for Windows developed by Microsoft
Digital Forensics Framework	Unix-like/Windows	GPL	1.3	Framework and user interfaces dedicated to Digital Forensics
EPRB	Windows	proprietary	1435	Set of tools for encrypted systems & data decryption and password recovery
FTK	Windows	proprietary	6.0.1	Multi-purpose tool, FTK is a court-cited digital investigations platform built for speed, stability and ease of use.
Open Computer Forensics Architecture	Linux	LGPL/GPL	2.3.0	Computer forensics framework for CF-Lab environment
CAINE Linux	Linux	free/open source	8.0	Gnu/Linux computer forensics live distro.

Name	Platform	License	Version	Description
OSForensics	Windows	proprietary	3.3	Multi-purpose forensic tool
PTK Forensics	LAMP	proprietary	2.0	GUI for The Sleuth Kit
Registry Recon	Windows	proprietary	2.2.0.0047	Forensics tool that rebuilds Windows registries from anywhere on a hard drive and parses them for deep analysis.
SafeBack	N/a	proprietary	3.0	Digital media (evidence) acquisition and backup
SANS Investigative Forensics Toolkit - SIFT	Ubuntu		2.1	Multi-purpose forensic operating system
The Coroner's Toolkit	Unix-like	IBM Public License	1.19	A suite of programs for Unix analysis
The Sleuth Kit	Unix-like/Windows	IPL, CPL, GPL	4.1.2	A library of tools for both Unix and Windows
Windows To Go	n/a	proprietary	n/a	Bootable operating system
Wireshark	cross-platform	GPL	n/a	Open-source packet capture/analyzer, backend library used is [win]pcap.
Netherlands Forensic Institute / Xiraf	n/a	proprietary	n/a	Computer-forensic online service.

Memory Forensics

(Alphabetical) Memory forensics tools are used to acquire and/or analyze a computer's volatile memory (RAM). They are often used in incident response situations to preserve evidence in memory that would be lost when a system is shutdown, and to quickly detect stealthy malware by directly examining the operating system and other running software in memory.

Name	Vendor/Sponsor	Platform	License
Belkasoft Live RAM Capturer	Belkasoft	Windows	Free
WindowsSCOPE	BlueRISC	Windows	proprietary
OSForensics	PassMark Software	Windows	proprietary
Volatililty	Volatile Systems	Windows & Linux	Free (GPL)

Mobile Device Forensics

Mobile forensics tools tend to consist of both a hardware and software component. Mobile phones come with a diverse range of connectors, the hardware devices support a number of different cables and perform the same role as a write blocker in computer devices.

(Alphabetical)

Name	Platform	License	Version	Description
Belkasoft Evidence Center	Windows	proprietary	8.3	
Magnet AXIOM	cross-platform	proprietary	1.0.1	A software platform for acquisition, analysis and sharing from Magnet Forensics

Name	Platform	License	Version	Description
MicroSystemation XRY/ XACT	Windows	proprietary		Hardware/Software package, specializes in deleted data

Software Forensics

Software forensics is the science of analyzing software source code or binary code to determine whether intellectual property infringement or theft occurred. It is the centerpiece of lawsuits, trials, and settlements when companies are in dispute over issues involving software patents, copyrights, and trade secrets. Software forensics tools can compare code to determine correlation, a measure that can be used to guide a software forensics expert.

Name	Platform	License	Version	Description
CodeSuite, by SAFE Corporation	Windows	proprietary	n/a	A suite of patented tools for comparing computer source code and executable code to detect plagiarism, pinpoint copyright infringement, highlight trade secret theft, and measure intellectual property. It can also be used to track software development changes through numerous revisions.

Other

Name	Platform	License	Version	Description
HashKeeper	Windows	free	n/a	Database application for storing file hash signatures
Evidence Eliminator	Windows	proprietary	6.03	Anti-forensics software, claims to delete files securely
DECAF	Windows	free	n/a	Tool which automatically executes a set of user defined actions on detecting Microsoft's COFEE tool

References

- M Reith; C Carr; G Gunsch (2002). "An examination of digital forensic models". International Journal of Digital Evidence. Retrieved 2 August 2010

- Various (2009). Eoghan Casey, ed. Handbook of Digital Forensics and Investigation. Academic Press. p. 567. ISBN 0-12-374267-6. Retrieved 27 August 2010

- Carrier, B (2001). "Defining digital forensic examination and analysis tools". Digital Research Workshop II. Retrieved 2 August 2010

- Aaron Phillip; David Cowen; Chris Davis (2009). Hacking Exposed: Computer Forensics. McGraw Hill Professional. p. 544. ISBN 0-07-162677-8. Retrieved 27 August 2010

- Maarten Van Horenbeeck (24 May 2006). "Technology Crime Investigation". Archived from the original on 17 May 2008. Retrieved 17 August 2010

- GL Palmer; I Scientist; H View (2002). "Forensic analysis in the digital world". International Journal of Digital Evidence. Retrieved 2 August 2010

- K S Rosenblatt (1995). High-Technology Crime: Investigating Cases Involving Computers. KSK Publications. ISBN 0-9648171-0-1. Retrieved 4 August 2010

- A Yasinsac; RF Erbacher; DG Marks; MM Pollitt (2003). "Computer forensics education" (PDF). IEEE Security & Privacy. Retrieved 26 July 2010

- M Reith; C Carr; G Gunsch (2002). "An examination of digital forensic models". International Journal of Digital Evidence. CiteSeerX 10.1.1.13.9683. Missing or empty |url= (help); |access-date= requires |url= (help)

- Warren G. Kruse; Jay G. Heiser (2002). Computer forensics: incident response essentials. Addison-Wesley. p. 392. ISBN 0-201-70719-5. Retrieved 6 December 2010

- Olivier, Martin S. (March 2009). "On metadata context in Database Forensics". Digital Investigation. 5 (3–4): 115–123. doi:10.1016/j.diin.2008.10.001. Retrieved 2 August 2010

- Various (2009). Eoghan Casey, ed. Handbook of Digital Forensics and Investigation. Academic Press. p. 567. ISBN 0-12-374267-6. Retrieved 27 August 2010

- Michael G. Noblett; Mark M. Pollitt; Lawrence A. Presley (October 2000). "Recovering and examining computer forensic evidence". Retrieved 26 July 2010

- Christian Hlavica, Uwe Klapproth, Frank Hülsberg et al: Tax Fraud & Forensic Accounting. Gabler Verlag, Wiesbaden 2011, ISBN 978-3-83491-429-3

- Rick Ayers, Wayne Jansen, Nicolas Cilleros, and Ronan Daniellou. (October 2005). Retrieved from Cell Phone Forensic Tools: An Overview and Analysis. National Institute of Standards and Technology

Permissions

We would like to thank the editorial team for lending their expertise to make the book truly unique. They have played a crucial role in the development of this book. Without their invaluable contributions this book wouldn't have been possible. They have made vital efforts to compile up to date information on the varied aspects of this subject to make this book a valuable addition to the collection of many professionals and students.

This book was conceptualized with the vision of imparting up-to-date and integrated information in this field. To ensure the same, a matchless editorial board was set up. Every individual on the board went through rigorous rounds of assessment to prove their worth. After which they invested a large part of their time researching and compiling the most relevant data for our readers.

The editorial board has been involved in producing this book since its inception. They have spent rigorous hours researching and exploring the diverse topics which have resulted in the successful publishing of this book. They have passed on their knowledge of decades through this book. To expedite this challenging task, the publisher supported the team at every step. A small team of assistant editors was also appointed to further simplify the editing procedure and attain best results for the readers.

Apart from the editorial board, the designing team has also invested a significant amount of their time in understanding the subject and creating the most relevant covers. They scrutinized every image to scout for the most suitable representation of the subject and create an appropriate cover for the book.

The publishing team has been an ardent support to the editorial, designing and production team. Their endless efforts to recruit the best for this project, has resulted in the accomplishment of this book. They are a veteran in the field of academics and their pool of knowledge is as vast as their experience in printing. Their expertise and guidance has proved useful at every step. Their uncompromising quality standards have made this book an exceptional effort. Their encouragement from time to time has been an inspiration for everyone.

The publisher and the editorial board hope that this book will prove to be a valuable piece of knowledge for students, practitioners and scholars across the globe.

Index

Printed in the USA
CPSIA information can be obtained
at www.ICGtesting.com
JSHW051424221024
72173JS00006B/1397

9 781632 407252